Biography-Driven Culturally Responsive Teaching

Biography-Driven Culturally Responsive Teaching

SOCORRO HERRERA

Foreword by
Edmund T. Hamann

Teachers College, Columbia University
New York and London

Worksheets and supporting instructions for the following instructional aids and strategies are available for free download from the Teachers College Press website: www.tcpress.com

- Hearts Activity, Figure 2.2, page 23
- CLD Student Biography Card, Figures 5.4 and 5.5 and Appendix B, pages 64, 65, 153
- Content and Language Objectives, Figures 7.2 and 7.3, pages 91, 92
- DOTS Chart (Determine, Observe, Talk, Summarize), Appendix C, pages 154, 155
- Mind Map, Appendix D, pages 156, 157
- Vocabulary Quilt, Appendix E, pages 158, 159
- Ignite, Discover, Extend, Affirm (IDEA), Appendix F, pages 160, 161
- Thumb Challenge, Appendix G, pages 162, 163
- Uncover, Concentrate, Monitor, Evaluate (U-C-ME), Appendix H, pages 164–166

Permissions credit lines for reproduced figures appear below the individual figures.

Published by Teachers College Press, 1234 Amsterdam Avenue, New York, NY 10027

Copyright © 2010 by Teachers College, Columbia University

Text Design: Lynne Frost

Library of Congress Cataloging-in-Publication Data

Herrera, Socorro Guadalupe.
    Biography-driven culturally responsive teaching / Socorro Herrera.
        p.   cm.
    Includes bibliographical references and index.
    ISBN 978-0-8077-5086-5 (pbk. : alk. paper)
        1. Linguistic minorities—Education—United States.   2. Multicultural education—United States.   3. Education—Biographical methods.   I. Title.

    LC3731.H476 2010
    371.102—dc22   2009053250

ISBN 978-0-8077-5086-5 (paperback)

Printed on acid-free paper
Manufactured in the United States of America

17 16 15 14 13 12 11 10   8 7 6 5 4 3 2 1

For your limitless love and commitment to my craziness,
I will forever be grateful …

> *My Husband: Gilbert Davila*
> *My Children: Dawn, Kevin, Jesse, and Isamari*

> *Love you always!*

Contents

Foreword

ON THE FIRST PAGE, Herrera writes "We teachers," and from that point forward it is clear that this is a volume *by* a teacher and *for* teachers who want to become more adept at helping culturally and linguistically diverse learners succeed academically. Her work is our work. She draws our attention to two important facts. First, students come to our classrooms with biographies—with experiences, dispositions, and understandings that are the intellectual tool kits with which they will make sense of anything we want to draw their attention to or help them develop skills for. Second, students' biographies will continue to matter—shaping aspirations, decision-making, and which repertoires they will draw upon—as they solve problems and negotiate lives long after they leave our classrooms. For that reason, we should help students figure out how to reconcile what we teach in our classrooms with who they are and propose to be. This volume lays out steps and strategies, along with convincing real-world examples, for *biography-driven instruction*. In short, it is a teacher telling fellow teachers what we can (and should) do.

In an age when there is much fretting about "best practices," Herrera's book is crucial in at least three ways. First, it helps bridge the gap between research and practice by pointing out how some key educational research understandings—for example, Vygotsky-derived constructivism or the "funds of knowledge" framing (González et al., 1995; González, Moll, & Amanti, 2005)—can guide what teachers do day in and day out in their classrooms. In my experience with preservice and in-service teachers, I see that many find the cultural responsiveness implicit in attending to students' backgrounds and experiences to be highly attractive. But until now, too often there has not been a teacher-friendly answer to the question *What should I do?*

Second, Herrera's biography-driven instruction offers a teacher-affirming reminder that there is no externally created (or creatable) "silver bullet" instructional package that can be imported into a classroom and will work for all students without adaptation. While there are a lot of good, empirically grounded ideas "out there" that we can and should deploy in our classrooms, these ideas never chart the full course of what we should do because they are incomplete until we teachers figure out how they matter to our students. *We* are the ones who get to know our students. *We* are the ones who can see our students react favorably to a particular exercise and who can respond enthusiastically (and in English) to their engagement. In one example presented in this volume (a 2nd-grade poetry unit described on page 45), a student responded to a class activity by creating a flag-shaped poem about her home country of Saudi Arabia, complete with lines in Arabic. The exercise allowed the student to reconcile who she is and where she came from with the language-learning task the teacher was promoting. Herrera's point is not that we should all have our 2nd-grade students make flag poems, but rather that a portion of instructional decision-making best remains in the hands of the classroom teachers. If a broad and clear goal is to have our 2nd-grade students recognize language patterns and possible word-play (in speaking or visual presentation of text), it is teachers who can test and probe and ultimately co-develop with their students the particular ways the task is to be accomplished (and this book offers a number of suggestions that can inform that testing and probing). "Best" responses will be intrinsically contextual and thus will vary, with *best* being partially a function of who the learner is. And what works "best" one year may well need to be modified or adapted to work well the next.

Third, Herrera helps us move beyond deterministic behaviorism without rejecting the notion that there *are* patterns and tendencies in how various learners learn. Too often in teacher talk and practice we hear that a given student is a "visual" learner or a "concrete thinker," as if that is the only way that such individuals can learn. As teachers, this can feel overwhelming—not just because it makes us worry about how we can attend to all of these differences but also because it can make us fear that if we lead a certain activity in a certain way we will not reach those students who learn in a different way. Herrera's point is more agentive. *Yes* some students will more easily understand and respond to activities framed one way versus another, so *yes* it behooves us to present themes in different and multiple ways. But it is also true that we have multiple routes to engagement with any learner, and those routes can reveal themselves if we invoke students' biographies—and not even everyone's biographies all the time.

I am reminded of a story told by a colleague, Dr. Elizabeth Lewis, who worked with a Phoenix middle school when she was a doctoral student at Arizona State University. For a geology unit on earthquakes, the cooperating teacher realized that she had a number of students who had family in Mexico City who had lived through that city's tragic earthquake of 1985. The teacher invited those students to conduct oral history interviews with their relatives to gather accounts of the disaster. Not everyone in the class had such relatives, so this was not the only task the teacher created to help students engage with the material. Nonetheless, when the histories had been collected, translated, and shared, everyone in the classroom had a more tangible and interested attachment to the topic, and everyone in the classroom had at least classmates whose relatives had lived through the quake. A geology lesson had become personally relevant, and there was a new repertoire of examples that the teacher and students collectively shared and that either could invoke as they tried to make sense not just of other parts of the geology unit but of later science lessons as well.

Herrera starts her last chapter with an important question: "At the end of this book and the end of your school day, it will be important to ask: What have I accomplished today to make the world a better place for all students?" That question exemplifies the umbrella-like social justice framing of this entire volume. It assumes that we teachers want to make the world a better place for all students. More importantly, the rest of the volume clarifies what "making it better" would look like: helping all students engage in their school learning by attaching that learning to their biographies and thereby making their biographies one of the resources that we teachers have as part of our tool kit. According to the constructivist framing of Vygotsky, students, like all other learners, make sense of the new by comparing it to the already familiar, to the already known. As teachers, we cannot be our most effective if we do not invoke students' background knowledge, if we do not promote making tie-ins to biography, and if we neglect the fact that our classrooms function as miniature communities. Elements of one student's life will often be more vivid and interesting to classmates than the more remote material in the textbook and thus can serve as a teacher's tool for promoting engagement. Biography-driven instruction promises to help us make our classrooms far more interesting—and also more successful—places.

—*Edmund T. Hamann*

Acknowledgments

MY WORK on this book has reminded me of the many people who bless my world with their talents, passion, and limitless giving. Melissa Holmes, Shabina Kavimandan, Sheri Meredith, and Jory Oulhiad shared without boundaries their insights, wisdom, and knowledge of culturally and linguistically diverse students. Throughout the process, they provided constructive criticism with compassion and guidance to stretch the limits of thinking, creativity, and perfection (from multiple perspectives). Without their support, my goal of putting my life's work into written format might never have been possible.

For the first time in my academic life I have had the privilege to work with my oldest two children, Dawn and Kevin. They have been my constant companions in schools from the very beginning of my teaching career. Today, they find themselves on their own academic tracks, yet both found time to read, edit, and provide loving feedback that served to strengthen my voice and commitment to finishing this project.

The Center for Intercultural and Multilingual Advocacy (CIMA), where much of the work with the teachers in this book has taken place, is filled with colleagues, graduate students, and undergraduate students—friends who were there filling in the pieces when the rest of us had little energy left to spare. Emily Banks and Dominika Ornatowska found literature and references in some remote places. Jennifer Brunenn's creativity with photography and formatting was simply genius. My love and thanks go to each and every one of them.

I am grateful to the BESITOS students at Kansas State University for sharing their lives, experiences, and unique perspectives with me as they navigate educational settings that have not always encouraged success. Through your dedication, perseverance, and determination to succeed, you will become educators and advocates for other culturally and linguistically diverse students in school districts throughout Kansas. Besos!

A heartfelt word of appreciation goes to the teachers across the country who contributed their creative voices and talent to this project. A week does not pass that one of you will not share a picture, quote, or student work that exempli-fies what biography-driven instruction is all about in classroom practice. Without your words and images of what is possible with culturally and linguistically diverse populations, this book would not have been possible. You have taken theory to the highest level of classroom practice and have stepped outside the box to provide *all* students with the education they deserve, regardless of current or past political agendas. *You are the people who make a difference!* I treasure your friendships and the willingness you have to share of yourself. To educators in the state of Kansas and across the country, I will forever be grateful.

Energy and excitement are what I find in the schools of the many administrators with whom I have had the privilege to collaborate during the process of writing this book. I humbly thank you for creating spaces and places where teachers are cherished and celebrated. I have personally witnessed your encouragement of teachers' professionalism by supporting them to *step outside the box* and do what is best for all students. It is through administrator support that the teachers described in this book have been able to soar beyond sociopolitical and other boundaries that often threaten teacher voice and action. Thank you for celebrating and encouraging your educators to participate in this project.

Regardless of the day or time, Jean Ward was only a phone call away during this process. It is difficult to find the words to express how I feel about her support. In the decade since we first met, she has never stopped believing that this book would be written. It brings warmth to my heart to think of the many times, across the country at multiple education conferences, we have had dinner together. She has always welcomed the "Latina way," smiling when a dinner turned into a CIMA family gathering. She has never hesitated to generously welcome anyone who came along. I knew then, as I know now, not only that would this book happen but also that she and I would be good friends for a long time. Jean, you are the guiding light for the words written in this book.

The team at Teachers College Press has quickly and patiently responded to all of my questions or concerns related to every aspect of this book. It has been a real privilege to collaborate with all of you.

Introduction

THE DIVERSITY OF STUDENTS in today's class-rooms challenges us as educators to invest our hearts and minds in our teaching efforts with each and every student. Yet with competing agendas tugging at our time, energy, and professional understanding of how best to address the needs of culturally and linguistically diverse (CLD) learners, we often struggle to make sense of it all and to have our voices heard above the rhetoric that surrounds teaching. This book has been written as a response to the voices of thousands of teachers I have had the privilege to work with across the United States—teachers who continue to step out of the box and teach with students and families in mind. Although the journey is difficult at times, their passion and commitment serves as their catalyst for clearing the path for the academic achievement of our CLD student populations.

The following is a brief overview of the path set forth by this book. It is a path that I hope will lead you to discovery of the great rewards that can be reaped through the use of biography-driven instruction—a model for enriching every CLD student's academic experience. Teachers dedicated to seeing their CLD students succeed in the classroom place the biographies of their students at the center of their practice. In this way, they are able to use students' knowledge, skills, and words as entry points to learning and as the foundation for culturally responsive teaching.

Chapter 1 describes models that have proven to be excellent guides for framing lessons and delivering instruction in our contemporary diverse classrooms. This chapter looks particularly at how the work of Vygotsky, with his emphasis on the importance of working from each student's "zone of proximal development," and the work of Krashen, which contextualizes this idea for CLD students, underpin the ideas of this book about the importance of using the biographies of all our students to make our instruction more effective and their learning more successful. This chapter also describes current programs being used across the nation to support English learners, and the ways in which biography-driven instructional techniques enhance these existing models without needing to replace them. In addition, this chapter foreshadows the four dimensions of learning that are discussed in subsequent chapters.

Chapter 2 explains how teachers can use CLD students' biopsychosocial histories to create optimal classroom learning conditions. The term "biopsychosocial" encompasses the entirety of the human experience, with considerations for the biological, psychological, and social aspects of a person's history. Understanding this concept is essential to the academic success of CLD students because students carry more than their backpacks to school. They carry with them intrinsic traits and lived experiences that shape their knowledge, skills, and learning styles. By delving into CLD students' culture, background, and emotions—and sometimes stepping outside of our own comfort zones—we teachers can begin to understand those elements that influence students' engagement and motivation to learn. When we incorporate CLD students' unique abilities and experiences in the classroom, we can better advance their academic and linguistic development.

Chapter 3 addresses the processes by which CLD students learn and acquire a second language and how that affects their academic progress. Just as a student's sociocultural history creates rules for living, laughing, and loving, in much the same way a student's linguistic background establishes a guide for how he or she understands verbal communication. We teachers must understand CLD students' cultures and English language learning processes to effectively plan instruction. Using the knowledge we gain through observation, we can determine how to most effectively plan instruction that allows students to view texts through the lens of their life experiences. Our efforts to this end will result in more meaningful lessons that will support students' retention of key concepts, language, and skills in permanent memory.

In Chapter 4, I address the question *Why do we think the way we think?* Vygotsky suggests that language and sociocultural experiences determine thought and development. When we understand the role of cognition and culture in shaping how our brains are accustomed to working, we can tailor our culturally responsive instruction, learning strategies, and assessments to ensure the best fit for our CLD students. Instructional moves, materials, and tasks that make sense to us educators, because of our own frames of reference, may be confusing, awkward, or even alienating to our students. We can more effectively promote students' learning of academic concepts, skills, and vocabulary when we value and build upon their ways of knowing, thinking, and applying.

Chapter 5 discusses the critical need for educators to provide CLD students with access, engagement, and hope. At times, even our best intentions can fall short of ensuring that all students have equal access to a rich, challenging curriculum. Our efforts to design and implement instruction that promotes the engagement of *every* student in the meaning-making process can move CLD students one step closer to ever greater gains in academic and literacy development. Key to this process is our demonstration of respect and care for each of our students, both as individuals and as learners in our classrooms. This chapter provides the CLD Student Biography Card as a helpful tool for getting to know your students and planning instruction that is culturally responsive and biography-driven.

Chapter 6 explores concrete strategies for creating a biography-driven classroom. By looking at the contextual and situational processes of teaching, which encompass the classroom ecology and in-the-moment learning dynamics, we can learn how to best create a learning community that supports CLD student achievement. Students' affective filters lower and they become more open to instruction and interaction when we create a climate that takes into account their voices, motivations, and mind-sets. In biography-driven instruction, we teachers begin each lesson as a participant-observer, uncovering what students already know and have experienced. Then we incorporate the various kinds of knowledge students bring to the classroom into our teaching, using their funds of knowledge (home assets), prior knowledge (community assets), and academic knowledge (school assets) to guide our actions and decisions. Putting student knowledge to use in the classroom sparks new learning and supports academic achievement for all learners.

Chapter 7 looks at the teacher's job as one of continuous discovery—recognizing students' assets and potential and using what students bring culturally and linguistically to facilitate learning. It addresses the difference between this kind of facilitation and the more traditional practice of simply transmitting knowledge. Optimal instruction for CLD students begins when we consider students' biographies and background knowledge in planning lessons, and then make efforts to be transparent in our teaching by explicitly telling students what we expect them to take away from the lesson. When we share content and language objectives with students, we create a sense of hope and expectation among CLD learners. This chapter also explores how the brain processes information and provides considerations for vocabulary lessons that can support students in storing newly acquired information in their permanent memory.

Chapter 8 provides teachers with tools to scaffold instruction for CLD students, giving students the support they need to stand on their own while learning and to show others what they know. This kind of support begins with active listening and creating comprehensible input that aligns with students' individual biographies. Strategies, as differentiated from one-time activities, can help us provide such comprehensible input. Cognitive, metacognitive, and social/affective strategies can aid learners in present learning situations as well as in future endeavors. Such strategies help students gain a sense of ownership and responsibility in their learning and develop interpersonal skills as they collaborate to make sense of new concepts. By having students work together in pairs or small groups, we provide CLD students with low-risk opportunities to practice their language skills and share their unique cultures and perspectives. These opportunities for interaction and discussion help us as we monitor and navigate students' states of mind (e.g., anxiety, fear, boredom) during instruction.

Chapter 9 helps us see assessment in a new light, emphasizing the need to celebrate what students *do* know and *can* do. Standard forms of assessment tend to show what students do *not* know and are *in*capable of doing. Consider for a moment CLD students' emotional states when they take a test or see their resulting grade. Students learn through trial and error and through discovering meaning in ways that are relevant to them. Memorizing information for standardized tests rarely results in learning that lasts. By using formative assessments before and during the lesson, we can discover what and how students are learning and determine how we can best modify instruction to guide students from the known to the unknown. Reviewing and providing closure at the end of the lesson gives students one more chance to confirm their learning, helps alleviate any anxiety they might feel, and gives us teachers a chance to evaluate how the class as a whole has met the learning objectives. When it comes time for summative assessment, we can take into account students' individual biographies as we tailor assessments to yield the most informative data about the content and language development students have achieved.

Chapter 10 provides insights from educators in the field, who relay how biography-driven instruction has had an impact on CLD students in their schools and classrooms.

These educators discuss their unique student populations and the benefits of culturally relevant pedagogy for the entire learning community. These administrators and teachers share their thoughts about the importance of dialogue, collaboration, and critical reflection as they continually work to transform their programs, models, curricula, and instruction to enhance learning opportunities for CLD students. By listening to their stories, we can better visualize what biography-driven instruction might mean for our own professional settings.

IN DEVELOPING the model for biography-driven instruction, I have been informed by wide-ranging educational research and theory as well as my own experiences as a teacher of CLD students, working with teachers in diverse classrooms nationwide, and, decades ago, as a CLD student myself. In this book, I have strived to present what I have learned in the most straightforward and practical manner possible, elaborating on important theoretical constructs that underlie the suggested strategies without ever losing sight of what really works in real classrooms. Altogether, this amounts to a large volume of new information!

At times, it may seem impossible even to think about how to integrate biography-driven instruction into a teaching practice that already is subject to so many competing demands. Should this frustration begin to set in, I encourage you to keep in mind the metaphor of the journey that is employed throughout this book. When we travel in a new place, the best way to get to know the landscape is to go step by step, keeping our senses attuned to the details of what we encounter along the way, paying close attention to how it makes us feel. What interests us? Frightens us? Excites us? What challenges our current ways of thinking, or makes us want to go back for another look? If we try to speed through everything all at once, jet lag and frustration will surely result. But if we take our time and remain focused on deliberately reaching our goal, a life-changing discovery may open before us.

CHAPTER 1

Taking Current Perspectives to *i*+1

THE POPULATION of English language learners (ELLs) has increased nationwide. Between the academic years of 1995–1996 and 2005–2006, the ELL student population increased by 57.2 percent, while the total student enrollment increased by only 3.7 percent (NCELA, 2007). The diversity of the ELL population makes these students' educational dynamics more complex. Students who speak a language other than English come with biographies as unique and varied as the more than 400 languages represented in our classrooms today. Currently, Spanish speakers make up the highest percentage of ELL students in U.S. schools, constituting 79% of the ELL population; speakers of Asian languages represent the second largest group, although with a much lower percentage (Kindler, 2002).

Labels for students who are acquiring English as an additional language have shifted over time. Labels that describe the student's language skills from a deficit perspective have ranged from limited English proficient (LEP) to English language learners (ELL). Both of these labels have been used by the U.S. Department of Education primarily to describe students whose native language is something other than English and who have difficulty performing academically in the classroom with regard to speaking, reading, and writing. Terms such as these limit the way we think about teaching and learning. By focusing solely on the acquisition of English skills, we devalue the role of the student's native language in the entire learning process.

Students often are given the label of ELL, or a similar designation as defined by the state in which they are receiving services, based on a point-in-time test that tells very little about their capacities to be successful in school. Moreover, this kind of labeling disregards the great variance that exists among students of this population. By contributing to the tracking of learners in lower-level classes that may not hold the same level of expectations as those held in grade-level or content-area classes, such labeling furthers the marginalization of these students within our school system.

Each student who arrives in a classroom brings with him or her a history or biography that is much more meaningful than points scored on one test. These students carry with them experiences, native languages, academic backgrounds, and other resources that can inform the decisions made about placement and programming. Within this population we find students who speak perfect social English when they arrive, but converse in another language at home. We have students whose parents refuse services to avoid the stigma of a label, and we have students who are exited too soon from services and not monitored for performance in the grade-level classroom. Yet, due to insufficient professional development specific to the needs of ELL students, many teachers I meet have learned about the linguistic and cultural needs of their students only after they have already pre-referred the students to a special education program. Figure 1.1 presents the range of labels used to describe CLD students.

For the purpose of this book and the work I do in the field, I find the term *culturally and linguistically diverse (CLD)* to be much more representative and inclusive of this population. For teachers, it serves as a reminder that when the student's culture differs from that of the school, there is a high probability that their language may also be in conflict with that of the school curriculum. It also reminds us that in our efforts to address language acquisition processes and challenges, we can draw upon a diverse range of knowledge, skills, and talents that students already possess.

As the number of students from diverse backgrounds continues to grow in our schools, it is more important than ever to find ways of providing equitable educational opportunities for all learners. Although we can choose from among multiple paths to take on this quest, answers to many challenges already exist within our own classrooms. At times, however, influences beyond our control can affect our efforts to provide CLD students with a high-quality education that promotes both their linguistic and their academic development.

FIGURE 1.1

Labels for Students Learning English as an Additional Language

Term	Definition/Connotation
CLD: Culturally and Linguistically Diverse	This term emphasizes the multiple dimensions of bilingual and multilingual students who are in the process of acquiring English. *CLD* has a more positive connotation than many other terms used to refer to these learners.
ELL: English Language Learner	This term has a more positive connotation than *NEP* or *LEP* because it highlights the *process* of acquiring English rather than the lack of English having been acquired. However, *CLD* is still preferable to *ELL* because it emphasizes the cultural and linguistic assets that students contribute to the classroom, school, and community.
ESL Student: English as a Second Language Student	This is a generic term applied to students who are in the process of acquiring English. However, it can sometimes be a misnomer, as English is the third, or even fourth, language acquired by some students.
FEP: Fluent English Proficient **FES:** Fluent English Speaker	While *FEP* and *FES* have more positive connotations than the terms defined below, they de-emphasize/neglect the cultural and linguistic assets of students, focusing solely on the English skills that students possess. *FEP* and *FES* are terms frequently found in government documents.
LEP: Limited English Proficient **LES:** Limited English Speaker	These terms refer to students who are in the process of acquiring English. However, they focus on the "lack" of English that a student possesses rather than valuing the totality of students' linguistic knowledge and skills. In this way, *LEP* and *LES* emphasize the perceived linguistic inadequacies of learners when compared with other students. *LEP* and *LES* are terms commonly used in government documents.
NEP: Non-English Proficient **NES:** Non-English Speaker	*NEP* and *NES* are used to refer to students at the beginning stages of English language acquisition. These terms de-emphasize the process of acquiring English and highlight what students are not able to do versus what they *can* do. These terms are commonly found in government documents.

The Influence of Politics on CLD Student Education

Politics have long defined what education should look like for CLD students, beginning with the landmark case *Lau v. Nichols* (1974). In this case, the Supreme Court ruled that we do not ensure an equitable education "merely by providing students with the same facilities, textbooks, teachers, and curriculum; for students who do not understand English are effectively foreclosed from any meaningful education." Since then, the debate has continued, with no consistent finding that would give educators the answer to the question they are asking: *What is the single best way to educate CLD students?*

The debate instead has followed the political winds of elected officials. More than a decade ago, bilingual education programs were largely removed from schools, even those where students were outperforming their peers across the country. This shift in educational programming was driven by the politically charged Unz Initiative of California (also known as "English for the Children"), which resulted in the state's passage of Proposition 227 in 1998. Current agendas push for a more rushed approach, limiting the time services can be provided to CLD students before they are sent to classrooms with teachers who are likely to have limited understanding of their linguistic and academic needs. Disregarding everything that has been learned to date through rigorous, longitudinal research (e.g., Thomas & Collier, 2002) about the best programs for CLD students, the debate continues to revolve around the politics of the day and leaves many students behind in the process. Meanwhile, legislative and judicial decisions continue to affect the efforts of administrators and teachers. Appendix A presents a brief overview of the cases and decisions that have affected the education of CLD students.

One result of this nationwide movement of students as quickly as possible into heterogeneous grade-level and content-area classrooms is that many teachers who are unprepared for teaching CLD students now need perspectives and strategies to help them make these students successful. This book was written for those classroom and content-area teachers, as well as for English as a second language (ESL) professionals. So what then does it take to educate CLD learners? First, it requires the recognition that there is no *one* answer to this question. Rather, we see positive academic results when whatever programs and instructional models we provide also take into account the unique population being served, the human resources available, and the best interests of the student, family, and teacher.

Existing Programs and Models Provide a Starting Point

The wide range of language programs in the United States speaks not only to the linguistic diversity in the country, but also to the overabundance of names for these programs. Particular terms can be used to describe a wide variety of program types. Current academic programs for students who are learning English, although clearly described by the literature, come to life based on the interpretation of the people who implement them. Figure 1.2 (see pages 8 and 9) provides an overview of current program types, along with a description of how the biography-driven instructional approach described in this book can inform and enrich each of them. Each of these programs selects and implements curricula based on the needs of the population being served or the politics of the school, district, or state in which they operate. Models of instruction differ within each of these programs, and such models are described later in this chapter.

While looking at Figure 1.2, keep in mind that there are many benefits of each program type that are additive in nature, as highlighted in a report by the Center for Applied Linguistics, entitled *Guiding Principles for Dual Language Education* (Howard, Sugarman, Christian, Lindholm-Leary, & Rogers, 2007). In this report, the authors differentiate between *additive bilingual programs,* where the goal is for students to "add on" English as an additional language, and *subtractive programs,* where the primary purpose is to transition students from their native language to English, thereby "subtracting" their first language from their knowledge base.

The authors of the report underscore the benefits of additive programs, stating that additive bilingual programs are associated not only with student achievement in the content areas, in both English and the native language, but also with increased self-esteem and more positive cross-cultural attitudes (Howard et al., 2007). On the other hand, subtractive language programs have been shown to have detrimental effects on CLD students' school performance and on their learning of a second language. Subtractive programs that lead to native language loss correlate with lower levels of second language proficiency, diminished academic achievement, and even with the development of psychosocial disorders (Howard et al.).

At this point, you might be saying to yourself, "I understand that research supports additive program types, but I teach in a subtractive one. What am I supposed to do?" While program type can be a constraint, it need not dictate all aspects of instruction. By focusing on the holistic development of our CLD students and by using their biographies to guide instruction, we can respond to their sociocultural, linguistic, cognitive, and academic needs in a more comprehensive manner, despite the program type in which we work.

Highlights of Effective Instructional Models

Current models of practice offer great promise for teachers' work with CLD students and provide a helpful backdrop for conceptualizing the pedagogy I propose in this text. These models frame what a lesson should look like during delivery and outline teacher skills necessary for implementation. The following is an introduction to each model, including references that can guide you to additional information and a more complete understanding of how the models are designed to work in the classroom.

Cognitive Academic Language Learning Approach (CALLA)

CALLA emphasizes the need for CLD students to develop the academic language skills and knowledge of content-area concepts needed for success in the grade-level classroom. This model incorporates instruction of multiple types of learning strategies that students can use as they make personally relevant connections to the lesson, monitor and assess their learning, and practice their English language skills. Figure 1.3 (see pages 10 and 11) provides a more in-depth look at this model.

Specially Designed Academic Instruction in English (SDAIE)

SDAIE originated in the state of California (California State Department of Education, 1994). This model focuses on the need to provide grade-level curriculum to students who have achieved intermediate to advanced levels of proficiency in the English language. SDAIE incorporates numerous strategies designed to make academic content more comprehensible for CLD learners. Figure 1.4 (see page 12) provides an overview of this instructional model.

Sheltered Instruction Observation Protocol (SIOP)

SIOP (Echevarría, Vogt, & Short, 2000) puts greater emphasis on accommodating students' linguistic backgrounds in lesson planning and instruction. The prior cultural, language, and learning experiences of students are made an *integral* part of the learning process. Content and language objectives for each lesson are identified and explicitly addressed with students throughout the lesson. In addition, vocabulary key to student understanding is identified and previewed with students before the lesson begins. Figure 1.5 (see page 13) elaborates on the SIOP model of instruction.

Bringing CLD Students to the Center of Instruction

As we continue to experience changes in the makeup of our classrooms, the *How to?* question becomes ever more relevant to our practice. We often look for answers in professional developments and come away discouraged, wondering how the take-away techniques could possibly affect change in the academic success of our CLD students. The active role of CLD students themselves in the learning process has often been absent from consideration or only superficially discussed. This book seeks to fill that gap by emphasizing approaches to planning, delivering, and assessing instruction in ways that include the CLD student, and each of our students, at the center of our practice and that work in grade-level and content-area classrooms.

Torgesen et al. (2007) reflect on how teacher "interventions" are only as successful as the degree to which teachers know and understand students' assets and needs during instruction. This involves investigating what CLD students know and applying such knowledge and skills to their process of learning linguistic and academic content. What kinds of teaching and learning dynamics provide us with the greatest level of information about students? How can we use this information in our teaching to achieve our curricular goals? In this book, I propose a *biography-driven instruction model* that provides educators with the guidance they need to tailor their pedagogy in ways that promote the success of all students—especially CLD students—in their classrooms.

The Foundations of Biography-Driven Instruction

The biography-driven instruction model has evolved from the work of Thomas and Collier (e.g., Thomas & Collier, 1997), Moll (e.g., Moll, Amanti, Neff, & González, 1992), Krashen (e.g., Krashen, 1984/1994), and Vygotsky (e.g., Vygotsky, 1978), individuals whose findings continually remind educators of the power of students' assets in the classroom. It also incorporates what we know from research (e.g., Jensen, 2006; Sousa, 2006; Willis, 2006) regarding how the brain learns. The model gives us a practical way for applying what others (e.g., Gay, 2000; Ladson-Billings, 1995; Nieto, 2000; Ogbu & Simons, 1998) have shared about culturally responsive teaching. In addition, through its emphasis on integrating student knowledge with the school curriculum, the biography-driven instruction model creates opportunities for teaching and learning in the "third space" (Gutiérrez, Baquedano-López, & Tejeda, 2003) that is formed in effective, inclusive classrooms where teachers negotiate the school's "official space" and the "unofficial space" of students' lives outside classrooms to create a third space that draws on assets of both to promote learning. The theme that unites these theory- and research-based strands is the necessity of fully including CLD students at the center of our educational efforts by first getting to know them as individuals and then using the resulting insights and information to inform our instruction.

Krashen and the Input Hypothesis

Stephen Krashen's findings regarding how people develop a second language have long guided teachers' practice. At the core of this research, Krashen (1984/1994) explains, is the *input hypothesis* that language is acquired "by understanding input containing i+1; that is, by understanding language that contains input containing structures that are a bit beyond the acquirer's current level" (p. 54). Teachers might think of Krashen's small "i" as the snapshot of an individual student in the present moment of development. In light of this widely accepted theoretical construct, one would expect classroom plans and processes to be organized around the biography of the student, and that pedagogy would be orchestrated to place second language learners in contexts and situations designed to carry them linguistically to i+1, where they are stretched just beyond the current limit of their language acquisition. Currently, however, there appears to be a gap between what we have learned from Krashen's input hypothesis and what is happening in classrooms that serve CLD students.

FIGURE 1.2

Language Instruction Program Types

**Subtractive Instructional Programs—
Students' Native Language Development Is Not Fostered**

Transitional Bilingual Education (TBE)	• Goal of gradually transitioning CLD students from content-based instructional programs in students' native language to an English-only environment; also known as "early exit programs" (Ramirez, 1992). • Has a subtractive effect—as students' levels of English language proficiency increase, their native language fluency decreases (Díaz-Rico, 2008). • Short-term and transitional (2–3 years), not allowing students sufficient time to develop the necessary grade-level cognitive academic language proficiency (CALP) in their native language or in English before being transitioned to English-only instruction (Berman et al., 1992; Díaz-Rico, 2008). • Students become dominant in English and their native language capabilities diminish, having potentially detrimental effects on academic language development in English (Díaz-Rico, 2008).
Pull-Out English as a Second Language (ESL) Programs, English Language Development (ELD) Programs	• Provide CLD students with instructional support (e.g., scaffolding, cooperative learning, other "sheltered" techniques) outside the grade-level classroom to transition students to an English-only instructional program without native language support (Faltis & Hudelson, 1998; Linquanti, 1999). • ESL teachers not required to be fluent in students' native languages; emphasis placed on the teacher employing techniques to make input in English comprehensible for CLD students. Effective ESL/ELD programs based on grade-level curriculum and incorporate both language and content objectives; less effective programs rely on the incorporation of language objectives and treat language learning as a process isolated from content-area learning (Berman et al., 1992; Faltis & Hudelson, 1998). • ESL programs are the most widely implemented program type in the United States, but research has also shown them to be the least effective (Thomas & Collier, 1997). • Potential disadvantages, particularly when students are "pulled out" of the grade-level classroom: (a) very costly for school districts to implement; (b) do not capitalize on CLD students' academic knowledge in their native language; (c) can lead to CLD students being stigmatized by others; (d) CLD students miss out on the academic content being taught when they are away from their grade-level classroom (Linquanti, 1999).
Push-In ESL Programs	• Use many of the same teaching techniques as ESL pull-out, such as scaffolding instruction. • CLD students remain with grade-level peers for the full day, receiving support and clarification within the classroom. Depending on program design, an ESL teacher might team-teach or assist the classroom teacher in making lessons comprehensible for CLD students, or an instructional aide might also provide differentiated support. • Benefits include less segregation due to language differences, integration, and exposure to grade-appropriate content material. • Goal of transitioning students to English (www.hunter.cuny.edu/nycbetac/questions.html).
Structured English Immersion (SEI)	• Takes on numerous forms depending on the political, economic, and sociocultural aspects of the community. • Classes in which CLD students, preferably who share a common native language, are taught within the same classroom unit. All instruction in English, but teachers may possess receptive skills in students' native language. • *Example:* Arizona's SEI programs are aligned with the state's relatively strict English-only education laws (A.R.S. §15-751). SEI classrooms defined as those that teach English language development (as opposed to content-area material) for 4 hours per day (www.ade.state.az.us).

Content-Based ESL and Sheltered English Instruction (SI)	• Content-based ESL comprised solely of CLD students; taught by ESL educators. • Goals that characterize content-based ESL instruction: (a) develop students' English language skills; (b) prepare students for entry into grade-level classroom (Echevarría, Vogt, & Short, 2008). • Content-based ESL addresses grade-level topics in addition to English language development. • Concerns about the potential of content-based ESL to be remedial in nature if content in these courses is characterized by topics that students might not have been exposed to if they are new to the U.S. school system (Echevarría et al., 2008). • SI seeks to integrate grade-level content topics simultaneously with language instruction. • In SI, content-area teachers modify instruction to make content comprehensible for CLD students (Echevarría et al., 2008). • SI classes usually taught by grade-level teachers, not ESL teachers.
Additive/Developmental Bilingual Programs— **Development of Students' Native Language and Second Language (e.g., English) Is Fostered**	
Developmental Bilingual Education	• Also known as "late-exit bilingual" or "maintenance" programs; implemented in a wide variety of ways. • Teaches content-area subject matter in both the CLD students' native language *and* in English. • Rooted in the belief that CLD students bring cultural and linguistic assets to be incorporated into the classroom environment (Cummins, 1998). • Encourages involvement of parents, who may not speak English fluently. • Typically begins in early years of schooling (K–1st grade) and continues as long as is feasible in the school district.
Two-Way Immersion Programs	• A form of bilingual education; also known as "two-way bilingual" or "maintenance bilingual" programs. • Designed with the linguistic and academic needs of both CLD students *and* native English speakers in mind. • Typically takes place during elementary school years. • Main goals: (a) students obtain high levels of proficiency in native language; (b) students develop high levels of proficiency in second language; (c) both groups attain academic proficiency at grade level; (d) students develop respect and positive cross-cultural attitudes (Howard & Christian, 2002). • Criteria include: equal number of students in each of the groups (i.e., native English speakers and language minority students). These two groups are integrated and interact in *content-area* lessons (Howard & Christian, 2002).
Heritage Language/ Indigenous Language Programs	• A heritage language learner is "a person studying a language who has proficiency in or a cultural connection to that language" (Kelleher, 2008a, p. 5) and comes from a home in which a language in addition to English is spoken or understood (Valdés, 2000). • Heritage language refers to the home and/or ancestral language of students; applies to students across a range of language proficiency, from no/low proficiency to high proficiency (Valdés, 2001). • More than 6,000 heritage language schools in the United States, teaching 145 different languages, including 91 indigenous American Indian languages (Kelleher, 2008b). • Heritage language programs can be community-based (i.e., organized and funded through private organizations) or take place within the public K–12 sector (Kelleher, 2008b), although they are frequently categorized as two-way immersion programs. • Indigenous language programs promote the learning of American Indian languages. Most American Indian languages are in danger of becoming obsolete if steps are not taken to preserve and support them (Wright, 2007). • Children learn only 10% of the 175 existing American Indian languages (www.cal.org). • The Bureau of Indian Affairs funded 184 elementary and secondary schools, on 64 reservations in 23 states, for more than 48,000 students in 2007–2008 (www.doi.gov/bia/).

FIGURE 1.3	
Cognitive Academic Language Learning Approach (CALLA)	
Basic Premises	CALLA, which takes into account theories on cognition, is founded on the following key ideas: • Learning strategies should be explicitly taught to CLD students; most students will benefit from this instruction. • Knowledge of academic language is critical for CLD students' success in school. • ESL curricula should incorporate grade-level content concepts to prepare CLD students for the grade-level (mainstream) classroom.
Components	**Three Types of Learner Strategies** CALLA instruction incorporates the usage of three strategy types: metacognitive, cognitive, and social affective. • *Metacognitive strategies* are those that "enable one to anticipate or plan for a task, determine how successfully the plan is being executed, and then evaluate the success of the learning and the plan after learning activities have been completed" (Chamot & O'Malley, 1994, p. 61). Some examples of these strategies include directed attention, selective attention, organizational planning, self-monitoring, and self-evaluation. A learner can apply metacognitive strategies widely across many domains. • *Cognitive strategies* can be classified into rehearsal, organization, and elaboration strategies. Whereas metacognitive strategies can be applied widely across many domains, cognitive strategies are connected to the completion of individual tasks and include classification/grouping, note-taking, summarizing, inferencing, and elaboration of prior knowledge. • *Social/affective strategies* refer to both students working with one another to enhance language and content learning as well as students using self-talk to guide learning. These strategies are concerned with lowering students' affective filters (Krashen, 1982) or reducing their anxiety so that they are more likely to learn the content at hand. Questioning for clarification is another social/affective strategy that learners can use to aid their own learning.

Application of the input hypothesis to classroom practice requires that the teacher have knowledge of the following aspects of the learner:

- Native language
- Proficiency in speaking, reading, and writing the native language
- Stage of English language development
- Preferred interaction style
- Cultural discourse patterns
- Cultural relevance of the topic at hand

The student's ability to attend to potential input during the teaching and learning process depends on the existence of suitable learning contexts and conditions within the classroom. Teachers striving to create opportunities that support students in progressing one step beyond their current level of performance must not only understand the theoretical underpinnings of second language acquisition, but also reflect upon how a student's biography influences language learning. Chapter 3 of this book elaborates on how Krashen's findings can assist this process.

Vygotsky and the Zone of Proximal Development

The work of Lev Vygotsky also has contributed to our understanding of how to take students from their current point of development to the next level, but unlike Krashen, in his research Vygotsky adopts a perspective that involves all types of academic learning. Vygotsky's formulation of ideal learning conditions is termed the *zone of proximal development* (ZPD), which is defined as "the distance between the actual developmental level as determined by independent problem solving and the level of potential development as determined through problem solving under adult guidance or in collaboration with more capable peers" (1978, p. 86). Vygotsky posits that all individuals have the potential to learn and that learning is highly dependent upon the particular context, situation, and social interac-

Components *(continued)*	**Phases of CALLA Instruction**
	CALLA instruction is conducted in five phases: preparation, presentation, practice, evaluation, and expansion (Chamot & O'Malley, 1994).
	• *Preparation Phase.* During this phase, the teacher takes time to explicitly discover what students already know about a particular concept. Here, the teacher might also discover that students are familiar with certain concepts in their native language, but they have conceptualized them in a manner different from how they will be taught in the upcoming lesson. In this phase, the teacher presents both the content and language objectives for the new topic and employs activities such as brainstorming, creating graphic organizers, and role-playing to stimulate student interest in the subject matter and encourage prediction-making.
	• *Presentation Phase.* In this phase, the teacher purposefully scaffolds new information being presented based on what the teacher learned about students' prior knowledge during the preparation phase. Special attention is paid to making new information meaningful to students by illustrating how the information relates to students' prior academic learning. Throughout this phase, the teacher models ways students can ask for clarification if they do not understand certain concepts, as well as ways to respond to higher order comprehension questions.
	• *Practice Phase.* In this learner-directed phase, students are encouraged to work cooperatively to enhance their content and language learning simultaneously. A particular emphasis is placed on the development of students' CALP as they work in cooperative groups using hands-on activities. In the practice phase, the teacher provides guidance and encourages cooperation over competition as students work together.
	• *Practice Phase.* In this learner-directed phase, students are encouraged to work cooperatively to enhance their content and language learning simultaneously. A particular emphasis is placed on the development of students' CALP as they work in cooperative groups using hands-on activities. In the practice phase, the teacher provides guidance and encourages cooperation over competition as students work together.
	• *Evaluation Phase.* This phase consists of students evaluating their own performance through the use of cognitive and social/affective strategies such as summarizing and checking predictions put forth in the preparation phase. Importance is placed on students' self-evaluation as opposed to teacher evaluation of their performance.
	• *Expansion Phase.* In this final phase, students take part in activities that help them integrate personal meaning with the new knowledge they are gaining and reflect on how some of their previous thoughts on the topic might need to be revised. The teacher also helps students see how new knowledge can be applied in various contexts. He or she facilitates activities that promote students' application of new learning across contexts.
Supporting Research	The CALLA model of instruction is driven by cognitive theory (Anderson, 1976, 1983, 1985) and its application to second language acquisition processes. According to cognitive theory, learners are active participants in the learning and meaning-building process: "learners select information from the environment, organize the information, relate it to what they already know, retain what they consider to be important, use the information in appropriate contexts, and reflect on the success of their learning efforts" (Chamot & O'Malley, 1994, p. 13).
What Biography-Driven Instruction Can Contribute to CALLA	• Emphasizes strategies that are cognitively anchored to students' cultures • Provides consistent opportunities for students to record their initial schematic, especially cultural, connections to the topic so that they can modify/elaborate upon these connections throughout the lesson • Utilizes students' native language as a springboard for both linguistic and academic development

FIGURE 1.4

Specially Designed Academic Instruction in English (SDAIE)

Basic Premises	SDAIE (California State Department of Education, 1994) refers to the sheltering of *academic, content-area material* for CLD students at intermediate to advanced levels of English proficiency. Like CALLA, SDAIE promotes content-rich, cognitively challenging, and grade-appropriate instruction for CLD students. SDAIE is the precursor to the more formalized Sheltered Instruction Observation Protocol (SIOP®) model. SDAIE emphasizes the simultaneous nature of both language and content-area development.
Components	SDAIE promotes the use of hands-on activities, visual clues, cooperative learning, and guarded vocabulary in order to make content comprehensible for CLD students. More than 25 specific strategies are listed on the California State Department of Education Web site (http://pubs.cde.ca.gov/tcsii/documentlibrary/englishlearners.aspx#fn4). Some of these strategies include modifying texts to increase comprehensibility, enlisting the help of peer/adult tutors, and relating new material to real-life examples. Through implementation of these features, CLD students are provided with access to grade-level content while developing their English language skills.
Supporting Research	Research supporting sheltered instruction includes Vygotsky's (1962) theory of social cognitive development and Krashen and Terrell's (1983) theory of comprehensible input. According to Vygotsky, social interaction is a critical aspect of children's cognitive development. Vygotsky stresses the importance of students working with a "more knowledgeable other" (i.e., teacher, tutor, peer) who provides the necessary direction to guide the learner toward new learning. Krashen and Terrell underscore the role of comprehensible input in the language acquisition process by stating that CLD students must receive input (both oral and written) just slightly more advanced than their current level of English language proficiency in order for learning to occur. This is referred to as the $i+1$ level.
What Biography-Driven Instruction Can Contribute to SDAIE	• Challenges teachers to create conditions and situations that allow students to share what they bring to the lesson and that support students in taking ownership of the learning process • Supports teachers in strategically and systematically addressing the linguistic and academic needs of students at all stages of second language acquisition • Guides teachers to use comprehensible input to ensure cognitively demanding instructional conversations, while continually monitoring students' states of mind

tion. Aljaafreh and Lantolf (1994) describe the ZPD as "the framework, par excellence, which brings all of the pieces of the learning setting together—the teacher, the learner, their social and cultural history, their goals and motives, as well as the resources available to them, including those that are dialogically constructed together" (p. 468).

Commonalities in the Contributions of Krashen and Vygotsky

It is easy to understand how comparisons of these two great thinkers have come to be part of discussions regarding the education of CLD students. Current conversations have drawn a parallel between Vygotsky's ZPD and Krashen's $i+1$ construct (Ellis, 1997; Nyikos & Hashimoto, 1997). According to Guerra (1996), Krashen's i "is what

Vygotsky called the actual development of the child" and "the $i+1$ stage is the equivalent to Vygotsky's zone of proximal development. It refers to the kind of input that is at a level of difficulty which immediately follows the i stage" (p. 7).

Using these two theories, in conjunction, to inform practice has the potential to move CLD students one step beyond—both linguistically and academically. However, to maximize this potential, we must guard against oversimplifying what it means to determine the i, or the actual development of the student. We must value multiple perspectives on what counts as "knowledge" rather than allowing our view of a student's current level of development to be limited by the results of standardized tests.

Even before we think about strategies and tactics for taking theory into practice, we must examine the attitudes

FIGURE 1.5

Sheltered Instruction Observation Protocol (SIOP®) Model

Basic Premises	Originally developed as a research and supervisory tool, the SIOP® protocol was first used to document teachers' implementation of key features of sheltered instruction. Teachers then suggested that the SIOP protocol be used as a lesson planning tool and delivery system, and this led to the creation of the SIOP model. SIOP lesson plans are based on the premise that "language acquisition is enhanced through meaningful use and interaction" (Echevarría et al., 2008, p. 16). According to Echevarría et al., "Sheltered instruction is an approach for teaching content to English learners (ELs) in strategic ways that make the subject matter concepts comprehensible while promoting the students' English language development" (p. 5).
Components	SIOP® is comprised of eight components: (a) lesson preparation, (b) building background, (c) comprehensible input, (d) strategies, (e) interaction, (f) practice/application, (g) lesson delivery, and (h) review/assessment. Within these eight components are 30 features that describe each one in further detail. The components and features focus broadly on teaching declarative knowledge (i.e., facts), procedural knowledge (i.e., the steps that students take to accomplish an academic task), study skills, and learning strategies (see description of CALLA, Figure 1.3, for examples of these strategies). Teachers who implement SIOP ensure that information related to content, activities, classroom procedures, and so forth is comprehensible to students. They use multiple strategies and techniques as they scaffold instruction and connect what students know with new knowledge and skills. For example, they support less advanced language learners with more proficient language peers during student grouping, and they draw on the native language as a bridge to students' English language acquisition and academic success. Teachers who use SIOP emphasize student development of all literacy domains (i.e., listening, speaking, reading, writing) during every lesson. They explicitly guide students to use learning strategies as they grapple with new language and content. At the end of each lesson, teachers review key vocabulary and concepts.
Supporting Research	Similar to SDAIE, the SIOP® model is based on Vygotsky's (1978) research regarding the importance of social interaction and personal meaning construction during the learning process. The creators of SIOP explain that "In effective SIOP lessons, there is a high level of student engagement and interaction with the teacher, with other students, and with text, which leads to elaborated discourse and critical thinking" (Echevarría et al., 2008, p. 17). Another aspect of SIOP lessons is the inclusion of activities based on Gardner's (1993) Theory of Multiple Intelligences.
What Biography-Driven Instruction Can Contribute to SIOP®	• Utilizes students' home and community-situated discourse patterns as a bridge to academic language development • Allows the student's biography and linguistic assets to inform instructional decisions related to preassessment, grouping configurations, assessment, and so forth • Supports students' connections from the *known* (background knowledge) to the *unknown* (new material) through techniques such as teacher revoicing

and beliefs guiding our current efforts with CLD students. Take a moment to reflect upon the following questions:

- What factors influence the way your daily instruction looks?
- How do you document the actual developmental linguistic and academic levels of your students?
- What types of observations do you make throughout the lesson to gain insight into how CLD students understand (or do not understand) vocabulary, concepts, and tasks?
- How do you use grouping configurations to promote social interaction and learning?
- What kinds of strategies do you use to move students from their existing knowledge and skills to a thorough understanding of new curricular material?

In classrooms where cultural and linguistic diversity is the norm, it is essential that instruction be designed to take *all* learners beyond their current level of development.

According to Vygotsky (1956), "Instruction is good only when it proceeds ahead of development. It then awakens and rouses to life those functions which are in a stage of maturing, which lie in the zone of proximal development. It is in this way that instruction plays an extremely important role in development" (p. 278). The type of activity or strategy selected to begin the lesson is important to "rousing" each learner's developing understandings and skills, as well as his or her past experiences and existing knowledge. As learning starts to move forward, the students and the teacher continually connect the past to the present, and the present to the future, through social interactions. For this reason, teaching and learning that are organized around Krashen's and Vygotsky's constructs necessarily involve planning, teaching, and assessing with the biographies of the learners in mind.

Research into How the Brain Learns

If the zone of proximal development and $i+1$ prepare us for asking questions about what contexts and situations are best for taking students—regardless of background—to the next level linguistically and academically, current brain research sets the stage for teachers' understanding of the kinds of learning conditions that support the brain in perceiving input, making sense of it, and effectively storing it for future use. According to Sousa (2006), "The total of all that is in our long-term storage areas forms the basis for our view of the world around us. This information helps us to make sense out of events, to understand the laws of nature, to recognize cause and effect, and to form decisions about goodness, truth, and beauty" (p. 52).

Students bring this view of the world, which Sousa calls our *cognitive belief system,* when they enter school. Often teachers are not prepared to help students activate and bridge from the world view constructed in their past to the present, and from the present to the future. Yet working in the present and disregarding the past puts CLD students at a disadvantage from the start. We must prepare lessons that take learners from what they know to an understanding of the unknown, new information. Engaging the brain requires that learners be motivated and supported to learn. This, according to Sousa, requires teachers to use strategies that promote students' personal connections to the curriculum and that hold every student accountable for his or her learning.

Although this book cannot hope to fully do justice to cognitive science by providing an in-depth guide to what brain researchers tell us about the self in relation to learning, it offers introductory ways to think about how CLD

FIGURE 1.6

Monitoring Our Inclusive Practice

- Get to know the biographies of your students. Who are they?
- Listen to what students have to say, and use their voice as your point of departure to make lessons meaningful.
- Create an environment that values interaction for both social and academic tasks.
- Select strategies that maximize students' self-knowledge, create low-risk learning environments, and support students in integrating new information with their existing understandings.
- Make time to affirm and celebrate language, culture, and learning.

---

students' background knowledge relates to our classroom ecology—that is, to the students, the teacher, the community, and all the other dimensions and dynamics of classroom practice. Manipulating the ecology in effective ways then becomes a matter of asking questions that are not so much *What do I need to make my CLD students academically successful?* but rather *Who is here?* and *What does this mean for my teaching practice?* Jensen (2006) poses the following suggestion: "Think less in terms of what *one thing you can do* and start thinking in terms of *creating conditions for contrast*" (p. 207). In saying this, he refers to the need for us to create places where students are always anticipating the challenge and excitement of the new learning that lies ahead. Figure 1.6 suggests ways to create these conditions in practice, which will be discussed in detail throughout this book.

What the teacher does before, during, and after the lesson creates the "contrasting environments" to which Jensen refers—environments that provide opportunities for students' exploration, learning, and growth. These kinds of environments are possible only when the classroom provides conditions and situations that are "substantially richer" than what the student already is exposed to or knows. Much like the constructs of Krashen and Vygotsky, brain research reminds us that in order to "invite" the brain to learn, the teacher must value what each student brings to the learning situation and create engaging circumstances to challenge each brain. I call this process "getting oxygen to the brain," and it requires that teachers:

- Keep students "on their toes" as they engage in the lesson.
- Allow students to negotiate the curriculum in multiple ways and through interaction with multiple people.

- Work with students to co-create new models for information by integrating the curriculum with the knowledge that each member of the learning community, regardless of background, brings to the learning endeavor.

Strategies and activities can be used to support students as they construct meaning by activating what they know and work with others to build understanding. Ultimately, our guidance should result in students using their newfound or elaborated knowledge and skills to analyze, synthesize, evaluate, and create ideas relevant to their learning. This is what taking students "one step beyond" is all about. Information that is linked to the past, experienced in the present, and taken into permanent memory is more likely to be available to the learner in the future.

Unfortunately, many classrooms where CLD students find themselves today do little to invite students, with their unique histories, experiences, knowledge, and personalities, to engage in learning. Jensen (2006) says it best when he reminds us:

> Many students struggle through school, never finding out what their learning styles are, their passions, their strongest talents, or their preferred modes of communication. This puts them at a tremendous disadvantage because it is their strengths that will help them cope and even thrive in this world. (p. 209)

The standardized test movement challenges professionals to strategically and systematically select strategies that respond to the needs of all learners, rather than succumb to the more "drill-and-kill" approach that has become prevalent, where students are asked to "repeat after me" in lessons that are so scripted that even the teacher's brain struggles to remain engaged. Such lessons leave little hope that students will be motivated to learn. In classrooms where the culture and language of CLD students are not valued, the brain often shuts down, and little or no thinking takes place.

For optimal thinking and learning to occur, all aspects of the classroom must be designed with the learner in mind. When we think about the classroom only in terms of a physical environment—for example, as related to arranging desks in a certain way because it meets the demands of "the way I teach"—we limit our opportunities to create brain- and student-compatible places where activities and strategies can bring school and learning to life for CLD and other students. Furthermore, when envisioning ways to create contexts and situations conducive to learning, it is helpful to think about the lesson in three distinct phases: *activation* (before), *connection* (during), and *affirmation* (after). I offer a brief introduction to these phases here; each will be further elaborated in subsequent chapters of this book.

- ***Activation.*** If we believe, as brain research tells us, that new information is learned only if the new information can be attached to something that is known or has meaning for the learner, it becomes critical that teachers look for ways to *activate* CLD students' background knowledge. Strategies implemented before the lesson can provide opportunities for students to share, or make public, what they know about the curricular concepts, language, and skills being covered. But what good is it to ignite, or activate, background knowledge, and then leave it in the dust as we proceed into the lesson to introduce new concepts? Successful activation requires that we remain present to observe when and how the student activates the brain, listening for insights about his or her knowledge that can be taken into the lesson. To support students in making meaningful links to new learning, we must first learn what they know!

- ***Connection.*** Cognitive research tells us that the human brain has roughly a 30-second holding pattern for new information that enters (Sousa, 2006). This means that if a student determines that the information is of little or no importance, it's gone. If, in the activation phase, we have made note of the knowledge and associations that students already possess related to the lesson, we can more easily find ways during the lesson to make the curriculum relevant to the students. In this way, students are more likely to retain new information in their memory for a substantially longer period of time, long enough to actively make sense of it. During the lesson, the teacher takes on the role of facilitating learning and creating conditions that encourage learners to practice and apply new vocabulary and concepts in meaningful and interactive ways. It takes multiple meaningful exposures, with different people and for a variety of purposes, for students to come to a thorough understanding and take ownership of the new information.

- ***Affirmation.*** Regardless of an individual student's linguistic or academic starting point, all learners need to have their learning affirmed. The importance of this principle cannot be overstated. Affirmation must be given in a way that lets students know their effort during the lesson was worth it: "Look at what you have learned!" By providing time in the "after" phase of the lesson for one final review and rehearsal of the new information, we prepare students to individually demonstrate their learning. Then, at the end of the lesson, we can ask students to complete assessment tasks, knowing that we have provided students with the tools and understandings they need to succeed. Students do not want to be asked to produce something that is out of reach—they want a chance to show others what they learned. Acceptance and affirmation lead learners to not fear taking risks in their learning, because they already know the teacher and their peers value them as learners. When we expect everyone to learn and hold everyone accountable for learning—*believing and communicating to students that everyone has potential*—we will begin to see the results we work so hard to achieve!

Brain research provides insights that can help us as we strive to create the conditions that allow students to reach their zone of proximal development, or receive $i+1$ input. Such research enables us to better understand how learners perceive, work with, and store new information. The key to all of these processes is our knowledge of each student's biography. Rather than relying solely on the results of standardized tests to tell us what students know and can do, the most effective educators of CLD and other students employ strategies that delve into students' long-term memories to expose the wealth of their knowledge and experiences, which combine to form the fundamental core beliefs and understandings that affect their interpretation of new material. Using these student understandings to guide our subsequent decisions about instruction and assessment results in biography-driven decision-making.

The use of relevant strategies before, during, and after the lesson will support students' comprehension and storage of new content and language input. As Willis (2006) states, educators must learn how to "hone strategies to guide students' brains to more effective focusing; sustained attentiveness; and active learning, storing, connecting, and retrieval of learned material" (p. ix). In this way, we can enable students to move from memorizing isolated facts to internalizing understandings that are personally relevant in the present and available for the future. No one can be forced to learn. We can only encourage, support, and thus motivate students to join the community of learners on their educational journey.

Culturally Responsive Teaching

No one would intentionally deny students the opportunity to bring their "historical self" into the classroom. Nor would we ever want to deny students their language or culture while we teach. However, creating a learning ecology that is culturally relevant and responsive to CLD students requires more than good intentions. To do so effectively, requires thoughtful planning, continuous learning, and perhaps most importantly, conscious reflection on our most deeply held beliefs and assumptions. Many have written of what it means to teach in culturally responsive ways (e.g., Gay, 2000; Ladson-Billings, 1995; Nieto, 2000; Ogbu & Simons, 1998).

Each of these educators and researchers agrees about the need for:

- Holding high expectations
- Valuing families' and students' ways of being
- Creating contexts where all voices are provided an opportunity to be heard
- Creating classroom ecologies that care and respect the student, regardless of background
- Using what is learned about students' biographies to plan lessons that are meaningful to the learner

Working in schools, I am guided by the ideas and words of Geneva Gay, who describes what it means to be culturally responsive in classroom practice. She states:

Culturally responsive teaching is defined as using the cultural characteristics, experiences, and perspectives of ethnically diverse students as conduits for teaching them more effectively. It is based on the assumption that when academic knowledge and skills are situated within the lived experiences and frames of reference of students, they are more personally meaningful, have higher interest appeal, and are learned more easily and thoroughly (Gay, 2000). As a result, the academic achievement of ethnically diverse students will improve when they are taught through their own cultural and experiential filters. (2002, p. 106)

I am continually reminded that we cannot hope to achieve our goal of having CLD students learn within their zone of proximal development, or through $i+1$ input, unless we know who they are and what they dream of becoming in the future. Every student has dreams. When classrooms become places where failure is seen as just another opportunity to learn, students risk without fear. According to Gay (2000), "Culturally responsive teaching is a means for unleashing the higher learning potentials of ethnically diverse students by simultaneously cultivating their academic and psychosocial abilities" (p. 20). This can only happen in contexts that care for and respect the uniqueness of every student.

In culturally responsive classrooms, teachers not only make decisions about their teaching based on their students' biographies, they often take on the challenge of doing so in socio-politically charged environments. Such environments draw out the courage of educators, enabling them to become advocates for doing what is right for CLD students. Thanks to the courage of such teachers, all students can be challenged and supported to become critical thinkers and learners who look forward to taking the next steps in reaching their dreams.

Teaching and Learning in the Third Space

In classrooms across the country, CLD students and their teachers are brought together to make sense of the multiple institutional agendas and expectations of schooling. In these classrooms, spaces are created that can be transformative or oppressive, depending on how teachers make decisions and organize learning environments. When educators work to move beyond the status quo, CLD students' biographies, knowledge, and Discourse are valued and utilized beyond superficial attempts to "celebrate" students' culture and language. Gee (1990) defines *Discourse* (with a capital D) as commonly shared "ways of using language, of thinking, believing, valuing, and of acting" (p. 143). Discourse shapes our way of knowing as we interact and build relationships with our families and communities, including our classroom communities.

Gee's conceptualization of Discourse is closely linked to the idea of *funds of knowledge* (Moll et al., 1992), which highlights the wealth of knowledge and resources that students accumulate from their homes, families, and communities. Discourse and funds of knowledge, although tied to a student's culture, are situated within a student's unique, individual biography. Teachers who capitalize on students' ways of knowing and interacting with the world understand that CLD students' assets have the potential to accelerate learning and create true teaching and learning communities.

More often than not, however, CLD students' assets are left untapped because the classroom does not provide a place for them to become part of the curriculum. Teachers often have not been prepared to recognize this kind of information or use it to differentiate instruction. Kris Gutiérrez and colleagues (e.g., Gutiérrez, 2008; Gutiérrez, Rymes, & Larson, 1995) provide some thought-provoking ideas on conceptualizing a "space" within the classroom where the negotiation of disparate assets, demands, expectations, and needs becomes possible. Uncovering, discovering, and utilizing students' funds of knowledge and Discourse during instruction enables us to bring together what Gutiérrez et al. (2003) refer to as the "official space," characterized by the teacher's Discourse and the school curriculum, and the "unofficial space," characterized by the students' background knowledge and thoughts related to the curriculum, to create "third space" classroom conditions that make it possible for students and the teacher to jointly negotiate Discourse and knowledge in ways that make the curriculum truly relevant to the student. This third space is an indicator of culturally relevant and responsive classrooms.

According to Gutiérrez et al. (2003), the third space can be described as a place in which "alternative and competing discourses and positionings transform conflict and difference into rich zones of collaboration and learning" (p. 171). Taking students to their zones of proximal development requires more than superficial ways of thinking about and using prior knowledge. When teachers create conditions and situations in which they activate, connect, and affirm the multiple dimensions of CLD students' biographies, third spaces become the norm.

Making It Happen! How This Book Can Guide Your Next Steps

Now more than ever it is important to understand teaching and learning from a more sociocultural and humanistic perspective, using a "lens" that focuses our attention on the student and not on current political agendas. As educators, each of us wants to do what is best for all students; yet we can often become overwhelmed with all that comes our way from the sociopolitical climate we work in, the school culture we find ourselves in, and the magnitude of the curricular and assessment demands that are imposed upon us.

For too long we have danced around what it means to be "student centered" when it comes to instructional practices for this growing population. In this book, I make more explicit what it means to teach CLD students. This book adds to the discussion of sheltered instruction, differentiated instruction, and other methods and philosophies that work to enhance educational opportunities for all students.

The first goal of this book is to provide educators with a strong foundation for understanding the following four critical dimensions of the learner's biography:

- *Sociocultural Dimension.* This dimension represents what a student brings to school from the "resources" he or she has learned from birth. Although these understandings and skills may differ from prevailing definitions of what "counts" before a child enters school, for the CLD student they represent the treasures of his or her life. Exploration of this dimension must move beyond simple interest surveys and toward an understanding and utilization of students' funds of knowledge, as they relate to the content of our daily lessons.
- *Linguistic Dimension.* Language is not a static number on a test. Rather, language is the dynamic tool we use to express our thoughts and to communicate about, and comprehend the daily interactions that surround us. Becoming prepared to educate CLD students involves the skill of listening beyond the spoken word, where our efforts to understand become a gift that allows us entry into the student's heart and mind. Many say that our language cannot be separated from our culture. Our instruction can profit more from active listening and making connections to a student's culture than from knowing a student's particular score on a test.

- *Cognitive Dimension.* Have you ever been fascinated in watching a student and wondered how it was that they creatively solved the problem at hand without you? When we teach, questions related to students' approach to problem solving can seem perplexing at times. Yet, we know that all individuals take different paths when making decisions, solving a problem, or sharing a story. A student's culture has great influence on his or her way of thinking, knowing, and applying information. If throughout lessons we provide a "gallery" for students to "exhibit" their thoughts and learning, we provide an opportunity for their culture and language to make themselves visible that otherwise would not likely exist in the school.

- *Academic Dimension.* Academic success can usually be equated with the level of access that has been afforded to the individual, particularly if quality education has been denied due to a student's level of linguistic ability or socioeconomic background. How is it then that we can profess to provide an equitable opportunity for every CLD student who enters school? Every CLD student has the potential to learn and become proficient in the English language. If we rely less on the test and focus more on the learner, then we may move forward toward creating places where every child's potential is realized.

This book places these four dimensions at the center of decision making for reaching the zone of proximal development with our CLD students. By really learning about the biography of the student, and placing that understanding at the center of the context provided by our knowledge of culturally relevant pedagogy and brain research, we set the stage for the selection of tools and strategies to meet the CLD student halfway during instruction. The strategies provided in this book go a step beyond the measures currently taken in most classrooms to make CLD students an integral part of the meaning-making process. This book is intended to provide educators with tools for reflection on their current habits of practice with CLD students, from the creation of classroom ecology to the use of what students share in making decisions about how to assess students' linguistic and academic growth.

In biography-driven instruction for CLD students, *the journey truly is the destination.* Just as it is for our students as they navigate new content in our classrooms, *every successful step along the way constitutes its own arrival.* As you undertake this journey, I encourage you to think about what you already do in your teaching that is connected to the perspectives and strategies recommended here, while remaining open to other approaches you may never have considered before. It is not possible, nor is it necessary, to perfectly incorporate every new idea as soon as you are introduced to it. Rather, begin the journey with a simple willingness to shift perspective. This openness to re-envisioning what is possible has the potential to set your feet on the path to enhanced classroom practice, and your heart on the academic success of all students.

CHAPTER 2

Biography-Driven Instruction

EVERY JOURNEY we make begins with an understanding of the basic reasons why we are making the trip. It might be for business, pleasure, a family visit, or in response to an unexpected event. The journey of becoming competent in working with culturally and linguistically diverse students in the classroom is no different.

For most of us, part of the decision to become a teacher hinged on our interest in children as individuals—in the unique character of the students we could imagine ourselves teaching. Our vision of these students was framed by our own experiences in classrooms and the community in which we were socialized. However, the reality we may have faced when we arrived in our first classroom, and the reality we more frequently face in our classrooms today, is usually far removed from the initial "myth" in which we believed. Part of what has changed in our classrooms is the presence of greater numbers of CLD students, who both challenge and reward our best teaching efforts. The journey toward becoming a more effective teacher of CLD students begins with the intent to raise our own awareness of how the uniqueness and individuality of each learner can factor into student learning.

This chapter introduces and describes the elements that comprise the *biopsychosocial* history of the CLD student. This complex term encompasses the many facets that define the individuality of each student in a classroom. This chapter also describes the four interrelated dimensions of the CLD student biography that were introduced at the end of Chapter 1—the sociocultural, linguistic, cognitive, and academic dimensions—and explores the sociocultural dimension from two different perspectives. The goal in this chapter is to move beyond school-initiated definitions and notions of the sociocultural dimension and toward culturally relevant pedagogy. Culturally relevant pedagogy, as described by Gay (2000), places students at the center of teaching and learning. When we take the risk of stepping outside the boundaries often set for us in schools, we provide opportunities for students to express knowledge and understanding that is more deeply rooted in their culture, language, and life experiences. In this way, we, as part of an educational system, begin the journey of accelerating CLD students' academic development.

This chapter guides you to explore the following questions:

- How is the sociocultural/emotional dimension tied to my teaching and students' learning?
- What role does politics play in classroom teaching?
- How does the climate of the school/classroom make a difference in academic learning?

For every concept you will learn in this chapter, there is an *exception to the rule.* Every thought and action will take its own unique path based on the biographies of the students in your specific setting. As you read this chapter, remind yourself that it is *you* who will use the information to create your own road toward optimal learning. By exploring the biographies of your students and the context in which they live and learn, you will come to realize the many unique opportunities you have for reaching every CLD student in your classroom.

Biopsychosocial History

The concept of biopsychosocial history can best be understood by thinking about the many facets of our own lives. Within our own unique complexity, we educators can begin to understand the CLD student. *Biopsychosocial history* is simply a term used to describe the most basic elements of human experience, which include the *biological, psychological,* and *sociological* aspects of an individual (Engel, 1977; Gates & Hutchinson, 2005; Herrera, Murry,

& Morales Cabral, 2007; Saleebey, 2001). We do not have to know how to spell *biopsychosocial* or commit the order of the component parts to memory. We *do* have to know and understand how these aspects impact the motivation, engagement, and learning of each and every one of us. Students come to us with their own unique cultural and linguistic backgrounds. Within these backgrounds, we can find the key that unlocks their potential for academic success.

Biological Aspects

As educators, we have little to do with the biological dimensions of the students in our classrooms. These aspects are determined well before the time the students arrive in school. However, we can be concerned and ask questions such as:

- Has the student had an eye examination?
- Has the student had a hearing test?
- Does the student have any special needs?

CLD students may not have had access to regular checkups to ascertain their physical needs, and such circumstances can have implications for their learning.

Migrant children, for example, have a high incidence of hearing loss due to lack of medical care at a young age. Often ear infections go untreated, and this can lead to students' difficulty in learning to read using current programs based on knowledge of English sounds, such as phonics. Additionally, many English sounds are "pruned," or discarded by the brain as unneeded, when not used by age 10 (Jensen, 2000). Such pruning has implications for students' reading and comprehension in the future. Although we cannot control biological factors, we can observe and seek attention for the medical needs of our students. Frequently, schools provide students with hearing, speech, and vision exams. If such services are not available at the school, referrals to appropriate clinics or organizations can be given.

Psychological Aspects

Most CLD students who arrive in our classrooms from another country did not ask to leave their community, their native language, and their culture to come to a new and exciting place. Frequently, CLD students must transition

Asking students to respond to questions that provide insights into their lived experiences and states of mind as they participate in school activities helps us connect to their emotional and psychological needs.

—*Mohamad Abdullah, Elementary, Kansas*

quickly from an environment that includes friends and close family ties to an environment a great distance from "home." They must deal with uncertainty on a daily basis. We educators, therefore, must prepare ourselves to understand and navigate the state of mind a student may find himself or herself in during instruction. We can begin to understand and respond to a student's state of mind by:

- Learning about past schooling experiences through a "Getting to Know You Journal"
- Asking students to discuss or write about feelings related to the old and new school, community, or country
- Learning about the reasons parents decided to move to the new community
- Designing grouping configurations based on linguistic proficiencies, country of origin, empathy level of peers, and affective needs of the CLD student

Students are asked to brainstorm about the events and experiences they consider most important in their life. The teacher then connects the things that the learning community has in common.

—*Jamie Williams, Bilingual 3rd Grade, Iowa*

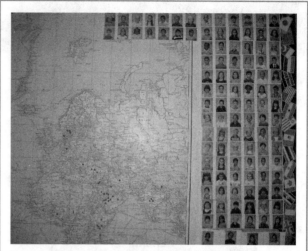

Every student has a place of origin. Immediately upon entering Hillcrest Elementary, members of the school and extended community are presented with the amazing diversity that makes the school such a dynamic and exciting place.

We may feel as though we are probing into the lives of our students and asking for information they consider private. Although this can be a concern, learning more about a student's life can inform us as educators about the sociocultural and resiliency factors that may be supporting or inhibiting the student's learning. Therefore, do not be afraid to gently learn from your student and his or her family about their fears, frustrations, and successes. Sharing our stories and reaching out is what connects us as human beings—and as teachers and learners.

Sociological Aspects

We rarely think about the influence that society has on what we teach, how we teach it, and why we teach it. Yet societal influences, which are often political, have implications for us as teachers and for CLD students as learners. How often do we feel disappointed by decisions made about the program and curriculum that must be used or about the assessments that will be used to assess the level of our students' academic growth? These decisions about programming, curriculum, and assessment that influence what happens to students are often dictated by the politics of the day or district mandates driven by individuals who may not understand the needs of CLD students and families.

In the midst of this outside pressure, we must continually reflect on why we teach. For most of us, our commitment to teaching might involve the desire to reach students and develop the citizens of our country and world. By asking ourselves the following questions, we become better able to navigate the politics of our school, community, state, and nation, and we ready ourselves to move forward in doing what we were prepared to do—teach students.

- Is the surrounding community welcoming toward immigrants and those who bring diverse languages, cultures, and religious beliefs?
- Is my school welcoming toward CLD students?
- Is appropriate programming available?
- Is my classroom community welcoming toward CLD students?
- Do I critically reflect on and discuss media portrayal of CLD families and students with my class?
- Do I know where I stand and what I believe about teaching CLD students?

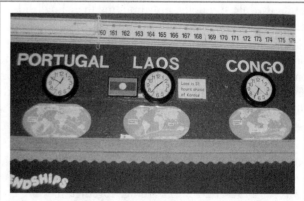

Hillcrest teachers move beyond the halls of the school and use what they learn from families and the community to create an accepting classroom environment by highlighting students' countries of origin, traditions, and individuality.

—*Denise Johnson, 2nd Grade, Kansas*

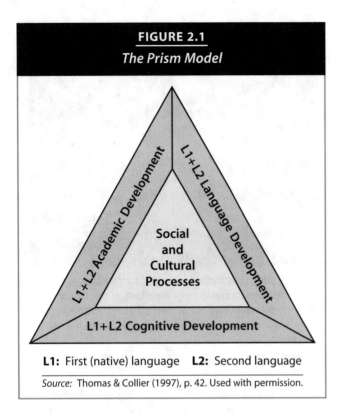

FIGURE 2.1
The Prism Model

L1+L2 Academic Development

L1+L2 Language Development

Social and Cultural Processes

L1+L2 Cognitive Development

L1: First (native) language   **L2:** Second language

Source: Thomas & Collier (1997), p. 42. Used with permission.

So . . . Now What?

Educators who are putting together the puzzle of understanding their diverse student population realize that, in addition to the factors I have discussed, CLD students still face the process of becoming proficient in the language of schooling—English. This complex process is described in detail in Chapter 3. These educators also understand that CLD learners need to keep pace with grade-level curricular content while simultaneously building their English language capacities.

In considering what educators need to understand in order to use their students' backgrounds to provide differentiated instruction, we first turn to the research of Thomas and Collier (1995, 1997, 1999, 2002). Their multisite, multi-dimensional longitudinal work has guided my efforts as a researcher and educator for the past decade. Thomas and Collier (1995) outlined four dimensions that greatly influence CLD student success in school. The four dimensions—*sociocultural, linguistic, cognitive,* and *academic*—form the basis for all teaching and learning. Together, they are encompassed in the *prism model,* which is depicted in Figure 2.1. These four interdependent and complex dimensions are the foundation for understanding linguistic and academic growth of students.

Building upon this foundational work, I have collaborated with others to expand on the dimensions of the prism model to develop the concept of the *CLD student biography*

(Herrera & Murry, 2005; Herrera et al., 2007). The CLD student biography is a concept that accounts for the challenges and processes associated with each of the four dimensions. To be successful, we educators must explore and understand these dimensions through multiple lenses— like a photographer trying to fully represent the many dimensions of a subject.

The CLD Student Biography

We must use what we learn before, during, and after our lessons to assess students' language and academic growth and to strive to understand them from both a school and a cultural perspective. To begin, take a few minutes to assess your current understanding of what the sociocultural, linguistic, cognitive, and academic dimensions represent in classroom practice. Figure 2.2 provides a brief activity that can help guide your self-assessment. As you learn more about the first dimension of the CLD student biography, begin to ask yourself how you might plan, teach, and observe student behavior through the prism of your new insights and learning.

The Sociocultural Dimension

Transitions: Viendo hacia un futuro

Un futuro
 Un futuro de historia
  Todos tenemos historias
   Por eso estoy aquí
    We all have stories
     I am here
      Get to know me and you will see
       I have a different point of view.
          —*BESITOS/Herrera Terry (2004)*

The complex variables that influence our way of life, our definition of love, and what makes us laugh also influence a student's motivation and engagement to learn. This *sociocultural dimension* of the CLD student biography is at the heart of language acquisition and learning (see Figure 2.3). The sociocultural dimension includes the adjustment and development processes that students go through as they learn to respond to unique, idiosyncratic ways of being and behaving both in and out of school. Sociocultural development is driven by:

- *Social institutions,* including the home, school, and societal interactions
- *Affective influences,* including self-esteem, anxiety, and motivation
- *Social interactive phenomena,* including bias, prejudice, and discrimination

FIGURE 2.2
Hearts Activity

1. Take a piece of paper and draw hearts on the page to mirror those illustrated here.
2. For each layer of the heart, do the following:
   - **Outside Layer of the Heart.** Record the words that come to mind when you hear the words *sociocultural, linguistic, cognitive,* and *academic.*
   - **Middle Layer of the Heart.** Record tools and strategies you use in practice to learn about these dimensions of your students.
   - **Center of the Heart (or outside the heart for additional space).** Write about an experience from your classroom practice that comes to mind when you think of the sociocultural, linguistic, cognitive, and academic dimensions of the CLD student biography.
3. Read the rest of the chapter and consider connections to your own practice, as reflected in your completed heart.

Available for free download and printing from www.tcpress.com

Independently and together, each of these factors creates a variety of complex language and learning issues, including student/teacher/family interactions, a student's learning process, and other dynamics of teaching and learning.

Traditional School-Initiated Responses

In response to these dynamics, school environments have long focused on learning about the sociocultural dimensions of a child's life by using tools that provide information related to the culture and language of the student, family, and community. Some of the most typical efforts include:

- Learning about the traditions of different ethnic groups and celebrating important aspects of that culture
- Making sure the environment and curriculum in some way mirror the lives of the students in the classroom
- Using the student's native language when necessary to increase communication
- Using interest inventories to learn about the students and their families

Many educators have broadened their horizons by going further through:

- Learning the language(s) of their students, or at least enough vocabulary to demonstrate interest and respect

FIGURE 2.3
The Prism Model

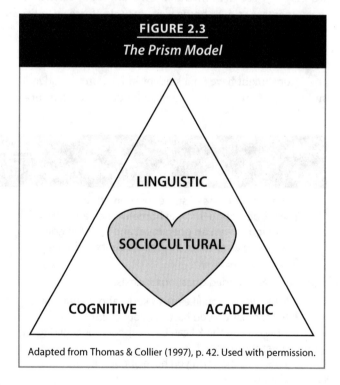

Adapted from Thomas & Collier (1997), p. 42. Used with permission.

- Visiting the communities where their students live
- Conducting interviews with community members to learn about the students and families in the community

One of the most important ways teachers learn more about their students is through home visits. A home visit can illustrate and strengthen a teacher's understanding of the multidimensional facets of students' lives. Home visits enable teachers to become more aware of:

- Family structures and roles
- Students' learning styles, acculturation levels, and language development at home
- Communication patterns within the family

When teachers enter households not with the purpose of discussing a student's reason for absences or failure to thrive at school but as genuine ethnographic researchers wanting to gather information, they are able to dip into the palette of opportunities to create an all-encompassing portrait of their students. By learning about and drawing upon families' household resources, networks, and survival strategies, teachers can play the role of cultural mediators between the school culture and the home culture.

Home visits allow us to see nontraditional forms of literacy development and evidence of student skills we may not see demonstrated on traditional classroom assignments. At times, home visits may also force us to live in the moment and delve deeply into the challenges of overcrowded living, multiple jobs, and beginning levels of proficiency in English. If we consider the influences these conditions might have on a student in relation to academic success, access to English language models, and accultura-

Here the teacher uses the interactive word wall as a source for defining and clarifying vocabulary words. The wall uses English and the students' native languages to make connections.

—*Jennifer Welk, Kindergarten, Kansas*

tion, we may begin to understand the student behaviors and responses we witness in our classrooms. In addition, home visits help us see our students as creative explorers who are dynamic and adept members of their families and communities. Through newfound understanding of the variables that bring our students love, life, and laughter, we are better able to create a sense of belonging among the learners in our classrooms.

FIGURE 2.4

Tips for Teachers Conducting Home Visits

1. Go into the homes of students as an ethnographer. That is, do not go into the home with an agenda; rather, go in with an open mind and with the goal of learning as much about the students and their families as possible.

2. Pose open-ended questions such as:
   - What would you like me to know about your child?
   - What goals do you have for your child?
   - How do you think I can best support your child to meet these goals?
   - What questions do you have about me and/or my classroom?

3. Encourage parents to share information about their children informally (e.g., likes, dislikes, personality traits, strengths, areas where they might need support).

4. Advocate for home visits as a powerful tool for learning about your students while taking into consideration district guidelines.

5. If possible, identify and bring a paraprofessional or other volunteer who can translate if necessary.

6. Be sure to follow up with parents via verbal and written communication regarding the date and time of the home visit. Remember to work around *their* schedule.

7. After you have completed the home visit, take time to document your observations and insights as they relate to the sociocultural, linguistic, academic, and cognitive dimensions of the CLD student biography and think about ways you can bring these into the classroom.

FIGURE 2.5
Guide for Home Visits

Home visits (duration about 45 minutes to an hour) can provide an amazing source of information regarding the sociocultural, linguistic, cognitive, and academic dimensions of CLD students. When talking with caregiver(s), it is important to consider that most caregivers hold teachers in very high regard.

Observations During Home Visits	Sample Questions

• In some cultures, parents are not the ones who are directly responsible for their children; oftentimes, the grandparents are important caregivers (e.g., in families from India). Who is/are the student's primary caregiver(s)?
• What types of learning opportunities are available to the student at home?
• Do the parents/grandparents/siblings/extended family members read to the student?
• What role do stories play in the student's language development?
• What insights are revealed about the student's cultural learning style?
• What are the family's goals for the educational, vocational, and personal development of the student?
• What general expectations do the caregivers/parents have for the student? This often varies across cultures.
• What roles does the student play at home? Sometimes students perform the role of caregiver for younger siblings while parents work in the evenings.
• What is the level of acculturation of the child and his or her family?
• What are the cultural norms of the family (e.g., not looking another in the eye while speaking)?
	• *Ask open-ended questions:*
	  • What would you like me to know about [student's name]?
	  • What do you think he/she does especially well?
	  • What would you like to see [student's name] accomplish this year?
	• *Ask about the student's language opportunities at home:*
	  • Does the student get to go to the grocery store? Make a grocery list?
	  • Does the family discuss television shows (e.g., novelas)?
	  • Does the family discuss trips taken during Christmas/winter break/summer break?
	  • Are there any books that the family reads together?
	  • Do the parents/siblings/extended family members tell stories? For what purposes (e.g., to entertain, to teach lessons) are the stories told?

The following excerpt exemplifies the kind of insights educators can gain from a home visit:

As I visited the parents, something else I found very intriguing was that Dad usually gave Amla and Amaan choices about their culture versus American culture. Many festivities that we have are not celebrated in Jordan—Halloween, music activities, etc. Dad said he gave Amla a choice in those situations. He said if she wants to participate in music at school, it would not be a big problem. Amla always asks her dad what he would want her to do and he replies he would prefer her not to, but it is her choice. So she does not participate in music here at school or celebrate Halloween. She remains very true to her country and culture and is very proud of where she is from and her family background.

This actually made me realize that the students truly are living two worlds at the same time and are so adept at making choices. If that is the case, then why don't I present Amla with situations where she can make different choices about content in the classroom.

—*Brooke Jones, Elementary Teacher*

Think about what you just read and ask yourself, "How can home visits take me one step beyond in my own teaching?" Although making home visits can be challenging because it often requires going into spaces that are outside our comfort zone, doing so can prove pivotal to our discovering student assets and eliminating barriers in our classroom practice. Figures 2.4 and 2.5 provide tips and an example guide for conducting home visits.

Home visits, as well as the other aforementioned ways of learning about the sociocultural aspects of a student's life, have long been documented in the research and practical literature of the field (Herrera et al., 2007; McCarthey, 2000; Reid, 1996). Educators who use what they have

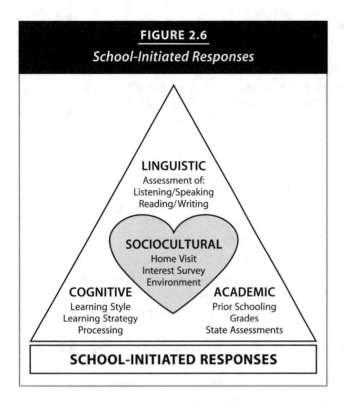

FIGURE 2.6

School-Initiated Responses

LINGUISTIC
Assessment of:
Listening/Speaking
Reading/Writing

SOCIOCULTURAL
Home Visit
Interest Survey
Environment

COGNITIVE
Learning Style
Learning Strategy
Processing

ACADEMIC
Prior Schooling
Grades
State Assessments

SCHOOL-INITIATED RESPONSES

learned about CLD students and families in their teaching move beyond the "institutional curriculum" to one that is more inclusive, participatory, and ultimately transformative. By capitalizing on students' cultures, educators increase the likelihood of students' active engagement in learning. Figure 2.6 depicts the school-initiated responses common to the sociocultural dimension, as well as those related to the linguistic, cognitive, and academic dimensions, which are discussed in Chapters 3, 4, and 5.

Socioculturally Speaking: *i*+1

The aspects of the sociocultural dimension discussed thus far affect our decisions for planning instruction, buying curricular materials, interacting with students, and teaching lessons. Yet, traditional ways of learning about the sociocultural dimension of students tend to yield somewhat limited information for teaching lessons, because they frequently provide a "point-in-time" understanding of a student's way of life outside school. Without additional sources of information to provide context for a particular event or particular data, our understanding of a student may be limited to the interpretations we make of what was learned in that moment.

Given the pace of life in schools, we do not give much thought to allocating some of our time before the lesson to learning about how the student's life experience might manifest itself in the lesson we are going to teach. Little attention is given to how a student's emotions might relate

to the vocabulary or topic to be taught. The following sections move us one step further in considering new lenses we can use to observe the students in our classrooms so that we will be better able to feel and think *with them* as we teach. Chapters 7, 8, and 9 provide practical strategies to help reveal the sociocultural picture of students' lives—a picture that reflects the heart of their experiences.

Life: The Wide Angle

In my current work in schools, I have been exploring the effect that a student's life has on his or her engagement in the classroom and motivation to risk sharing about the ways he or she personally relates to a lesson. *Life* can be defined as the entirety of what an individual has experienced and what he or she is experiencing in the present. These experiences determine our psychological, sociological, linguistic, and academic thoughts and actions. At the end of each day, many students leave school to participate in home and community situations that often do not fit within our own frame of reference; yet these experiences can enrich our teaching.

As you read the following vignette, consider ways this student's experiences could contribute to your classroom learning community:

> After school Cecilia walks home from her 6th-grade classroom with her four brothers. A long afternoon awaits her because she has to make sure dinner is cooked for all the family. She also must make sure that the house is ready, because six members of her mother's family will be joining them this evening. The relatives just lost their jobs in Colorado and will

Sharing our past experience with others and then taking our combined perspectives to text increases the likelihood that what we are learning will be more meaningful.

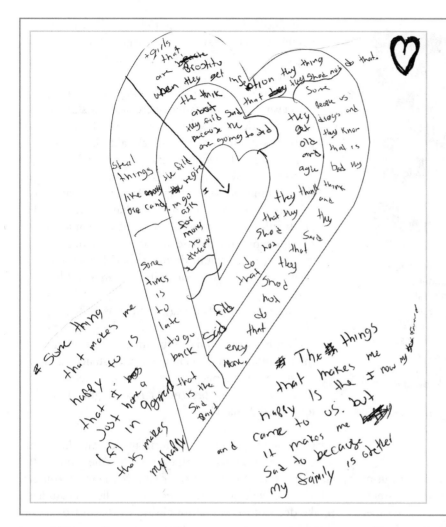

—James Callahan, High School, Kansas

**Hearts Activity:
One Teacher's Perspective**

I used this activity to introduce *Bleachers*, by John Grisham. One of the major themes is regret. I introduced the word and then we started on the outside with examples. The middle heart was used to document feelings associated with regret. Students used the center heart (or outside of the heart) to write about personal regrets or fond memories.

Working individually, in pairs, or in small groups, the students were able to understand what it means for a text to have a "theme." By providing them an opportunity to link the story to their own experiences and share with each other, the activity promoted sociocultural connections and language development as they discussed with each other what they wrote. For preproduction and early production (students not ready to write in English), I had them write in their native language and then get assistance from a peer who could translate. This lowered the students' anxiety and they were more engaged. I observed the students thinking in ways that connected themselves to the standard I was trying to teach, one that is difficult to get across in traditional ways.

be living with Cecilia's family until they can decide what will happen next. Cecilia lives in an efficiency apartment with her brothers and parents (and soon the six members of her extended family). She looks forward to everyone getting together because that means staying up until early morning, laughing, and listening to the adults tell stories about their struggles in the United States. Often Cecilia wonders how losing a job can be amusing. For now, she needs to focus on getting ready. She needs to rearrange the furniture and figure out where everyone is going to sleep before *mama y papa* come home from work. She also needs to figure out how to make the potatoes, meat, and flour feed 12 people instead of six. She looks forward to all the craziness of everyone being together again, if only for a short time.

Life happens, and we all must play the game with the cards we are dealt. As children, we rarely ask questions about what is happening. It is what we know and live, and it can bring love and laughter to our life.

Given the right tools, we as educators can create environments where we can become part of the fabric of our students' lived experiences. We can draw on our CLD students' experiences, knowledge, and problem-solving skills and frame them within the contexts of our academic world. For example, given the scenario just described, we could certainly find ways to integrate aspects of Cecilia's life into mathematical explorations of dividing portions, discussions of efficient use of electricity and other resources, and so forth. We can provide what I call a "canvas of opportunities" for students to think about and talk about, and we can celebrate their contributions. These opportunities help create the classroom conditions needed for students to become valued members within the academic learning community.

Love: The Group Shot

Our life is filled with emotional and social aspects that often influence our attitudes, thoughts, and behaviors. The ways we demonstrate *love*, and what we love, are heavily

By creating classroom contexts and opportunities before the lesson that are risk-free and that allow students to disclose what they bring to the lesson, we gain valuable insights that we can use during instruction. The vocabulary quilt (see Appendix E) is one strategy that provides the opportunity for such disclosure by allowing each student to make connections with the content, see other's connections, and reveal connections to teachers that can help the teacher bridge from what students know and clear up misunderstandings.

—*Kendra Herrera, 3rd Grade, Texas*

influenced by the life we have experienced in and out of school. Often we as teachers wonder how it is that parents can make certain decisions related to our students. At times we may think, "Can they truly love them? If they do, why don't they make decisions that make sense? Why do they not support them in learning English? Why do they not read to them at night? Why do they send their children thousands of miles away to a new and unknown country to live with friends and extended family? Why do they take them out of school for so long? How can this be love?" Consider the following vignette about Angelica. How would you interpret and react to the family's decision about Angelica's education?

Since arriving in the United States at the age of 13, Angelica had been the perfect daughter. As the oldest of four children, she was the first to learn English and thus became the language broker of the family. When things went wrong because of her father's drinking, she was there every Monday to translate with the judge. When it came time to ask *el patron* for the family's paycheck at the end of a long week in the fields, it was Angelica who was there to deal with the sarcastic remarks about the "kids" not earning their pay. There was no dating, no talking on the phone, no, no, no, to anything that was "American."

"You know those girls are not like you," her mother would say, "They have no morals, no rules." (Remember, every immediate family has its own unique value system.)

In school Angelica excelled, always keeping up with everything, no matter where her year started or where it ended. Her senior year came and it was time to graduate with honors and make a decision about which college she would attend. Her counselor was excited about the many possibilities and the scholarships coming her way. This was Angelica's dream. So, when Angelica came and told her that she would not be attending college and that instead she would continue to work, the counselor was devastated. How could Angelica's family do this to her? How could they take away this opportunity? Did they not love her?

The answer for Angelica's family was quite simple: Her parents loved her so much that they wanted to protect her from all harm that might exist outside their familiar environment and circumstances. Sending Angelica to a place that was beyond their scope of understanding represented a risk too great to take for their only daughter.

Gaining insight into what it meant for Angelica's parents to live in a new country with new rules, and at the same time try to protect their children from harm, can give us a new perspective about why families and students make decisions that are not always within our own cultural boundaries of understanding. It becomes our role to step out of our comfort zone, care about how our students define what they love, and explore the histories of our students and their families. Such efforts can help us understand the love-centered motives behind others' actions and illuminate ways we can work *together* with families to support our students. Gay (2000) finds that teachers who really care about students' humanity move beyond the parameters defined in school and toward a more caring way of teaching.

Laughter: The Close-up

What does not make you laugh can sometimes make you cry. Which would you prefer to do? We often look at students' lives and wonder how they can be so resilient given the many life challenges they face. Through my own lived experiences and the stories my students have shared over the years, I have come to realize that laughter and humor are deeply embedded in the resiliency and persistence of my successful students. It is their stories filled with faith and laughter that can make teaching meaningful in ways that are often absent in our teacher preparation programs and professional development training. Consider the following teacher reflection on how Jaime's experience with *el coyote* provided a link to content concepts.

> I remember Jaime's story to his friends about the time he crossed from Guatemala. The many adventures that he had experienced culminated with him and his family being left in Mexico, thinking they had reached the United States. I only understood bits and pieces of the story the first time I heard it, given my initial "disinterest" in what was being talked about and my concern that the conversation was too loud for my own comfort level.
>
> Later that semester, the border crossing story resurfaced. The laughter of the group surrounded Jaime's tale of his family's entry into the United States years earlier, when the person helping them cross into the United States (*el coyote*) had left them at a Walmart just across from the U.S. border, still on the Mexican side. He had told them that this was a U.S. store and that a phone and food were available for them before they continued their journey to their destination. By the time he reached my class, Jaime's family was documented, and he found the story something to laugh about.
>
> I decided to "hook" into what I had learned from Jaime's story and make connections to globalization. As a class we discussed the fact that Walmart is no longer a chain of stores found only in the United States. Other students added to the discussion by chiming in with the names of additional companies whose influences have crossed national boundaries. Those were the connections that students in class never forgot.

Young and Hadaway (2006) point out that any type of "conceptual hook" with the experiences a student has had in the past increases the chance that the information will make it into the student's permanent memory. Memories closely related to personal life experiences make for great opportunities to create a community of learners that values each member's prior knowledge.

What makes us laugh is very much culturally bound, and the joy we experience in our community is heavily connected to our own ethnicity, socioeconomic level, and educational background. Gay (2000) asserts that planning instruction that takes into account the complex, interactive, and dynamic yet stabilizing force in human life—that is, a student's culture—paves the path to culturally relevant pedagogy. I believe that understanding the sociocultural dimension of each student beyond our standard school-initiated definitions and moving toward a pedagogy that encompasses and is defined by the content of life, love, and laughter can

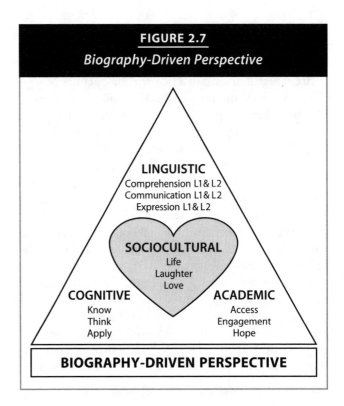

FIGURE 2.7
Biography-Driven Perspective

lead to a new way of using students' experiences to ensure their academic success. Figure 2.7 illustrates the dimensions of the CLD student from a biography-driven perspective.

Reflections on the Sociocultural Dimension

I began this chapter by discussing the importance of the biological, psychological, and sociological aspects of our humanity. In the context of classroom learning, these aspects play out in the four dimensions of the CLD student biography—the sociocultural, linguistic, cognitive, and academic dimensions. This chapter focuses on the sociocultural dimension. As educators, we must be attentive to the sociocultural dimension as it relates to both the assets that we can draw from and the challenges that may be keeping our students from moving forward. We can remember that prior to arriving in our classrooms, our students have already learned to love and learn within their own families and communities. Their lives are filled with experiences we can learn from and draw on in the classroom to transform their educational experience. Cummins (1996) best summarizes the influence of the sociocultural dimension on students' learning by noting:

> When students' language, culture and experience are ignored or excluded in classroom interactions, students are immediately starting from a disadvantage. Everything they have learned about life and the world

up to this point is being dismissed as irrelevant to school learning; there are few points of connection to curriculum materials or instruction and so students are expected to learn in an experiential vacuum. Students' silence and nonparticipation under these conditions have frequently been interpreted as lack of academic ability or effort, and teachers' interactions with students have reflected a pattern of low expectations, which become self-fulfilling. (pp. 2–3)

We educators must first recognize the gifts that our students possess, no matter how far removed they may be from our own reality and the reality of our school. The gifts are more varied than we can begin to imagine. By building on the background knowledge students bring to the classroom, we can provide conditions that will promote CLD students' motivation and engagement in the learning process.

The scenarios presented in this chapter no doubt may have left you with much to think about related to the challenges students face each day. We must move beyond thinking such ways of life inhibit students intellectually; on the

This is me when I graduated from preschool. It was so funny!

Ask students about the important and exciting events in their lives multiple times throughout the year.

contrary, for many students, the kaleidoscope of languages, cultures, and communities provides a source of energy to continue to move forward despite all the challenges life presents both in and out of school. Our charge then is to draw upon our students' gifts and assets and use those to bridge to the content we teach. Chapters 7, 8, and 9 provide practical ideas for making this a reality in our classrooms.

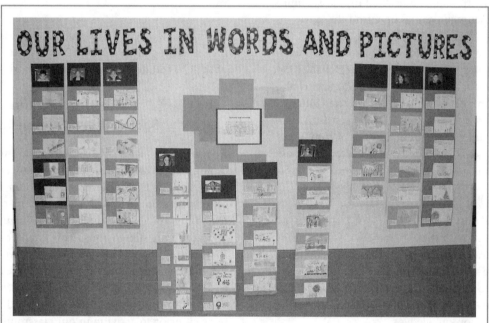

OUR LIVES IN WORDS AND PICTURES

Share these student events with the rest of the classroom and school. Create communities where every language, culture, and experience are celebrated and become a source of learning inside and outside of the school.

—*Dennis Stanton, Marie Kane, & Gayle Durbin, Elementary, Kansas*

CHAPTER 3

Language of the Heart

THERE IS no greater magic than having someone listen to and validate what we have to say. In Spanish, there is a saying, "cada cabeza es un mundo"—every head is its own world. When we communicate effectively, we succeed in crossing the distance from our world to the world of another. However, we do not always succeed in crossing that distance. Much gets lost in schools, where the culture and thought of educators often depart from those of CLD students. Currently, educational institutions tend to focus on learning about the linguistic proficiencies of students through the narrow lens of formal language assessment. This chapter first reviews school-situated aspects of language and then takes the educator into the heart of communication by exploring how language is inextricably tied to culture.

The Linguistic Dimension

My life made a complete turn.
Un cambio radical.
Questions rushed through my head.
Tengo que hacer un extra esfuerzo.
Para speak and read in English.
I felt like a part of myself was missing.
I am here today.
—*BESITOS/Herrera Terry (2004)*

As demographics have shifted and the number of CLD students has grown, great attention has been paid to what teachers should understand to be successful with these students. College courses and professional development trainings abound that aim to provide pre-service and in-service teachers with the fundamentals of second language acquisition and demonstrate how this process is relevant to classroom practice. Yet before we explore the process of second language acquisition, let us first briefly look at the way we acquire our first language.

We do not begin life as fluent speakers of our first language. With much encouragement and support, we spend our early years acquiring the basic sound patterns, vocabulary, sentence structures, and communicative skills that we later take for granted. We then continue to improve our linguistic capabilities through formal schooling and our interactions with others. Although by age six we have completed 50% of the process of acquiring our first language, we continue to spend the rest of our lives acquiring additional vocabulary and refining our language skills (Herrera & Murry, 2005).

The process of second language acquisition is markedly more difficult than that of first language acquisition. Second language learners rarely have the opportunity to spend years merely becoming acquainted with the sounds and structures of the new language. Rather, they are expected to quickly acquire enormous amounts of vocabulary, recognize and use complex sentence structures that may be very different from those used in their native language, and grasp subtle nuances of the new language that are key to in-depth comprehension and effective communication. Continuing the discussion of the four interrelated and complex dimensions of the prism model, I will now review the most commonly known aspects of teaching linguistically diverse students.

Traditional School-Initiated Responses

Both pre-service and in-service professional preparation provide information related to the fundamental concepts and theories, which set the stage for understanding second language development and teaching:

- Distinction between basic interpersonal communication skills (BICS) and cognitive academic language proficiency (CALP)
- Krashen's theory of second language acquisition (SLA)

- Acquisition–learning hypothesis
- Monitor hypothesis
- Natural order hypothesis
- Input hypothesis
- Affective filter hypothesis
- Stages of second language acquisition
- Distinction between common underlying proficiency (CUP) and separate underlying proficiency (SUP)
- Formal assessment of oral language proficiency
- Communicative and sociolinguistic considerations

The sections that follow provide a brief discussion of each of these concepts and theories as well as suggestions for their application in classroom practice.

BICS and CALP

When considering students' levels of proficiency in both their first and second language, we must take into account their listening, speaking, reading, and writing abilities in those languages. We must also differentiate between their level of basic interpersonal communication skills (BICS), commonly described as conversational playground language, and their level of cognitive academic language proficiency (CALP), which refers to the more decontextualized, abstract language that is often used in academic settings (Cummins, 1981). This distinction explains why the fact that CLD students might be able to converse quite effectively with their peers in English does not guarantee that they will grasp the English vocabulary needed to comprehend an academic lesson.

The BICS/CALP distinction has generally been associated with the need to teach academic language in systematic ways in order to increase students' academic achievement. The BICS/CALP distinction also has implications for planning instruction, interpreting assessment data, and understanding the reluctance of some students to fully participate in classroom activities. Figure 3.1 provides basic information about BICS and CALP that may be helpful in understanding CLD students.

Consider the following two tasks: (a) Tell me about your last family outing or vacation, and (b) Write a paragraph describing the solution formed in a chemistry experiment using the words *solute, solvent.* and *concentration.* Which task would require academic vocabulary, complex cognitive processing, and background content knowledge? The second task represents the type of work we often require of CLD learners in the classroom without providing adequate *scaffolding* that would support their CALP development and

FIGURE 3.1	
BICS and CALP	
Language as an Associative Function	**Language as a Cognitive Function**
BICS: **B**asic **I**nterpersonal **C**ommunication **S**kills	**CALP:** **C**ognitive **A**cademic **L**anguage **P**roficiency
Social communication/ playground language	Academic communication/ classroom language
Language processing and production are less cognitively demanding.	Language processing and production are more cognitively demanding.
The brain is focusing on ideas.	The brain is focusing on ideas and language production.
Similar to discussing familiar topics in one's first language.	Speaking in a second language requires a greater degree of mental effort.
The language learner's schema fits the experiential and conceptual knowledge as well as the linguistic and/or cultural context of the situation.	The language learner's schema does not fit the experiential and conceptual knowledge and/or the linguistic or cultural context of the situation.

Adapted from Herrera (2007), p. 30. Used with permission of KCAT/TLC, Kansas State University.

thus increase the likelihood of their academic success. As teachers, we can support students' CALP development by:

- Providing visuals to support the required task
- Teaching and posting the academic vocabulary
- Allowing peer-to-peer collaboration to paraphrase what was learned
- Using grouping configurations that allow practice of English vocabulary and concepts
- Allowing use of the native language in structured ways to pre-teach, clarify, or elaborate on critical academic vocabulary and concepts

Krashen's Theory of Second Language Acquisition

By shattering old myths, introducing new subtleties, and challenging the conventional wisdom, Stephen Krashen changed the way we think about language in the classroom. In his seminal works, Krashen (1981, 1982) describes his theory of second language acquisition by outlining five key hypotheses.

Acquisition–Learning Hypothesis. "A person cannot learn by grammar alone." Krashen distinguishes between the processes of *acquiring* and *learning* a second language. Acquiring a language is a largely subconscious process in which the learner picks up the language in a natural environment by using the language for a variety of real communication purposes. In contrast, learning a language requires conscious effort and involves being able to understand and apply grammar and other formal language rules.

Monitor Hypothesis. "Usage is the only path to fluency." Krashen demonstrates how it is only by *acquiring* a language that the learner gains fluency. For this reason, it is crucial to create a school environment that allows CLD students to hear and use the English language in meaningful contexts. Language *learning* merely assists individuals in self-monitoring and correcting their language production; it does not help learners use the language with natural ease.

Natural Order Hypothesis. "Errors are normal and often disappear on their own." Krashen describes how English language learners acquire the rules of the English language in a predictable order. He finds that regardless of age, students make certain grammatical errors as they progress through the stages of acquiring English. These errors are developmental and highly predictable. They are usually temporary and begin to disappear with modeling of the language. Therefore, it is important for educators to avoid "error correction" of CLD students' language production. An emphasis on mistakes can lead to student apprehension and prevent learners from moving forward in acquiring the English language. If an error persists for a long time (becoming what has been referred to as "fossilized"), then it may become necessary for the teacher to use explicit techniques to address the grammatical error.

Input Hypothesis. Beginning where they currently stand, learners advance step by step. First and second language learners need to receive *comprehensible input* as they acquire literacy skills. Comprehensible input is new language material that learners are able to understand, in spite of its unfamiliarity, because measures have been taken to ensure that connections are made between the new information and what the learners already know. Krashen's "i+1," discussed in Chapter 1, describes this kind of comprehensible, new material. The "i" represents the learner's existing linguistic capabilities and the "+1" signifies that the new material is one step beyond where the learner currently stands (Krashen, 1985).

Tying language and content to meaningful experiences is crucial because students cannot learn something that they do not understand. Consequently, successful educators focus their efforts, regardless of students' literacy levels, on the attainment of meaning. Teachers do this by actively engaging students in the learning environment and by using strategies that contextualize content (e.g., role

playing, experiments, field trips, visuals). As students learn from and about language embedded in rich and varied contexts, they develop their language proficiency.

Affective Filter Hypothesis. "It's hard to learn when you're scared." Learning a second language can be more difficult than acquiring a first language because second language learners often are inhibited by what Krashen refers to as an *affective filter*. CLD students are aware that they are not as proficient in their second language as their native-speaking peers. Therefore, they may struggle with anxiety about saying the wrong thing, making grammatical errors, or incorrectly pronouncing what they say. The affective filter controls the extent to which students are able to actually take in what they are supposed to be learning. If students feel comfortable in their learning environment and know their language efforts will be met with support, they are more likely to comprehend the material and take risks with their language production. However, in stressful situations, the affective filter of students is raised (much like a defense mechanism), and the result often involves a decrease in student motivation, engagement, and language production.

Stages of Second Language Acquisition

The process of second language acquisition mirrors the process of acquiring a first language in many ways. In both processes, the learner goes through a silent period—a period during which the learner is trying to internalize the common sounds, words, and patterns of the language. Although students in the silent period are actively acquiring language skills, they might use only nonverbal forms of communication (e.g., nodding, shrugging, or pointing) until they feel adequately prepared to take on the challenge of verbal communication. This preproduction stage of language acquisition may last for several months (Ovando, Combs, & Collier, 2006). Students then pass through the early production, speech emergence, intermediate fluency, and advanced fluency stages as they gain proficiency in the second language (Krashen & Terrell, 1983). (These stages are discussed further—in the context of assessing a student's progress in language acquisition—later in this chapter.) Figure 3.2 compares and contrasts first and second language acquisition processes.

CUP and SUP

The optimal learning environment for CLD students is one that leads to literacy skills in both the student's native language and in English. Why is it necessary to use students' native language when building their academic knowledge? In short, skills and knowledge gained in the native language transfer to the second language. The student's core of knowledge that is accessible through either language can be

FIGURE 3.2

Comparison of First and Second Language Acquisition

L1 Acquisition	L1 and L2 Acquisition	L2 Acquisition
• Parents or caretakers are the primary language models for first language learners. • First language learners have innumerable opportunities to interact with language models. • Most first language learners acquire a high level of first language proficiency. • First language acquisition is arguably internally motivated by an innate cognitive process, although environmental factors shape development. • Most people develop a first language.	• Through a process called overgeneralization, a language learner may indiscriminately apply a language rule to many different situations (e.g., *He goed to the store yesterday*). • Learners acquire language by interacting with others. • Learners go through a silent period. • Learners need comprehensible input. • A highly contextualized, language-rich environment will facilitate language acquisition. • Language acquisition is cognitively demanding. • Language acquisition involves conceptualizing information in new ways and developing new ways of processing information. • Language acquisition occurs in predictable stages. • Language acquisition is a dynamic process during which learners actively construct meaning using prior knowledge, experience, and context.	• Second language learners already have a language for communication and thought. • Second language learners can transfer knowledge about language (metalinguistic awareness) and thought processes from the first to the second language. • Peers and teachers are the primary language models for second language learners. • Second language learners have a greater repertoire of language learning strategies. • The second language learner may make language mistakes in the second language because he or she is applying rules from the first language to the second language. • Second language learners can code switch, which involves using both languages to create greater meaning than could be achieved by relying on only one language. • Second language learners can use cognates to comprehend new words in the second language. • Second language learners often need more time to process information. • Second language learners have greater prior knowledge and experience to rely on as they acquire the second language. • Second language learners often have fewer opportunities to interact with second language models. • Second language acquisition is arguably externally motivated by sociocultural factors, although innate cognitive processes facilitate the acquisition process. Not all people develop a second language. • Second language learners can lose a first or second language if they do not use that language. • Many people do not acquire a high level of second language proficiency. • Second language learners who reach high levels of bilingual proficiency tend to have greater cognitive abilities than monolingual language learners.

Source: Herrera & Murry, *Mastering ESL and Bilingual Methods,* Table 3.1 "Ways in Which First and Second Language Acquisition Compare and Contrast," p. 63, © 2005. Reproduced by permission of Pearson Education, Inc.

illustrated through the concept of *common underlying proficiency* (CUP) (Cummins, 1981). For example, regardless of the language educators initially use to teach the process of addition to students, the students will be able to perform the mathematical operation. The iceberg metaphor depicted in Figure 3.3 illustrates that while CLD students may not possess the English surface features to effectively explain how addition works, they might completely understand the concept of addition. They do not need to learn the concept twice, only the language to express their under-

standing in a new language. Unfortunately, some educators misunderstand students' background knowledge as being a *separate underlying proficiency* (SUP). The SUP viewpoint regards access to knowledge as limited to the specific language in which students originally learned the concepts or skills (Cummins, 1981). As a result of this misunderstanding, such teachers believe that curricular material must be retaught in English, and they often fail to notice the wealth of content knowledge that CLD students already possess.

Formal Assessment of Oral Language Proficiency

Ask a group of educators who are not ESL teachers what the formal assessments of their CLD students have shown in relation to their level of language proficiency, and often there will be silence in the room. With further prompting, the responses of those present likely will range from, "That is top secret information only available in the office for official use," to "That is the ESL teacher's information. I have too many students to keep up with that. I have the scores but I don't know what they mean," or "The students in my class have been exited so their scores don't really matter any more." My response is, "How will you know where you're going with your students if you don't know where they have been?"

Every district that has CLD students is required by law to administer a language test prior to assigning or placing a student in a program. These tests vary in the types of information they gather, yet whatever information is gleaned from the process can serve as a window into students' linguistic abilities. Figure 3.4 provides a list of the tests most used by states across the country to assess the linguistic and literacy abilities of CLD students, along with brief information that can guide you in understanding what the scores on each test mean. Often states choose to use tests that have been developed to meet the needs of students within their districts. We as educators can benefit from learning how CLD students are assessed and from using the results of those assessments to inform our understanding of each student's biography.

Standardized tests, along with informal observation of students' second language acquisition (SLA), help us to more effectively plan instruction. Thus, we need to be familiar with tools used to observe language development and get into the habit of using them daily in our classroom. Figure 3.5 provides an overview of the stages of SLA and student actions that may be observed by the teacher during each stage. As students progress through each stage, it is important that we recognize the steps of that progression so that we can appropriately scaffold and support their learning through our teaching strategies. Figure 3.6 illustrates what student production for a Thanksgiving activity can look like for each stage of SLA. Understanding the linguistic biographies of our CLD students increases our chances of successfully differentiating instruction to aid the progress of each student. In later chapters, we explore how knowledge of SLA stages is used to plan, teach, and assess student learning during every lesson.

FIGURE 3.3
The Iceberg Metaphor

Academic language starts with basic literacy skills, and the demands increase as a student continues through school. Fluency and literacy in the native language (L1) allow the optimal *transfer of skills* to the second language (L2). Therefore, the more literate and schooled a student is in his or her L1, the easier it is for the student to transfer skills and concepts from the L1 to the L2 with appropriate instruction and support. This is where the interdependence and relationship between the L1 and L2 can clearly be seen.

SUP: Separate Underlying Proficiency (L1 and L2 do not interact)

CUP: Common Underlying Proficiency (L1 and L2 do interact to promote L2 acquisition)

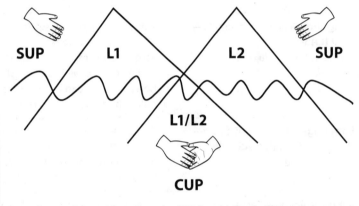

Source: Adapted from Cummins (1981), p. 24. Used with permission.

Communicative and Sociolinguistic Considerations

Just as the sociocultural dimension encompasses students' implicit, often unverbalized, rules for loving, laughing, and living, the linguistic dimension relates to their internal guide for comprehending the world of verbal communication, with all its hidden cultural messages. Before a student enters the classroom, avenues of communication already have been paved for appropriate ways of asking a question, responding, and making sense of what is communicated in different contexts. Hymes (1972) referred to this as "communicative competence." Teaching is often contextualized within the "norms" of the English language. These subtle aspects may differ from the modes of communication used by CLD students. Our students have learned how to express what they know, resolve conflict, react to nonverbal cues, and navigate their emotional state based on the cultural context to which they have been socialized. Effective cross-cultural communication is essential to the teaching and learning process.

To date, the standard focus in schools has involved:

- Supporting students' understanding of the grammatical rules of the English language by comparing English to the native language
- Supporting students' sociolinguistic knowledge by

teaching students to write for specific purposes, considering audience and setting
- Teaching students to use discourse in appropriate ways to ask questions and organize written thought
- Teaching students how to be strategic communicators in classroom settings

---

FIGURE 3.4
Language Proficiency Assessments

Language Assessment	Key Characteristics
Preschool Language Assessment Scale (Pre-LAS 2000) (Duncan & DeAvila, 1998)	This assessment is designed to measure the developing language and preliteracy skills of preschool-age children in order to inform the placement of these young language learners into the most appropriate classroom settings. It is available in English and Spanish.
Language Assessment Scale—Oral (LAS-O) (Duncan & DeAvila, 1990)	This assessment measures the listening and speaking skills of students in grades 1–6 and 7–12. Like the Pre-LAS, it is available in English or Spanish and is useful in assessing primary language development or to identify students for placement in, and exit from, bilingual or ESL programs. The LAS-O contains an optional observation form that can be completed by another examiner to further support or triangulate findings used to determine whether a student is ready for redesignation.
Language Assessment Scale—Reading/Writing (LAS-R/W) (Duncan & DeAvila, 1990)	This assessment measures reading and writing skills in English or L1 ability levels in Spanish. It may be used to identify students for placement in, and exit from, bilingual or ESL programs. The test combines selected response and writing sample evaluations to assess vocabulary, fluency, reading comprehension, mechanics, and usage.
IDEA Proficiency Test (IPT) (Ballard & Tighe, 2004)	This assessment offers oral, reading, and writing versions available in Spanish and English. It is designed to assess both social and academic language. Like other assessments of this type, the IPT may be used to measure primary language skills but is most often employed for the identification, placement, and (re)classification of CLD students who are acquiring English in appropriate classroom contexts.
Woodcock-Muñoz Language Survey Revised (WMLS-R) (Woodcock, Muñoz-Sandoval, Ruef, & Alvaredo, 2005)	This assessment is another popular measure of Spanish and English that comes with a computerized scoring program. This scoring program generates a narrative that describes the student's cognitive academic language proficiency in English or Spanish, or the relative proficiency between languages if both versions of the test are administered.
Maculaitis Assessment of Competencies II (MAC II) (Touchstone Applied Science, 2001)	This assessment evaluates the English proficiency of K–12 students through a variety of subtests designed to measure speaking, listening, reading, and writing. A 10-minute screening test can be used to assist schools with the placement of CLD students in any grade.
Stanford English Language Proficiency (SELP) Assessment (Harcourt Assessment, 2003)	This assessment was developed to measure and align the reading, writing, listening, and speaking skills of CLD students with curricular standards. This assessment measures both the academic and social language of students in grades K–12. A 5-minute screening version of the SELP also exists for students who lack sufficient English skills to take the full assessment. The screening version can be used to support decisions to appropriately exempt particular students from certain assessments, or as a quick placement screen pending more comprehensive assessment.

Source: Herrera, et al., *Assessment Accomodations for Classroom Teachers of Culturally and Linguistically Diverse Students,* Table 5.1 "Formal Assessments of Language Proficiency," p. 161, © 2007. Reproduced by permission of Pearson Education, Inc.

FIGURE 3.5
P-EP-S-I Ahh!

 P-EP-S-I Ahh! is a teacher-friendly mnemonic device to help you recall the stages of second language acquisition. Knowing which stage your CLD student is in will help you plan and implement instruction that supports English language acquisition and student achievement.

Acronym		Student Behaviors	Teacher Tips
P	Preproduction	• Gain familiarity with sounds, rhythm, and patterns of English. • Rely more heavily on picture clues for understanding. • Respond nonverbally by pointing, gesturing, or drawing.	• Pair students with more advanced learners. • Use many visuals, physical movements, gestures, and verbal cues to support and expand students' language acquisition process. • Avoid forcing students to speak prematurely by allowing for a silent period. • Try to help students use their background knowledge by making connections to their native language and previous experiences.
E P	Early Production	• Use one-word type utterances; may verbally identify people, places, and objects. • Manipulate objects and ideas mentally. • Start using knowledge of letter–sound relationship. • Use routine expressions independently.	• Provide students with an increasing number of visual cues to help them integrate phonics and context cues. • Use authentic and rich literature in classroom instruction. • Teach key vocabulary and concepts to increase students' comprehension. • Have students label or manipulate pictures and/or real objects.
S	Speech Emergence	• Understand grade-level concepts. • Engage in much more independent reading as a result of increased oral language proficiency. • Apply and manipulate writing according to their needs.	• Guard vocabulary and introduce concepts through the use of multiple strategies. • Model responses to literature for students by explaining, describing, comparing, and retelling. • Focus on communication in meaningful contexts and expression in speech and print. • Respond genuinely to student writing and hold conferences that highlight students' strengths and progress.
I	Intermediate Fluency	• Explore and utilize extensive vocabulary and concepts in content area. • Write and read a wider range of narrative genres and content texts with increased comprehension.	• Structure and guide group discussions to facilitate more advanced literature studies. • Provide for a variety of realistic writing experiences. • Continue to shelter instruction and check for understanding.
Ahh!	Advanced Fluency	• Produce language with varied grammatical structures and vocabulary. • Construct multiple hypotheses and viewpoints.	• Continue to support ongoing language development through integrated language arts and content-area activities.

Adapted from Herrera (2007), p. 29. Used with permission of KCAT/TLC, Kansas State University.

FIGURE 3.6

Stages of Second Language Acquisition Demonstrated in a Thanksgiving Activity

Preproduction

This student participated in all activities throughout the lesson and created this mind map to share with the teacher and her peers what she had learned.

Early Production

This picture illustrates the student's ability to label several of the things drawn.

Speech Emergence

In classroom writing, this student was able to use what she had drawn and written on the mind map to help her write down her thoughts.

Intermediate Fluency

With the mind map as a scaffold, this student was able to write very descriptively using vocabulary from her mind map.

Advanced Fluency

This student showed evidence through her mind map and writing that she was reaching a level of proficiency equal to that of her native English-speaking peers. With support, she was beginning to produce writing with varied and more complex grammatical structures.

—2nd-Grade Classroom, Kansas

These and other support systems have been employed to help students navigate and become competent users of the English language. What often is absent (and will be addressed in the subsequent chapters of this text) is evidence of teachers' valuing and bringing into the learning process CLD students' culturally embedded notions of communication, expression, and comprehension. Such scaffolding can increase students' communicative competence in a new culture and language.

Linguistically Speaking: *i*+1

For CLD students, communicative competence is situated in the discourse of their family unit and community ("primary discourse"). Primary discourse often is in conflict with that of dominant curricula and assessment tools in public education ("academic discourse"). According to Gee (2001), discourses can be defined as "ways of combining and coordinating words, deeds, thoughts, values, bodies, objects, tools, and technologies, and other people (at the appropriate times and places) so as to enact and recognize the specific socially situated identities and activities" (p. 721). My work with teachers and students relies heavily on observation of culturally situated discourse. I have found that culturally situated discourse has important implications for successful teaching and the advancement of student learning.

Communication

What might a language full of nouns tell us about a culture? How about a language full of verbs? A language with no past tense? No future tense? A language with no word for "read" or "write"? A language with six words for love?
—Linda Christensen (2000, p. 106)

From the moment young children begin to interact with their primary caregivers, they have models for every act of communication. They learn nonverbal cues, from a wink that means "I love you" to a motherly look that says "Just test me." According to Boggs (1985), the attitudes and behavioral patterns that are most important to children are those involved in communication. Given this information, how often do we teachers consider and use our students' culturally embedded communication patterns in our teaching? Is there a chance that we may interpret what we see based on our own cultural filters?

McDaniel, Samovar, and Porter (2009) note that in order to understand communication, we must also understand culture. In our classrooms, we must begin to move beyond framing communication as teaching the content/structure of language and toward understanding the sociocultural aspects of language development and communication. According to Boggs (1985):

> Communication entails much more than the content and structure of written and spoken language, and it serves purposes greater than the mere transmission of information. Sociocultural context and nuances, discourse logic and dynamics, delivery styles, social functions, role expectations, norms of interaction, and nonverbal features are as important as (if not more so than) vocabulary, grammar, lexicon, pronunciation, and other linguistic or structural dimensions of communication. (p. 301)

Boggs contends that the "form of exchange between child and adult and the conditions in which it occurs will affect not only what is said, but how involved the child will become" (p. 301). Exploration of how communication impacts student motivation and engagement can inform the way we conduct business in our schools.

Ask yourself the following questions:

- Do I consider culture when modeling student learning strategies that involve asking questions?
- Do I consider cultural patterns of communication when configuring my groups for different tasks?
- How do CLD students communicate with others in their first language (L1) versus English (L2)? Do these interactions vary based on the people involved (e.g., parents, peers, teacher, and others)?
- In what ways might culturally bound discourse patterns impact reading, writing, and class participation for my CLD students?

Consideration of the role culture plays in students' classroom responses can influence our interpretation of their behavior. According to Bowers and Flinders (1990), behavior can be understood as the communication of thoughts in culturally prescribed ways. Understanding that students use their culturally bound systems to communicate during the lesson moves us to recognize that we must structure and manage our own communication styles to establish conditions that will encourage students to bring their identities into every act of communication.

Expression

As an educator and researcher, I have elected to place special emphasis on how students' expressive behaviors and actions contribute to or hinder their comprehension of academic concepts. Classrooms are full of opportunities for students to express thoughts and ideas as teaching and learning unfold. As educators, we are always asking students to read with expression, respond to the prompt, define words, or write paragraphs. Seldom do we ask ourselves the following questions:

- Given the student's cultural background, is this the best way for him or her to express personal ideas?
- Does the student feel free to express his or her thoughts without fear of giving the wrong answer?
- Have I, as the teacher, considered my own ways of expressing what is expected and selected a way that will be best understood, given the biographies of my students?

Observing and reflecting on ways CLD students use language and communication systems to express their thoughts and ideas moves us one step closer to creating effective pathways for learning to take place. For example, according to Heath (2000), textbook questions often require students to provide straightforward answers to demonstrate learning. This type of questioning may lead to inappropriate answers from students whose primary discourse uses metaphor and imagination or emphasizes the generation of hypotheses. Expression of needs and learning is especially critical to the success of students whose first language is not English.

Consider the following scenario, and ask yourself if your interpretation of the student behavior would reflect the cultural norms of the classroom where you find yourself today.

> A few years ago I was asked to visit a kindergarten classroom where a teacher wanted me to observe a child she thought was in need of special services. I was asked to participate during the whole-group rug/reading time so that I might observe the disruptive behavior the child, Jamal, was exhibiting while the teacher was reading. The problem seemed to be that Jamal did not wait to be asked questions by the teacher; rather, he would ask questions and make comments while the teacher was reading. The teacher had already used all her classroom management tools to try to get this student to be like the other students and wait to speak until she asked questions or asked for comments on the book.
>
> As I observed, she was absolutely right in her observations. Jamal was very engaged in what the teacher had to say and wanted to immediately add to or pose

questions related to what she was reading. After the lesson, I took Jamal aside and asked:

> *Herrera:* Did you enjoy the story?
>
> *Jamal:* I liked it a lot.
>
> *Herrera:* It was a great story! Why did you not wait for the teacher to ask you questions about the book?
>
> *Jamal:* I answered the questions.
>
> *Herrera:* Sometimes you talked when the teacher had not asked a question. Why?
>
> *Jamal:* M'am, because in my church when you feel it, you just have to tell it!

I will never forget this exchange or the many similar exchanges I have experienced since then. CLD students generate "expressive acts" that are consistent with their own frames of reference. Educators do the same and have expectations of their students consistent with these frames of reference. We may interpret student behavior as nonattentive, evasive, or disrespectful and proceed to respond according to what we perceive. Although a student's behavior may be outside the lines of *classroom management,* that is, outside our *expectations* for student participation and ideas about what is acceptable and what is not, we must remember that as different cultures become part of our classroom fabric, it becomes necessary to *bridge* ways of expressing thoughts and feelings in new ways.

By using strategies that provide opportunities for students to express thoughts, ideas, and learning in multiple ways, we can begin to observe for the often subtle messages that our students send about their culturally embedded ways of expressing their understanding and knowledge. In the case of Jamal, the teacher might have gained greater understanding about his behavior and guided his participation by asking the following types of questions during strategy implementation:

- Jamal, I see that you get really loud and excited about the vocabulary quilt. Is there something you really like about this activity?
- Jamal, what could we do to have you wait to share all the exciting things you know until we finish with the quilt?
- Jamal, I am wondering what you thought about this word. Do you think you could raise your hand and tell me in a quiet voice what you are thinking?

Spending time with Jamal's small group during the activity would support his transition from culturally appropriate to classroom-appropriate ways of responding to learning. Understanding his behavior through the lens of his cultural response would set the stage for rerouting his actions by

talking to him about his excitement during participation. It may take time to move from a student's cultural/home response to classroom-appropriate behavior, but the time invested will be well worth it. The process may even provide new ideas for class participation that all students might enjoy. Chapters 7, 8, and 9 further discuss explicit ways of supporting student expression.

Comprehension

In schools, the ultimate goal of teaching is for students to comprehend what was taught and to take that information on to the next level. That is, students must store new knowledge in their permanent memory so that it is accessible in the future. In the classroom, we teachers often go about the act of teaching using all the prescribed methods and materials and sprinkling them with our own techniques to achieve the goal of having everyone learn. Yet frequently we are surprised at the interpretations our students have come to by the end of the lesson. We ask, "How did this happen?"

According to Säljö (1996) and Wertsch (1998), learning and meaning-making are seen as inseparable from the learner's situational and sociocultural circumstances. Hiebert (1991) supports this by stating that we are beginning to depart from a conceptualization of "literacy" as text-driven and move toward a view of literacy as the active transformation of texts. In the past, meaning was thought to be derived from text; however, new ways of thinking find that meaning is created through interactions of the reader with the text. Furthermore, Eisner (1998) reminds us that literacy "is not limited to text" (p. 15). Rather, it is related to the individual's ability to construe meaning from any of the forms used in the culture to create and convey meaning.

Providing opportunities for students to voice what they have learned before moving forward gives each student one last chance to *get it right*. In this picture, Mr. Aguilar asks selected students to share their personal perspectives about the topic and relate those perspectives to the new information they have gained.

—*Billy Aguilar, High School, California*

Consider the following scenario and note your initial reaction to the students' discussion.

A few years ago I had the opportunity to observe and co-teach in a middle school where the teacher had been reading *The Scarlet Letter* by Nathaniel Hawthorne. Because they were deep into the book by the time I visited the class, we decided to use a strategy called "The Relevance Scale" to have the students review for me what they deemed important from the story. Each group was assigned a chapter and asked to find the three most important details and be ready to share. As each of the groups debated what they were going to share with me, I noted from my observations how their sociocultural background was influencing what they considered important.

At the end of the lesson, the students were asked how the details they had selected as most important might differ if they were from another culture or country. Following is a glimpse of the path that students' responses took:

Student 1: Well, you know, I think if you sleep with someone else it doesn't matter, so why would that be important?

Student 2: Well, in my family a woman who does that is trash and no one would accept her.

Student 3: Well, then I think her sleeping around is important and she should be punished.

Student 2: My family and I would vote for that.

Student 1: Well, do we think we need to know that she slept around?

Many of the groups followed the same pattern of discussion, identifying relevance according to their own culturally bound ideas of what was important and why. After much discussion and debate on the students' *culturally situated* thoughts on the novel and class consensus building related to the overarching themes of the novel (e.g., compassion, withholding judgment), the teacher took the discussion to the present day. He asked student groups to consider the identified themes in relation to current environments or situations where inhumane actions, lack of compassion, and so forth have repercussions on the present-day lives of people. An assessment of student comprehension in this scenario would need to consider the pathways of thinking and analysis that each group took to arrive at the universal themes of the novel and apply those themes to various situations in the world today.

As we plan and deliver instruction designed to promote CLD students' comprehension of curricular content, we must find ways to elicit students' interpretation of text through the lens of their life experiences. We can then use these insights to better scaffold instruction and guide students toward the knowledge and understandings we want them to possess and be able to apply to future learning. The following questions can guide us as we move beyond school-initiated responses to linguistic diversity and consider differences related to how students comprehend new information:

- What kinds of opportunities do students have to individually respond to visuals in order to share from their own point of view?
- When introducing unfamiliar concepts, in what ways are connections that are culturally familiar to CLD students used to explain the new material?
- How are CLD students encouraged to communicate with their peers about their life and experiences so that all students can make multiple connections to content?

Reflections on the Linguistic Dimension

Increasing the academic achievement of our CLD students means thinking about language from multiple angles. Currently in schools, we focus heavily on understanding language from "one side of the coin," that is, language learning that emphasizes grammar, vocabulary, pronunciation, and limited sociolinguistic aspects. Moving beyond this limited focus means creating situational and social contexts in which we can learn through observation about the ways students communicate, express, and comprehend classroom instruction based on their cultural and linguistic socialization.

Considering students' linguistic capacities to communicate and express themselves, Delpit (1988) states that it is important that we "coach those voices to produce notes that will be heard clearly in the larger society" (p. 296). Mays (2008) further challenges us, saying, "Educators who take the time to learn the primary Discourse of their students are helping to close the achievement gap and value the voice of ELLs often stifled by the academic Discourse predominately used in schools today. Can you hear them? Each one has something to say" (p. 418). When we fully consider the linguistic dimension of the CLD student biography, we recognize that language, literacy, and learning are greatly influenced by the culture and community in which a student has been socialized. We begin to understand the importance of providing opportunities for students to participate in the learning process and demonstrate their understanding in ways that differ from those traditionally found in schools. Our ability to act on newfound insights about the linguistic dimension of our CLD students is bolstered by reflection on our current habits of mind and action.

CHAPTER 4

Culture-Driven Thought and Learning

What we talk about; how we talk about it; what we see, attend to, or ignore; how we think; and what we think about are influenced by our culture.

—*Porter and Samovar (1991, p. 21)*

THE THIRD and most overlooked dimension of the CLD student biography is the cognitive dimension. Cognition can be thought of as a broader yet more precise term for "thinking." It encompasses how a student's brain processes and learns what is taught (Ortega, 2009). For each of us, our thought process is part of who we are as individuals, and how we respond is based on our biographies. Often as teachers we fail to see or cannot understand why CLD students take their own path in writing, responding, or engaging in activities that have been explicitly modeled in the classroom. Knowing that students' thought processes are influenced by their biographies can give us insights into their actions, especially if we are aware of the impact of the cognitive dimension on the learning process.

The Cognitive Dimension

The cognitive dimension is often neglected, for a variety of reasons, including:

- Limited knowledge of the role cognition plays in acquiring a second language
- Limited understanding of the influence culture has on ways of thinking
- Limited perspectives on how cognitive processes can be demonstrated in the classroom
- Limited understanding of how to account for varying levels of language proficiency when designing cognitively challenging tasks

Often teachers may view cognition through a limited lens, leading to flawed interpretations of what is possible during instruction. For example, L2 learning issues (e.g., comprehension, pronunciation, or length of time needed for second language acquisition) frequently are viewed as a hindrance to academic success or as a sign that, given the English proficiency of the learner, he or she may not be able to participate fully in classroom activities that require certain cognitive processes. For example, many teachers cite the "silent period" as a reason for not asking questions of newly arrived students (Mohr & Mohr, 2007). Consider Jorge's story:

When I arrived in the United States I was eager to begin school and learn English. My father, a U.S. citizen, had great dreams of my receiving an education that would lead to something. At first I was happy when many of the teachers would skip me when asking questions or ask questions that required me to answer yes or no. After a few weeks I figured out that the teachers thought I was not capable of thinking, that my not speaking English was somehow connected to my intelligence level. I wanted to scream and say, just because I don't speak English does not mean I cannot think. I am so happy that some teachers made things happen for me. Here I am today at the University, having come to the United States just three years ago.

Many CLD students have had K–12 schooling experiences similar to those of Jorge. They often are not challenged cognitively during instruction and instead are taught lower-level skills (Chamberlain, 2005; Gaddy, 1999; Nieto, 2000). According to Waxman and Tellez (2002), lower teacher expectations may lead second language learners to lower achievement throughout their educational experience.

Considering different perspectives on the role of cognition in second language acquisition can help educators better understand the theoretical foundations of instructional practices used with CLD students. With a more thorough understanding of *why* we do what we do, we can more effectively reflect on our current practices as we continue to move forward and enhance our instruction with CLD students.

Evolving Thought on Cognition and Second Language Acquisition

This chapter's general overview of theories of cognition is intended to provide a foundation for understanding how cognitive theories of learning shape effective classroom practices for second language learners. Undoubtedly, research efforts will continue to expand our knowledge of factors and processes that influence how CLD students acquire linguistic and academic knowledge. My hope is that this section will give educators a context within which to reflect on their own perspectives on cognition and the role it plays in learning.

In the past, thought on second language acquisition reflected *behaviorist theories* and considered the acquisition of language a stimulus–response activity based on the establishment of habits. Current views on the acquisition of language have largely emphasized *information processing theories,* in which "the human mind is viewed as a symbolic processor that constantly engages in mental processes" (Ortega, 2009, p. 83). Although the thinking on second language acquisition and cognitive processing has changed, there are still classrooms that use a noncommunicative, linear, drill-and-practice approach to teaching. This way of thinking tends to place limits on the academic achievement of learners. Movement away from stimulus–response ways of teaching allows us to explore *performance* rather than behavior to assess student learning. In classrooms where diversity is part of the classroom fabric, an in-depth analysis of student performance enables us to attend to the needs of individual students throughout the learning process.

According to information processing theories, students' processing of knowledge used for learning can occur through both automatic and controlled operations. As the term implies, automatic processes "require small effort and take up few cognitive resources"; as a result, multiple automatic processes can take place at the same time (Ortega, 2009, p. 83). When students are learning in a language they understand (i.e., the native language), some of their learning occurs with little cognitive effort, particularly when they have background knowledge related to the topic. However, for CLD students who are learning in a language that is unfamiliar to them, cognitive processing is often much more controlled, or conscious, on the part of the learner.

Consciously controlled processes require greater cognitive resources, are voluntarily controlled by the learner, and

Classrooms where students sit in straight rows and work only on individual assignments provide little opportunity for students to make public what they are thinking, why they think the way they do, and how they are making sense of the information presented during the lesson.

are intricately linked to goal-directed motivation. Because these processes require the learner's attention, only one process can be carried out at any given moment. As Ortega (2009) notes, "performance that draws on controlled processing is . . . more vulnerable to stressors" (p. 84). The student's capacity for performance of automatic versus controlled processes in the classroom has significant implications for teachers of second language learners. Performance in the classroom is enhanced when the teacher aligns instruction and the ecology of the classroom to meet the cognitive processing needs of diverse learners. Teachers can do this by:

- Creating risk-free or low-risk opportunities for students to share what they know
- Considering the impact of students' emotions on learning
- Considering the culture of CLD students when introducing potentially foreign concepts
- Setting up situations in the classroom where student talk occurs often
- Allowing students to use their native language to make sense of new information and check their comprehension of new language and content
- Observing student conversations for insights into how students process information
- Using resulting insights and information about student learning to modify instruction or student groupings, as needed

The information processing theory known as *skill acquisition theory* has had a great deal of influence on instructional practices for second language acquisition. Ortega (2009) explains: "Skill acquisition theory defines learning as the gradual transformation of performance from controlled to automatic. This transformation [or *automatization*] happens through relevant practice over many trials" (p. 84). It is important to note that the process of automatization is skill specific. If practice emphasizes receptive comprehension in the second language, then comprehension skills will be the focus of automatization; if practice emphasizes L2 production, then production skills will be the focus (Ortega). Therefore, a balance of attention to both receptive (i.e., listening and reading) and productive (i.e., speaking and writing) skills is needed for CLD students.

Imagine, for a moment, that you are a second language learner in a grade-level classroom. During instruction, you are not provided with the support you need to acquire the academic vocabulary of the lesson or to use what you already know to comprehend the lesson. Instead, you are forced to move quickly through the lesson with little time to link ideas and make sense of what you are being asked to do. CLD students often experience this kind of scenario with reading programs in which they are asked to merely "mirror" what the teacher is asking them to do, without opportunities for meaningful and relevant practice. What often results is little development of student knowledge with regard to either language or content. Communicative, constructivist settings, on the other hand, provide students with opportunities to actively discuss and create meaning during learning.

Segalowitz (2003) posits that a qualitative change takes place when automaticity has been achieved. Automaticity means more than the learner simply becoming faster at a skill, or accumulating skills mastered through practice (Ortega, 2009). Rather, Ortega explains, "prolonged and repeated practice *changes the knowledge representation itself* [italics added] by making the stored knowledge become more elaborated and well specified" (p. 85). Such is the case, for example, with vocabulary learning. When a word becomes automatic, a reader is able to readily decode it when reading. Because teachers are concerned with the degree to which students' knowledge of a given word reflects both strength (i.e., ability to automatically recognize the word and to use the word) and depth (i.e., elaborated, structured understanding of the word and the subtle nuances of its use across contexts), it is important to focus CLD students' attention on the cognitive processes they engage in to comprehend words.

The most recent developments in understanding the cognitive processes involved in second language acquisition

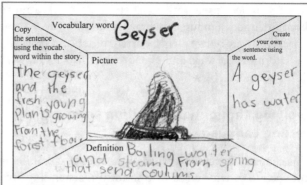

Using this multidimensional square strategy, the teacher provides the student with multiple opportunities to cognitively process the meaning of the target vocabulary word.

—*Emily Seaman, 4th Grade, Kansas*

relate to *emergentist theories,* which evolved from information processing theories. Emergentist theories emphasize the learner's desire to make sense of the linguistic environment in which he or she interacts (Ortega, 2009). The learner's brain strives to (a) identify recurring examples of language use; (b) make guesses based on the best possible evidence, context clues, most current relevant information, and so forth; and (c) adjust accordingly based on whether a given prediction is confirmed or disconfirmed (Chater & Manning, 2006; Ellis, 2002, 2006a, 2006b, 2007). In classroom practice, this can occur only through multiple exposures to vocabulary, content and context-embedded activities, and the use of multiple grouping configurations where CLD students can encounter different perspectives and different ways of expressing the same information.

Emergentist theories emphasize usage-based learning, which Ortega (2009) defines as the idea that "language use and language knowledge are inseparable, because we come to know language from using it" (p. 104). Ellis (2007) describes the language learning process as "a dynamic process in which regularities and systems emerge from the interaction of people, their conscious selves, and their brains, using language in their societies, cultures, and world" (p. 85). I believe we teachers have much to gain from understanding how researchers' knowledge and theories have changed over time regarding how language is acquired and processed, and the implications of such changes for classroom practice.

Traditional School-Initiated Responses

Within the classroom context, teachers have defined and have attempted to address the cognitive dimension of CLD students in the following ways:

- Varying the complexity and difficulty of the task CLD students are asked to accomplish
- Using learning style inventories to discover students' learning style preferences
- Using cognitive learning strategies to support student learning

The sections that follow provide a brief introduction to these school-situated responses to the cognitive dimension, which teachers often employ to address CLD students' development of academic content and English language proficiency.

Cognitive Complexity and Difficulty of Task

The cognitive demands any academic task places on a CLD student are complicated by additional linguistic demands. Providing contextual clues such as visuals, manipulatives, and concept-related objects can help students as they try to make sense of the language in order to understand the content. Figure 4.1 provides examples that demonstrate the range of contextual support and degree of cognitive involvement in communicative activities. Any student who is continually asked to participate in cognitively demanding tasks without time to periodically allow the brain to "relax" will likely lose the motivation to continue to be engaged in the lesson.

By varying the complexity of tasks, educators can increase CLD student engagement and understanding of the lesson. Students who are learning a new language need opportunities to be challenged at varying levels while they are learning new material. Selecting strategies that allow for variance in cognitive demand increases the likelihood that each student will be able to more fully participate in classroom activities. Figure 4.2 illustrates how a lesson on insects was designed to incorporate tasks that varied in cognitive complexity.

When teachers reflect on ways to vary the cognitive complexity of a task, they often look to Bloom's taxonomy, which was originally conceptualized to include the following six levels, organized in order of increasing complexity: knowledge, comprehension, application, analysis, synthesis, and evaluation (Bloom, Engelhart, Furst, Hill, & Krathwohl, 1956). Anderson et al. (2001) revised the taxonomy; the revised version is depicted in Figure 4.3. In describing the differences between the two versions, Sousa (2006) notes that the revised taxonomy "changes the labels to verb

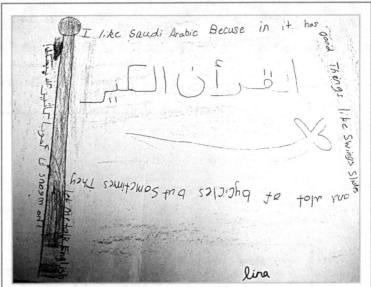

I read *Candy Corn* and *Just Around the Corner* by James Stevenson to the whole class. As a follow-up, I showed them how to write a shape poem—choose a topic and then write the poem in a representative shape. Then I asked them to write their own.

In an earlier lesson, we had read some Spanish poetry and listened for the rhythm and rhyme, noting that we could hear the play with words even in another language. As a class, I had the students chorally read some of the easier poems. As a result, some of the children wanted to write poetry in their own languages.

One student immediately decided that she would write a poem about Saudi Arabia. She wrote the poem in the shape of a flag, and she added lines in Arabic. Her poem shows pride in her culture and language and an awareness of English even in her home country. When she was done, she also wrote in Arabic about her relationship with her brother.

Although I know almost nothing about Arabic and was not able to read what this student wrote, I think it is still essential to provide students with opportunities to think and write in the language in which they are most fluent, which is their native language. Students can illustrate what they wrote, with the hope that some meaning will be apparent from the illustration. Then I can have follow-up conversations with them in English about what they wrote.

—Leellyn Tuel, 2nd Grade, Kansas

form, renames three levels, and interchanges the top two levels. The dotted outline suggests a more open and fluid model, recognizing that an individual may move among the levels during extended processing" (p. 250). Because we teachers want students to be able to use the information they are learning for future purposes that are personally relevant, it is fitting that *Create* now receives emphasis as the highest level of complexity.

Sousa (2006) urges educators to remember the distinction between *complexity* and *difficulty* when putting Bloom's taxonomy to use with learners in classroom practice. As he explains, "Complexity establishes the level of thought while

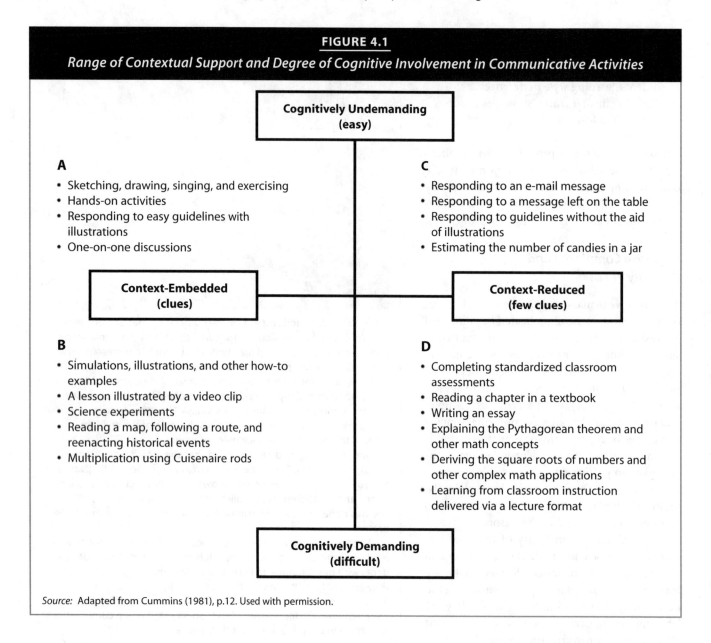

FIGURE 4.1

Range of Contextual Support and Degree of Cognitive Involvement in Communicative Activities

Cognitively Undemanding (easy)

A

- Sketching, drawing, singing, and exercising
- Hands-on activities
- Responding to easy guidelines with illustrations
- One-on-one discussions

C

- Responding to an e-mail message
- Responding to a message left on the table
- Responding to guidelines without the aid of illustrations
- Estimating the number of candies in a jar

Context-Embedded (clues)

Context-Reduced (few clues)

B

- Simulations, illustrations, and other how-to examples
- A lesson illustrated by a video clip
- Science experiments
- Reading a map, following a route, and reenacting historical events
- Multiplication using Cuisenaire rods

D

- Completing standardized classroom assessments
- Reading a chapter in a textbook
- Writing an essay
- Explaining the Pythagorean theorem and other math concepts
- Deriving the square roots of numbers and other complex math applications
- Learning from classroom instruction delivered via a lecture format

Cognitively Demanding (difficult)

Source: Adapted from Cummins (1981), p.12. Used with permission.

difficulty determines the amount of effort required within each level" (p. 257). Often teachers think the tasks they have designed will lead to more complex thinking, when in reality the tasks only require greater effort at the same lower level of thinking. For example, asking students to name the seven continents is equally complex as asking students to name all the countries on each of the seven continents. Both of these tasks require students to *remember*. The second task, however, is much more difficult.

Sousa (2006) also addresses the need for us to understand that student ability is more closely related to difficulty than to complexity. Even slower learners can think complexly; it simply takes them more time to learn the concept and to sort the subcomponents or supporting understandings when deciding which aspects of the concept need to

be retained for future use. Unfortunately, the time allotted to instruction of a given concept frequently does not afford slower learners the opportunity to fully learn the concept and perform the needed sorting. As Sousa notes, "This explains why fast learners are usually fast retrievers: They have not cluttered their memory networks with trivia" (p. 257). They have had ample time to both learn and sort.

Similarly, for CLD students who have language acquisition needs in addition to those generally associated with learning grade-level content, sufficient time must be allotted for processing curricular concepts. In practice, this means that we teachers must identify the core concepts of our curriculum that are absolutely essential for all students to learn. By emphasizing depth rather than breadth of content coverage, we increase the likelihood that all students will

FIGURE 4.2
Student Tasks That Vary in Cognitive Complexity

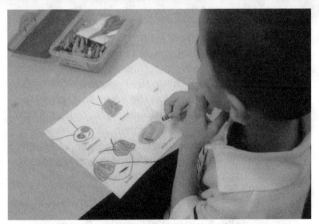

Cognitively Undemanding & Context-Embedded

In this part of the lesson, students were asked to draw the body parts of an insect. Students were able to look at examples of insects throughout this task.

Cognitively Undemanding & Context-Reduced

Students later worked in pairs to practice and discuss the vocabulary for the body parts of an insect. They listened to the teacher define the words, and they identified the corresponding terms on a vocabulary strip.

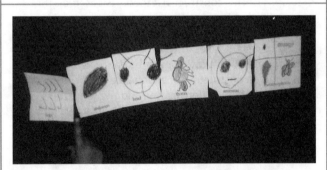

Cognitively Demanding & Context-Embedded

As the lesson progressed, the students were provided with the pictures they had drawn to share what they had learned in sequence. This task was context-embedded (pictures); however, it did require that the students discuss the information in sequence (cognitively demanding).

The abdomen has the important organs.

Cognitively Demanding & Context-Reduced

Students completed the lesson with a writing assignment in which the teacher provided them with a sentence strip on which a main idea of the lesson was written. The teacher then asked students to write a paragraph incorporating three supporting details related to the main idea on the strip.

—Erica Bonderson, Heidi Christensen, Judeen Matsuo, Amy Rojas, & Nichole Zoeller, Elementary, Iowa

have time to fully understand the content and build from there to become adept at creative and critical thinking.

Learning Styles

Students can vary greatly in their "typically preferred modes of processing information" (Sternberg & Grigorenko, 1997, p. 700). Ortega (2009) notes that such preferences are commonly referred to as "cognitive styles" or "learning styles." Such styles will influence the "ways in which they feel comfortable when perceiving, remembering and using information for problem solving and for learning" (Ortega, 2009, p. 205). A learning style refers to how a student consistently approaches problem-solving situations and demonstrates what he or she has learned, knows, or can do (Gay, 2000; More, 1989; Shade, 1989).

According to Guild and Garger (1985), in order to discover what students' learning styles may be, it is necessary

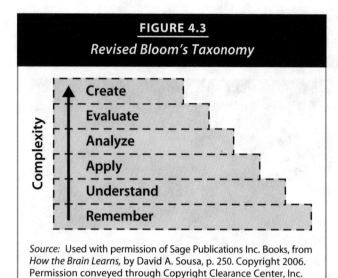

FIGURE 4.3

Revised Bloom's Taxonomy

Source: Used with permission of Sage Publications Inc. Books, from *How the Brain Learns,* by David A. Sousa, p. 250. Copyright 2006. Permission conveyed through Copyright Clearance Center, Inc.

FIGURE 4.4

Multiple Perspectives on Learning Styles

Dunn and Dunn Learning-Style Model

According to this model, learning style is described as the way an individual begins to focus attention on, take in, make sense of, and store new and challenging information (Dunn & Dunn, 1993, 1999). It is based on five elements designated as the environmental, emotional, sociological, physical, and psychological dimensions, which encompass more than 20 variables that can affect how a student best learns. Dunn and Dunn maintain that educators should administer diagnostic assessments to identify students' tendencies and strengths within these five dimensions.

Kolb's Experiential Learning Theory

According to Kolb (1984), "learning is the process whereby knowledge is created through the transformation of experience. Knowledge results from the combination of grasping experience and transforming it" (p. 41). This constructivist theory is based on the premise that learning is a continuous process shaped by the modes we use to construct knowledge from our experiences. It takes into account John Dewey's philosophy that "education must be conceived as a continuing reconstruction of experience ... the process and goal of education are one and the same thing" (Dewey, 1897, p. 79). Kolb categorizes learners into four types: assimilators, convergers, accommodators, and divergers.

Gregorc's Mind Styles Model

According to Gregorc (1984), individual learners will be more apt to perceive information in either a concrete or an abstract manner. Those with more concrete tendencies are likely to learn more effectively through their five senses, whereas more abstract learners prefer to visualize and imagine ideas. He emphasizes that everyone is capable of thinking in both ways, but people usually possess strengths in one domain over the other. Gregorc also states that people tend to think in either a sequential or a random manner. Sequential learners think in a more linear, step-by-step manner, whereas random thinkers chunk information in an unsystematic order. According to Gregorc, perception and ordering of information can be combined in the following four ways: concrete sequential, abstract random, abstract sequential, and concrete random.

to analyze what they do on a routine basis in interactions with people, situations, ideas, and information. A teacher's role, therefore, is to observe students to discover what learning style they most exhibit during the lesson, and to use that information to increase language learning and academic success. Guild and Garger suggest observing for the following kinds of information (p. 6):

- *Cognition:* People perceive and gain knowledge differently
- *Conceptualization:* People form ideas and think differently
- *Affect:* People feel and form values differently
- *Behavior:* People act differently

Bennett (1995) concurs with the findings of other researchers that, fundamentally, "learning styles" are the cognitive, behavioral, and affective responses of individuals when they are involved in learning. Learning styles change the way that tasks are perceived, acted upon, and ultimately accomplished. Many researchers have offered theories on different learning style types; Figure 4.4 provides a glimpse of some of the learning styles most widely mentioned in the field of education.

Missing from much discussion of learning styles is the influence of the CLD student's culture on the style he or she chooses to use within a learning situation. According to Laosa (1977), the student's culture will mold and shape his or her style. Where a student comes from as well as his or her learning expectations and experiences (both in and out of school) will have a direct impact on the learning style he or she chooses to use or uses unconsciously while learning. Furthermore, as students acculturate to the classroom/ school/community/country, they become more aware of

FIGURE 4.5		
Eight Dimensions of Learning Styles		
Dimension	**Characteristic**	**Examples**
Procedural	Preferred ways of approaching and working through learning tasks	Pacing rates; distribution of time; variety vs. similarity; novelty vs. predictability; passivity vs. activity; task-directed vs. sociality; structured order vs. freedom; preference for direct teaching vs. inquiry and discovery learning
Communicative	How thoughts are organized, sequenced, and conveyed in spoken and written forms	Elaborated narrative storytelling vs. precise responses to explicit questions; topic-specific vs. topic-chaining discourse techniques; passionate advocacy of ideas vs. dispassionate recorders and reporters; aimed at achieving descriptive and factual accuracy vs. capturing persuasive power and conveying literary aestheticism
Substantive	Preferred content	Descriptive details vs. general pattern; concepts and principles vs. factual information; statistics vs. personal and social scenarios
	Preferred subjects	Math, science, social studies, fine arts, language arts
	Preferred intellectualizing tasks	Memorizing, describing, analyzing, classifying, criticizing
Environmental	Preferred physical, social, and interpersonal settings for learning	Sound vs. silence; room lighting and temperature; presence or absence of others; ambiance of struggle or playfulness; ambiance of fun and joy or of pain and somberness
Organizational	Preferred structural arrangements for work and study space	Amount of personal space; fullness or emptiness of learning space; rigidity or flexibility in use of and claims made to space; carefully organized or cluttered learning resources and space locations; individually claimed or group-shared space; rigidity or flexibility of the habitation of space
Perceptual	Preferred sensory stimulation for receiving, processing, and transmitting information	Visual, tactile, auditory, kinetic, oral, or multiple sensory modalities
Relational	Preferred interpersonal and social interaction modes in learning situations	Formality vs. informality; individual competition vs. group cooperation; independence vs. interdependence; peer–peer vs. child–adult; authoritarian vs. egalitarian; internal vs. external locus of control; conquest vs. community
Motivational	Preferred incentives or stimulations that evoke learning	Individual accomplishment vs. group well-being; competition vs. cooperation; conquest vs. harmony; expediency vs. propriety; image vs. integrity; external rewards vs. internal desires

Source: Adapted from Gay (2000), pp. 151–152.

the ways of thinking and doing within this new context, and their learning styles may begin to shift to accommodate the new environment. During this time, it is important to be conscious of the need to create a space where the student does not feel pressure to fit into a certain style.

According to Gay (2000), "Overall characterizations of learning styles suggest that they are not monolithic, situationally idiosyncratic, or static traits. Instead, they are multi-dimensional, habituated processes that are the 'central tendencies' of how students from different ethnic groups engage with learning encounters" (p. 151). Gay discusses eight dimensions along which learning styles can differ. These dimensions are summarized in Figure 4.5.

Although Gay (2000) begins to move our understanding of learning styles toward a more dynamic and culturally embedded perspective, much research remains to be done.

	FIGURE 4.6	
	Chamot and O'Malley's Three Types of Learning Strategies	
Strategy	**Description**	**Definition**
Metacognitive Strategies		
Planning		
Advance organization	Preview Skim Gist	Previewing the main ideas and concepts of a text; identifying the organizing principle
Organizational planning	Plan what to do	Planning how to accomplish the learning task; planning the parts and sequence of ideas to express
Selective attention	Listen or read selectively Scan Find specific information	Attending to key words, phrases, ideas, linguistic markers, and types of information
Self-management	Plan when, where, and how to study	Seeking or arranging the conditions that help one learn
Monitoring		
Monitoring comprehension	Think while listening Think while reading	Checking one's comprehension during listening or reading
Monitoring production	Think while speaking Think while writing	Checking one's oral or written production while it is taking place
Evaluating		
Self-assessment	Check back Keep a learning log Reflect on what you learned	Judging how well one has accomplished a learning task

As knowledge in this area continues to grow, one thing is certain: CLD students' learning styles, including behavioral ways of learning, are tied to their biographies. Students' socialization experiences as unique individuals with ties to one or more cultures contribute to their ways of thinking and acting in the learning process (Guild, 2001). Students' knowledge and insights from such experiences have resulted in processes that have proven effective and functional in their homes and communities. These learning processes can become a resource for teachers during the lesson and may facilitate students' academic learning.

Student Learning Strategies

Whereas learning styles can be understood as the ways individuals process information, learning *strategies* "are conscious mental and behavioral procedures that people engage in with the aim to gain control over their learning process" (Ortega, 2009, p. 208). Understanding how these two are distinct prepares the teacher to create conditions wherein both are part of their practice and are aligned with the needs of individual learners. In the education of CLD students, the most widely recognized research on learning strategies was conducted by Chamot and O'Malley of George Washington University. Their research and writing (e.g., O'Malley & Chamot, 1990) documented types of learning strategies and their association with particular academic tasks. In Chapter 1 of this text, I discussed the CALLA method of instruction for CLD students. One of the central components of the CALLA model is the use of student learning strategies to support academic and language development of second language learners. An over-

Strategy	Description	Definition
Cognitive Strategies		
Resourcing	Use reference materials	Using reference materials such as dictionaries, encyclopedias, or textbooks
Grouping	Classify Construct graphic organizers	Classifying words, terminology, quantities, or concepts according to their attributes
Note-Taking	Take notes on idea maps, T-lists, etc.	Writing down key words and concepts in abbreviated verbal, graphic, or numerical form
Elaboration of Prior Knowledge	Use what you know Use background knowledge Make analogies	Relating new to known information and making personal associations
Summarizing	Say or write the main idea	Making a mental, oral, or written summary of information gained from listening or reading
Deduction/Induction	Use a rule/Make a rule	Applying or figuring out rules to understand a concept or complete a learning task
Imagery	Visualize Make a picture	Using mental or real pictures to learn new information or solve a problem
Auditory Representation	Use your mental tape recorder Hear it again	Replaying mentally a word, phrase, or piece of information
Making Inferences	Use context clues Guess from context Predict	Using information in the text to guess meanings of new items or predict upcoming information
Social/Affective Strategies		
Questioning for Clarification	Ask questions	Getting additional explanation or verification from a teacher or other expert
Cooperation	Cooperate Work with classmates Coach each other	Working with peers to complete a task, pool information, solve a problem, get feedback
Self-Talk	Think positive!	Reducing anxiety by improving one's sense of competence

Source: Table 4.1, pp. 62–63 from *The CALLA Handbook* by Anna Uhl Chamot and J. Michael O'Malley. Copyright © 1994 by Addison-Wesley Publishing Company, Inc. Reprinted by permission of Pearson Education, Inc.

view of the three primary types of strategies detailed by Chamot and O'Malley (1994) is provided in Figure 4.6.

Oxford (1990) also extensively researched learning strategies, developing a model that includes six groups of strategies and their associated subsets of strategies (p. 17). In total, Oxford discusses 62 strategies. Figure 4.7 depicts the relationships among the various strategies in Oxford's system.

Student learning strategies, when introduced and modeled by the instructor and gradually released for student learning, provide students with the necessary tools to take responsibility for and scaffold their own learning. This type of responsibility is often an expectation of the gifted student or is modeled by parents in homes where parents have a college education. However, because school may be students' first exposure to such strategies, it becomes essential

FIGURE 4.7
Oxford's System of Learning Strategies

Memory Strategies

Creating mental linkages
- Grouping
- Associating/elaborating
- Placing new words into a context

Applying images and sounds
- Using imagery
- Semantic mapping
- Using keywords
- Representing sounds in memory

Reviewing well
- Structured reviewing

Employing action
- Using physical response or sensation
- Using mechanical techniques

Cognitive Strategies

Practicing
- Repeating
- Formally practicing with sounds and writing systems
- Recognizing and using formulas and patterns
- Recombining
- Practicing naturalistically

Receiving and sending messages
- Getting the idea quickly
- Using resources for receiving and sending messages

Analyzing and reasoning
- Reasoning deductively
- Analyzing expressions
- Analyzing contrastively (across languages)
- Translating
- Transferring

Creating structure for input and output
- Taking notes
- Summarizing
- Highlighting

Compensation Strategies

Guessing intelligently
- Using linguistic clues
- Using other clues

Overcoming limitations in speaking and writing
- Switching to the mother tongue
- Getting help
- Using mime or gesture
- Avoiding communication partially or totally
- Selecting the topic
- Adjusting or approximating the message
- Coining words
- Using a circumlocution or synonym

Metacognitive Strategies

Centering your learning
- Overviewing and linking with already known material
- Paying attention
- Delaying speech production to focus on listening

Arranging and planning your learning
- Finding out about language learning
- Organizing
- Setting goals and objectives
- Identifying the purpose of a language task (purposeful listening/reading/speaking/writing)
- Planning for a language task
- Seeking practice opportunities

Evaluating your learning
- Self-monitoring
- Self-evaluating

Affective Strategies

Lowering your anxiety
- Using progressive relaxation, deep breathing, or meditation
- Using music
- Using laughter

Encouraging yourself
- Making positive statements
- Taking risks wisely
- Rewarding yourself

Taking your emotional temperature
- Listening to your body
- Using a checklist
- Writing a language learning diary
- Discussing your feelings with someone else

Social Strategies

Asking questions
- Asking for clarification or verification
- Asking for correction

Cooperating with others
- Cooperating with peers
- Cooperating with proficient users of the new language

Empathizing with others
- Developing cultural understanding
- Becoming aware of others' thoughts and feelings

Adapted from Oxford (1990), *Language Learning Strategies,* pp. 17–21, 1E. © 1990 Heinle/ELT, a part of Cengage Learning, Inc. Reproduced with permission. www.cengage.com/permissions.

in classrooms with diverse students that we, as teachers, take responsibility for including learning strategies as part of our daily practice so that all students have access to tools that lead to academic achievement.

To date, much of the research done on learning strategies has been inconclusive. According to Ortega (2009), strategy use by the individual is highly dictated and controlled by the teacher. This control manifests itself in the learning objectives and goals the teacher selects. Other factors that influence the learner's strategy use include:

- The student's motivation to learn the target language
- The particular learning task
- The cultural appropriateness of various strategies for the learner

Without a conscious inventory of these factors, the teaching of learning strategies may leave students, particularly CLD students, without any new skill or tool for uncovering, monitoring, or evaluating their own learning.

Although there is much to be learned about learning strategies and their true impact on the student, we do recognize that explicit strategy instruction can enhance the likelihood of CLD students' achievement of linguistic and academic success. The role that a student's sociocultural and linguistic biography plays in his or her selection and use of learning strategies, including when and how they are applied in different content areas and within different contexts, demands further research. By proactively seeking to understand how a CLD student has gained knowledge about the world, the types of thought processes he or she frequently uses to make sense of new information, and the ways he or she is most adept at applying information, the educator can gain insights into the learning strategies the student currently uses.

It is important to plan for and teach learning strategies that are aligned with the teaching objectives, curriculum, and CLD student biography. We must remind ourselves that merely teaching learning strategies will not result in greater learning. Rather, the strategies selected for instruction must lend themselves to supporting students' attainment of the objectives and understanding of the content.

In addition, learning strategies must be culturally responsive and relevant, as certain learning strategies may be inappropriate for some students (e.g., students from non-Western cultures may not be accustomed to providing corrective feedback to peers) (Ortega, 2009). In such instances, specific efforts should be made to provide explicit instruction and guidance in using the strategy to enhance learning. By incorporating use of multiple types of strategies in the classroom and continually reminding students that we all have "tricks" that support our learning, we can

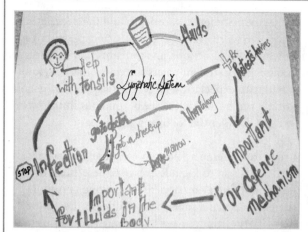

The use of mind maps (Buzan, 1983) as a strategy for allowing students to document what they know and to share what they have learned increases the chances that all students, even those who have not reached a high level of proficiency in English, will be active participants in learning. The mind map allows for both linguistic and nonlinguistic representations of student learning.

—*Jeremy Pride, Middle School , Kansas*

provide CLD students with assurance that strategy use should be flexible to their specific learning needs.

Pedagogy that values student biographies in the exploration and use of learning strategies requires a move away from pre-set, reductionistic taxonomies of how learning strategies are taught and used in classroom practice. Instead, by observing, listening, and documenting CLD students in action, we teachers can create more opportunities for students to integrate strategy use that is effective—based on how *they* as individuals know, think, and apply knowledge.

Cognitively Speaking: *i*+1

It is easy to get stuck in what has been researched or prescribed within our own teaching cultures and pay little attention to the cultural context of the student or the role of individual motivation in the learning process. Yet as Jensen (2008) reminds us, "In order to get learners to be creative and have greater subject interest, higher self-esteem, and the ability to be reflective, there must be intrinsic motivation" (p. 124). We are more likely to encourage that motivation, and to accomplish our teaching goals, when we focus on CLD students' ways of learning.

Multiple Ways of Knowing

The way we come to know things from an early age is a result of our interactions with the world around us. We learn to ask questions, respond, tell a story, and interpret the voices and actions of both the communicator and the message itself. Students' knowledge and their revelation of it reflect the words, understandings, and perspectives of those whose voices, actions, and thoughts they have learned to imitate. Every student enters the classroom with knowledge and with expectations about the way things are going to work. It can be difficult to see beyond our initial ways of knowing. Consider the following scenario:

I remember being asked to write, to tell my stories. My stories had to include everyone because in my family nothing ever happens to just one person. I remember when a snake bit my little brother in the fields. Lots of things were happening and they didn't happen in a line the way my teacher wanted me to tell them. My story happened in a zigzag, with many little things that I had to tell about before I could get to the point. These little things are what made my stories funny. In my family, you have to make your stories funny, even the serious ones. That's how we survived the really hard times, like not having a place to live, running out of gas, or praying for the chicken to lay an egg so we could eat. My families' stories are very funny. I *know* how to tell stories. Ever since I was little I could tell the best stories. My teacher didn't like the way I told my stories. She thought I needed to pay more attention to what the book said and tell my stories in a line. I still don't think she knows how to tell stories like I do.

In classrooms that I observe, I frequently find teachers trying to "fix" CLD students' ways of knowing. They ask students to imitate their actions, and often an interaction between the teacher and student can take multiple repetitions before the teacher gives up hope that the student will ever get it right. Seldom are questions asked about the student's way of knowing and how it has implications for the task at hand. As an outsider looking in, I am heartened when I see a teacher ask a student why he or she approached a task in a way other than what was prescribed by the curriculum.

The ways students come to "know," referred to by Byers and Byers (1985) as "the organization of the processes of human communication," is based on their particular culture and the "template for the organization of knowledge or information in that particular culture" (p. 28). The experiences CLD students have had in life will greatly influence their ways of knowing, and thus will have implications for what happens within the classroom. How students interpret information and respond when asked to answer a question or provide a written response will vary, as each student's knowledge and ways of sharing that knowledge

will reflect their unique histories. As Gay (2000) notes, students arrive in our classrooms with "internalized rules and procedures for acquiring knowledge and demonstrating their skills" (p. 150).

So what can a teacher do to ensure that CLD students' ways of knowing are central to their education? Here are a few suggestions:

- Listen closely to what is communicated both verbally and nonverbally.
- Look for patterns in responses. After multiple interventions, ask yourself if the type of intervention being used is culturally appropriate.
- Create the conditions for multiple ways of knowing to be allowed during the course of a lesson.
- Consider allowing cultural knowledge to be valued as highly as the prescribed answer.

Ways of thinking and knowing have implications for learning, feedback, and the way educators manage their classroom. Gay (2000) perhaps says it best when she reminds educators that "far from being simply a means for reporting experience, language is a way of defining experience, thinking, and knowing" (p. 80). Sapir (1968) similarly notes that "language is a guide to 'social reality' . . . [and] a symbolic guide to culture" (p. 162). In becoming culturally responsive educators, we must strive to ensure that our views on knowledge, thought, and the application of knowledge do not place limitations on our CLD students.

Why We Think the Way We Think

We teachers always are looking for ways to tap into what students are thinking as they listen, interact, and work with the information that is shared during the lesson. Most documentation of students' thought processes results from students' articulation of content understanding during the lesson or through their submitted work. What we often fail to do is observe and listen for cultural aspects of what students are thinking. According to Nieto (2000), there is an undeniable connection between students' thinking processes and the influences that have been shaped by their cultural background. Vygotsky (1962) discusses the interrelatedness of learners' thought, language, and culture. In his work, he states an "indisputable fact": "thought and development is determined by language . . . and the sociocultural experience of the child" (p. 51). Although culture cannot force us to think in a certain way, it does shape our way of thinking (McDaniel et al., 2009).

Ji, Zhang, and Nisbett (2004) explored such cultural influences on thought in a study on ways Chinese and

European Americans' reasoning styles differed. It appears that bilingual Chinese individuals are more "relational," whereas European Americans are more "categorical" when organizing objects. In the study, these differences remained, regardless of the language in which the participants were tested. Observation and research on differences in thinking when CLD students are asked to perform different tasks can lead to the identification of best practice strategies for CLD students of a given cultural background.

Students' ways of thinking are absolutely critical to literacy development. As I work with students from diverse backgrounds and we collaborate to make sense of text, I am continually reminded that we educators do not do enough to create places and spaces in our lessons where we can discover CLD students' ways of thinking. Consider the following quote and reflect on what it means for classroom practice:

> It is the culturally appropriate way of thinking, not the act of reading or writing that is most important in the development of literacy. Literacy thinking manifests itself in different ways in oral and written language in different societies, and educators need to understand these ways of thinking if they are to build bridges and facilitate transitions among ways of thinking. (Langer, 1991, p. 13)

If we teachers simply begin our lessons with the information that we want students to learn and focus on students' acquisition of the requisite skills, we forget one of the primary goals of literacy instruction: students should be able to read and write effectively for real purposes and for real audiences. This means that we must apprentice students to thinking about literacy acts in ways that are appropriate to the culture of formal education, and we must begin by valuing students' own ways of thinking about and enacting literacy.

Applying What We Know and Think

The ultimate goal of any lesson is for all students to reach a level of internalization of knowledge that allows them to apply that knowledge in the present and in future learning situations. This application of what has been learned is most often observed for during and after the lesson, when students are asked to respond to questions, complete a project, or write about the topic. Students' application of knowledge and thinking frequently is evaluated by teachers who, at these moments in the lesson, see their role as that of a judge who determines the extent to which expectations (often set arbitrarily without regard to students' biographies) have been met. When our perspectives on assess-

ment and evaluation are void of any understanding of how a student's biography may influence how he or she represents new learning, we educators may miss opportunities to celebrate success. Chapter 9 explores how classroom assessment that is centered on students' biographies can inform our teaching as well as encourage students to continue their learning efforts.

According to Bruner (1996), what we think and what we learn will always be situated within our cultural resources. Therefore, it is through our understanding of the particular culture of the student that we will find additional meaning in what students share about their learning with the rest of the classroom community. It is important to ask questions related to the cultural conflicts that may be present when we ask students to apply information in ways that may be inconsistent with their cultural paths of knowing, thinking, and applying. If what we ask students to do is inconsistent with their patterns, the resulting "evidence" that we have to evaluate may result in a shallow interpretation of a student's ability to apply new learning.

Although we should continually seek to open new avenues for application to students, we must do so in ways that first value the students' familiar ways of demonstrating learning and then guide them to new ways of applying what they know. For instance, students from Korea might be unfamiliar with the expectations traditionally associated with summarizing a chapter. They might repeat what the teacher has already mentioned about the topic, or copy some parts of the chapter. Korean students are accustomed to teachers pointing out what is important and needs to be memorized. Therefore, independent study or classroom tasks that require students to decide what is important about a topic or to identify the key information from a chapter can be confusing for these individuals. A teacher might help such learners as well as other students in the classroom to gain an understanding of the process of summarization by:

- First identifying key concepts from a passage or lesson and then asking students to locate textual explanations/support for each concept or to record points of the lesson related to each concept
- Providing explicit instruction on how to differentiate key information from supporting details
- Incorporating opportunities for students to work together to practice differentiating essential information from nonessential details (The Relevance Scale strategy, discussed in Chapters 3 and 9, can be particularly effective with CLD students.)
- Supporting students in individual summarization tasks by providing a graphic organizer to help guide their thinking

- Providing students with examples of written summaries and modeling for students how information contained on a graphic organizer can be used to develop a written summary of content knowledge

Consciously placing the biography of the student at the forefront of learning ensures attention to the impact that culture may have on CLD students' cognitive processing and their learning before, during, and after the lesson. According to Gay (2000), "the processes of learning—not the intellectual capability to do so—used by students from different ethnic groups are influenced by their cultural socialization" (p. 147). As Ramírez and Castañeda (1974) explain,

> The sociocultural system of the child's home and community is influential in producing culturally unique preferred modes of relating to others . . . culturally unique incentive preferences, . . . as well as a preferred mode of thinking, perceiving, remembering, and problem solving. All of these characteristics . . . must be incorporated as the principal bases upon which programs for instituting changes in the school must be developed. (p. 32)

Understanding cognition from a cultural perspective sets the stage for a different approach to planning, teaching, and assessing CLD students, and it has implications for the way we design learning tasks, interpret students' emotional and behavioral responses, and select and model learning strategies.

Reflections on the Cognitive Dimension

High expectations and cognitively challenging instruction must be hallmarks of our professional practice with every student. CLD students must be held accountable for their learning of grade-level content and their development of English language skills. At the same time, we must take into consideration students' learning style preferences and guide students in using strategies that will enhance the effectiveness of their learning processes.

The key for us as educators is to remember to use our students' biographies to center our instructional efforts. We can provide students with opportunities to share with us how they have come to know the world, in relation to what we are teaching. We can encourage students to openly share their ways of conceptualizing curricular concepts and relationships among concepts and words. As we gain insight into students' culturally influenced ways of thinking, we can better provide avenues that will allow each student to demonstrate fully his or her academic knowledge and linguistic skills, as well as progress they have made along the way.

CHAPTER 5

Academics

More Than a Grade on a Test

I **MAGINE WHAT LIFE** in schools would be like if academic achievement were viewed from the lens of student potential rather than a standardized score. Would the results for students who are failing improve? This chapter explores from a slightly different perspective what it means to look beyond standardized tests, test scores, and grades. It asks that we think about the kind of access that has been provided or denied to students, which is beyond their control. At the end of each day, one of the most important elements of teaching is giving students a reason to return the next day ready to engage and learn—that is, providing students with hope that tomorrow will be an even better day.

The Academic Dimension

The fourth and final dimension of the CLD student biography is the academic dimension. This dimension incorporates all content-area school instruction and learning from the first years of formalized education through adult education. With each progressive grade level, learners' language expands as their knowledge base increases. The optimal learning environment for CLD students is one that leads to literacy skills in both their native language and in English. Why is it necessary for students to use their native language when building their academic knowledge? Simply put, skills and knowledge gained in the native language transfer to the second language. This core of knowledge that is accessible through either language can be conceptualized as a student's common underlying proficiency (CUP) (refer to Chapter 3 for a discussion of CUP).

Traditional School-Initiated Responses

> Don't judge me
>   by my skin.
> Don't judge me
>   by my language.

> Don't judge me
>   by my test scores.
> Take a minute to talk to me
> And learn who I "really am."
>   *—BESITOS/Herrera Terry (2004)*

We teachers have been taught to make all kinds of decisions based on data that CLD students present at the time they arrive in our classrooms. Decisions are made related to the capacities CLD students have in reading, math, writing, and other academic areas. In my work with young adults, I have found—as reflected in the quote above—that there exists a need to use such data as a point-in-time measure of the gaps that *may* exist and to respond by developing culturally relevant and responsive lessons to address such potential needs. More importantly, however, we must *not* use the data to make decisions that have lifelong implications, such as placement of students in programs that further deny them access to high-quality instruction.

> I was placed in lower Math
>   Lower Language Arts
>   Because of this ONE test in the 6th grade.
>   *—BESITOS/Herrera Terry (2004)*

Traditional school-initiated responses to the academic dimension frequently reflect perspectives on academics that are defined simply by:

- Standardized test scores
- Grades
- School records

These sources of information often present a limiting, ethnocentric perspective on CLD students' academic abilities and achievement. Such a perspective may set the stage for instruction to be reductionistic in scope, leaving students further and further behind their grade-level peers. Students are placed in lower-level, drill-and-kill curricula and in programs that view learning in a linear fashion and do not accelerate, but instead remediate. Literature on this topic is saturated with voices decrying the consequences that reductionistic programs have on CLD students (e.g., Delpit, 1996; Gay, 2000; Ladson-Billings, 1994; Nieto, 2005). These authors urge educators to view CLD students' existing knowledge and skills as assets that can be used to accelerate academic growth and make decisions related to effective programming and instruction.

Frequently, the attitudes, beliefs, and lifelong assumptions that we educators hold regarding what is possible with CLD students can negatively impact the academic success and progress of these students. Expectations have a way of turning into the reality we see. If we believe, for example, that using heterogeneous groups when teaching will have negative implications for the advanced or "gifted" students, we translate this into the way we approach our practice. For every daily decision we make in classrooms, we must ask ourselves what "evidence" supports what we believe is true. If we have never taken a risk and gone against the stream of common practice, we may in fact be limiting the possibilities for CLD and all other students.

An audit of the way we feel, think about, and act on a situation involving our teaching with CLD students can reveal whether our initial thoughts were based on assumptions, misconceptions, past experiences with other students, or even just a "gut feeling" that stems from the school-situated information that is available to us. Consider the following teacher's critical reflection as she struggles with maximizing the resources available to support CLD students' participation in the grade-level curriculum.

> Why do CLD students get additional attention and accommodations for learning relative to those for non-CLD students who struggle with the same academic skills? At the elementary school where I teach, there is an extremely high population of CLD students. These students are given extra help with work during reading intervention times and pulled out during the reading block for small group instruction. Non-CLD students are not receiving the same attention or small group instruction. Both the CLD and non-CLD students are struggling with the same academic skills.

In this journal activity, Ms. Keith, an elementary teacher, shared that initially she felt upset, irritated, and disappointed. However, in reflecting upon this issue in practice, she recognized the following assumptions in her own thinking:

- I assumed the teaching of CLD students would be harder from an academic aspect (not understanding the concept) and not due to a lack of understanding of the language (vocabulary and meanings).
- I assumed that students who spoke and read English well didn't need the extra help with academic skills or understanding of various materials.

She also came to the following realization:

> Those students who speak and read English well do not always understand what they have read. They are not able to make a connection with their background knowledge of the material for full understanding. Slang words used in various reading materials are difficult for many CLD students to understand because they cannot make a mental picture or find the words in their native language. CLD students need to be given more strategies to understand the concepts.

This teacher realized, too, that her own background experiences as a child had colored her perspective about her CLD students. Today, Ms. Keith is committed to supporting her CLD students' academic achievement by finding and using strategies in the classroom that help both CLD and struggling non-CLD students.

Figures 5.1–5.3 detail the Reflection Wheel Journal process this teacher undertook as she examined an "event" from her own practice with CLD students. Her full journal entry is presented as an example of what this journaling procedure can look like in practice. When we make critical reflection a regular part of our professional practice, identifying and examining the assumptions we make in our efforts with students becomes second nature. The result is our increased capacity to make decisions that promote the success of CLD students in our classrooms and schools.

Academically Speaking: *i*+1

Throughout the previous chapter, the discussion focused on the role that culture plays in CLD students' processing of new information. We learned that culture is the lens that colors their interpretation of the input they are receiving, and that it has implications for learning. In the same way that this is true for CLD students, it is also true for teachers. The teacher's culture influences the way he or she teaches. As Gay (2000) notes, "Even without our being consciously aware of it, culture determines how we think, believe, and behave, and these, in turn, affect how we teach and learn" (pp. 8–9). Key to CLD students' success in school is the degree to which they are assured of access to

FIGURE 5.1

Reflection Wheel Journal: Process

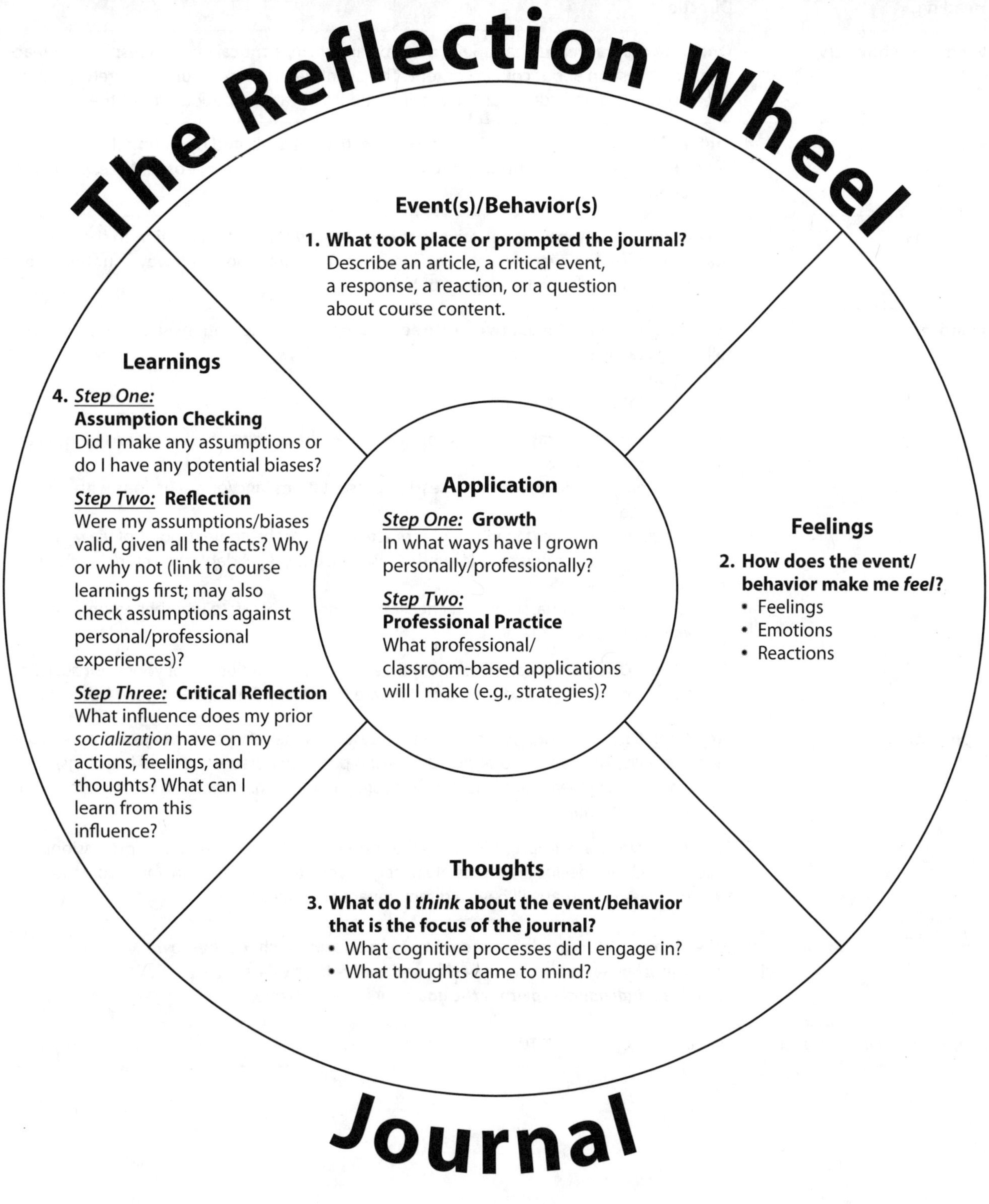

The Reflection Wheel

Event(s)/Behavior(s)

1. **What took place or prompted the journal?**
Describe an article, a critical event, a response, a reaction, or a question about course content.

Learnings

4. *Step One:* **Assumption Checking**
Did I make any assumptions or do I have any potential biases?

Step Two: **Reflection**
Were my assumptions/biases valid, given all the facts? Why or why not (link to course learnings first; may also check assumptions against personal/professional experiences)?

Step Three: **Critical Reflection**
What influence does my prior *socialization* have on my actions, feelings, and thoughts? What can I learn from this influence?

Application

Step One: **Growth**
In what ways have I grown personally/professionally?

Step Two:
Professional Practice
What professional/classroom-based applications will I make (e.g., strategies)?

Feelings

2. **How does the event/ behavior make me *feel*?**
- Feelings
- Emotions
- Reactions

Thoughts

3. **What do I *think* about the event/behavior that is the focus of the journal?**
- What cognitive processes did I engage in?
- What thoughts came to mind?

Journal

Adapted from Herrera (2007), p. 155. Used with permission of KCAT/TLC, Kansas State University.

FIGURE 5.2
Reflection Wheel Journal: Guide

Heading	Directions
Event(s)/Behavior(s)	**One or two paragraphs** that briefly describe an article, a critical event, a response, a reaction, or a question about course content. The event description should be purely descriptive; it should not include assumptions, judgments, or rationalizations about the event.
Feelings	**Bulleted list** of the feelings (*minimum of three*) that were elicited by/during the journal event. Feelings should be single words (e.g., happy, sad, confused, upset). No explanation is required.
Thoughts	**One or two paragraphs** of narrative that *describe your thoughts* in relation to the description provided in the event(s)/behavior(s) section. Thoughts should convey your thinking at the time you experienced the event/behavior.
Learnings	*Step One:* **Identify at least two or three assumptions**. Assumptions should start with the following lead-in statements: • I assumed . . . • A potential bias I had . . . *Step Two:* **One paragraph** (*minimum*) that checks the validity of assumptions identified in Step One. To do this: • Refer back to course readings, session presentations, and/or discussions with informed colleagues. • Consider the context in which you practice, and/or the context/point of view of the author(s) of what you read (or in the case of a critical incident, the actor(s) who took part in the event). • Elaborate on your assumption checking; do not simply state whether assumptions were invalid or valid. *Step Three:* **One paragraph** (*minimum*) that describes the influence of your prior socialization on actions, feelings, and thoughts. You are looking for links back to your background.
Application	*Step One:* **One paragraph** (*minimum*) that describes the way you have grown personally/professionally. You can elaborate by discussing personal perspectives and learnings, or you can discuss how you apply learnings professionally (e.g., continued research, collaboration with colleagues). *Step Two:* **One paragraph** (*minimum*) that describes your applications to professional practice. Include specific examples of strategies you can implement in your professional practice/classroom that will have a direct impact on students.

Remember: Reflection Wheel Journals are meant to help educators check their own
"habits of mind" by engaging in a specific series of reflective steps.
Therefore, *individual growth is the goal—never judgment!*

Adapted from Herrera (2007), p. 19. Used with permission of KCAT/TLC, Kansas State University.

FIGURE 5.3
Reflection Wheel Journal: Example

Ms. Keith, *Elementary, Kansas*

Event(s)/Behavior(s)

Why do CLD students get additional attention and accommodations for learning relative to those for non-CLD students who struggle with the same academic skills? At the elementary school where I teach, there is an extremely high population of CLD students. These students are given extra help with work during reading intervention times and pulled out during the reading block for small group instruction. Non-CLD students are not receiving the same attention or small group instruction. Both the CLD and non-CLD students are struggling with the same academic skills.

Feelings

- Upset
- Irritated
- Disappointed

Thoughts

I think CLD students do get additional resources that non-CLD students do not receive. It is upsetting to know I have to go through more red tape to get non-CLD students the academic help they also need. These students struggle with academics but do not qualify for Special Education classes because they are not low enough. I know there are monetary resources to provide these extra provisions for CLD students; however, it is irritating to know not everyone can benefit from it. I wonder if more funds could be found to benefit all students, not just those with a label, such as CLD students. It is disappointing to know a teacher has to put forth even more effort to see all students succeed without the additional resources for everyone to use.

Learnings

Step One: I assumed the teaching of CLD students would be harder from an academic aspect (not understanding the concept) and not due to a lack of understanding of the language (vocabulary and meanings).

I assumed that students who spoke and read English well didn't need the extra help with academic skills or understanding of various materials.

Step Two: Based on my assumptions about the language barrier and academic understanding, I have a different perspective with this class. If students do not have a true grasp of the English language, teaching CLD students various materials and skills would just be surface understanding and not go any deeper. According to Herrera and Murry's [2005] book, *Mastering ESL and Bilingual Methods,* CLD students face many sociocultural challenges. "The CLD student must adjust to a new country, city, or neighborhood . . . must adapt to a new education system . . . must cope with nuances of the school's culture . . . which can inhibit the performance of a CLD student in the classroom" (p. 13). Without taking into account these factors, how can I teach students academic skills for reading, math, science, and social studies, as well as social skills? Connections need to be made between the students' first language and their second language for deeper understanding. Language acquisition is the key to CLD students' success in the classroom, and using the Prism Model helps me take the whole student into account.

In assuming CLD students who speak and read English don't need additional help, another perspective has been shown. I have noticed from professional experience that those students who speak and read English well do not always understand what they have read. They are not able to make a connection with their background knowledge of the material for full understanding. Slang words used in various reading materials are difficult for many CLD students to understand because they cannot make a mental picture or find the words in their native language. CLD students need to be given more strategies to understand the concepts; by using techniques like picture clues, vocabulary will benefit CLD students and still benefit those who have a better grasp of the English language.

Step Three: Based on my own background, I grew up in the era of CLD students being given additional help that would benefit everyone. I remember feeling slighted because these students were excelling in the classroom and I was struggling, yet they got the extra time. At that time, I felt angry because I wanted the extra help. As an adult teaching in a predominantly culturally and linguistically diverse school, I have a different perspective from my adolescence. My background experiences colored my viewpoint of CLD students. I believe it is important for CLD students to get the additional resources to be productive members of society; understanding the culture and academics of the school is the first step.

Application

Step One: I have grown in a professional aspect. My eyes have opened to new ideas and viewpoints to benefit my students. The new perspectives I have been exposed to will benefit all my students. My school provides CLD students with additional resources to make them successful in the classroom and in society. What I need to do is take what the ESOL teachers in my building are doing and incorporate their strategies into my classroom lessons. Personally, I believe I have done a disservice to my first group of CLD students last year by not taking into account the diversity of my students. Last year, I used a few strategies in daily activities, however not to the extent my students truly needed. I hope I will be given many different strategies to engage my CLD and non-CLD students for academic success.

Step Two: I will make use of many of the strategies I have been taught so far in this class. The strategies are easy to adapt to the demanding curriculum already in place for my school district. My personal favorite strategy, the vocabulary foldable, is easy to use in many areas of academics, like reading, math, and science. Another strategy I have already used in my classroom is my life in pictures and words. I learned a lot about all my students with this. I need to take into account the grade level I am working with to change some strategies to accommodate my students' abilities. For example, the vocabulary quilt can be challenging due to the fact that many of my students do not have the academic and linguistic background to draw a picture of the vocabulary words. Many of the students are being exposed to these words for the first time in their reading books. But I can see how revisiting these words later in the week or later on would be a wonderful way to pull those vocabulary words out of working memory into permanent memory. I look forward to learning many more strategies for my students to use.

equitable educational opportunities, provided with learning environments that actively seek their engagement, and supported by teachers and other educators who inspire hope for their future.

Access

Often teachers comment on decisions families and students have made related to education with the remark, "I don't know what these families think—no one seems to place any value on education!" What many of these teachers have failed to see are the multiple ways of defining and valuing education. People are not all provided access to the same kinds of education, in the same ways, at the same time. Therefore, how education is perceived and valued will differ within each and every immediate community.

Most homes that CLD students grow up in are filled with the hope, faith, determination, and love needed to raise strong and healthy children. Often what is lacking are the resources to provide children with the materials that mainstream society believes are necessary for development of skills essential to academic success. Yet educators frequently fail to realize that even without such material resources, learning is still taking place, and this learning can provide "hooks" for what happens in school.

Access in school is made possible by valuing and encouraging use of the native language and by tapping CLD students' cultural knowledge and other strengths to make success in the grade-level curriculum achievable. According to Gay (2000),

> Much intellectual ability and many other kinds of intelligences are lying untapped in ethnically diverse students. If these are recognized and used in the instructional process, school achievement will improve radically. Culturally responsive teaching is a means for unleashing the higher learning potentials of ethnically diverse students by simultaneously cultivating their academic and psychosocial abilities. (p. 20)

Holding high expectations for CLD learners is essential to providing equitable access to education. Citing numerous authors (i.e., Babad, 1993; Brophy, 1982; Cooper & Good, 1983; Good, 1987; Jussim, Smith, Madon, & Palumbo, 1998; Weinstein, 2002), Rubie-Davies, Hattie, and Hamilton (2006) assert that "Several years of research into teacher expectation effects has provided clear evidence that expectations do exist in regular classroom situations and that they can positively and/or negatively influence student performance and achievement" (p. 429). Although most teachers assert that they hold high expectations for all of their students, there often exists a gap between what is espoused and what is demonstrated in their daily instructional practices.

The "Hearts" activity that was introduced in Chapter 2 is an excellent strategy for supporting students in making connections from self to text.

Rubie-Davies et al. maintain that teacher expectations "may be exemplified in the learning opportunities provided, in the affective climate created and in the interactional content and context of the classroom" (p. 430). Teachers of CLD students must remain steadfast in their commitment to supporting all students in meeting high standards, despite apparent challenges. Chapters 6, 7, 8, and 9 elaborate on ways teachers can orchestrate the kinds of instructional contexts and processes that are likely to turn their high expectations into reality for their CLD students.

Engagement

One of the questions I am most frequently asked by teachers as I travel across the country is "How do you motivate these students to learn? They seem to be interested in so little." From where I stand, this question represents some educators' continued focus on a search for external factors that limit CLD students' motivation. The question of motivation should be one that educators consider from the perspective of pedagogy, asking themselves, "Have I done enough to plan and deliver lessons that take into account the biographies of the students?" Planning lessons that spark a desire to learn and that allow CLD students to be equal contributors, regardless of their linguistic or academic ability, is essential to student engagement in the classroom. Therefore, we as educators must understand motivation and engagement in terms of our own discovery of how best to involve CLD students throughout the learning process.

How then does motivation relate to engagement? According to Wlodkowski and Ginsberg (1995), "Engagement is the visible outcome of motivation, the natural capacity to direct energy in the pursuit of a goal" (p. 17).

Without motivation, there is no engagement. Engagement cannot exist without the student being motivated to become part of the learning. Newmann's (1992) description of engagement captures what it means to be engaged in the lesson beyond the realm of stimulus response, that is, filling out a worksheet or idly sitting and waiting to be called on to answer a question. He defines engagement as "the student's psychological investment in and effort directed toward learning, understanding, or mastering the knowledge, skills, or crafts that academic work is intended to promote" (p. 12). The educator's task is to set up conditions during instruction that will promote students' investment in learning.

A primary concern is addressing the student's state of mind. Student feelings of anxiety, alienation, incompetence, frustration, or boredom must first be addressed in order that motivation and engagement toward meeting the objectives of the lesson can be promoted. Regardless of the sociopolitical climate of the times, the culture of the school, or any other threats to teaching, the teacher has the potential and control to create classroom conditions that will increase student motivation and engagement. Chapters 6, 7, and 8 explore in detail these aspects of classroom practice with CLD students.

Hope

> My teacher made me smart. She made me smart because she cares about me. She always tells me that I am learning so much and someday I'm going to be her superstar. My teacher makes me feel like I am so smart. I love my teacher because she cares about me.
>
> —*3rd-Grade Student*

CLD students are aware of their grades, test scores, and prior schooling experiences. What they need to see is that teachers care about them, as individuals, and have hope for their future. In their stories, second language learners often share feelings of isolation, a sense of disconnectedness, and thoughts of never being able to be part of the class because they often do not understand the teacher. Feelings of hopelessness can lead to a "Why try?" attitude that manifests itself in low motivation, engagement, and desire to learn. We educators can address this disconnectedness with learning through actions that demonstrate a sense of caring—first about the person we are teaching and, as a result, about the learning we are helping them achieve. A place where each individual is cared about can give students hope that the dreams and goals they have for the future are attainable. Too often the fast-paced nature of our school systems and the testing-oriented mandates pressure us to forget what we know from decades of research about creating places of care and hope in our schools.

Hope is essential to students' ability to cope with often unfamiliar, difficult, and unpredictable cultural and academic situations. Snyder et al. (1991) describe hope as having two distinct, yet reciprocal and additive, elements—agency and pathways—that support individuals in moving toward the goals they wish to accomplish. Agency refers to "a sense of successful determination in meeting goals in the past, present, and future" (p. 570). Pathways, on the other hand, are related to "the perceived availability of successful *pathways* related to the goals" (p. 570). In other words, hope is the feeling that there exists a road to walk on and that one is capable of the journey. These two components of hope work together in setting the stage for a student to have a sense of hope that he or she has what it takes to be part of the learning community.

Becoming aware of what we teachers do to orchestrate a learning environment that promotes (or hinders) a sense of hope is important to developing a pedagogy that is both culturally responsive and relevant to the CLD student. One of the most important ways we "give" or "take away" a sense of hope is in the way we provide feedback. In this era of testing mania, many students see their plight as having no hope for improvement, given the value placed on point-in-time standardized assessments. Consider, however, the way the teacher in the following scenario talks with the student and provides feedback that sends the message that there are multiple paths for attaining the goal of becoming a better writer.

> I always hoped to be a better writer and I knew that with practice I could accomplish anything I set my mind to do. When I was in the seventh grade my teacher, Ms. Porter, used to tell me: "Darling you write like you talk!" What she meant is that I could go on forever without putting in any kind of punctuation in my writing. I wrote to tell my stories or meet the assignments she was always giving. She made us write and write. Every time she handed something back it was another little mini-conference to talk about how I could make my grammar better, and every time I listened I was always hoping that my next paper would be better.
>
> What I liked best about Ms. Porter's corrections was that they always came with a "but." She would say, "I want you to keep working, working, working on that grammar, but in the meantime, don't ever hand in a paper without having someone edit your work. You know, there are these people out there called editors, and that's all they do is edit for people like you—people who have all the ideas and experience, who are unique and special like you. With that "but" she gave me hope that someday I would learn to write just like she wanted me to do; but regardless

FIGURE 5.4
CLD Student Biography Card: Front

CLD Student Biography Cards can support teachers in documenting student progress, making decisions about grouping configurations, and continually scaffolding to meet students' sociocultural, linguistic, cognitive, and academic needs.

Insert a photograph of the student (this is a helpful visual reminder for you as a teacher).

Name:

Age:

Grade:

Country of Origin:

Time in USA:

L1: _____
R: _____
W: _____

L2 Proficiency
(LAS/IPT/Other):
O: _____
R: _____
W: _____
SLA: _____

Student Processing:

Learning Style:

Prior Academic Experiences:

Preferred Grouping:

School-Situated

Sociocultural

Complete the student's **demographic information** by interviewing the student, his or her family, or a past teacher.

Linguistic

Step One: Determine (informally or formally):
L1: Student's First Language
R: First Language Reading Proficiency
W: First Language Writing Proficiency

Step Two: Determine the CLD student's English language proficiency (scores can be obtained from the district/school ESL teacher as needed).

O: English Oral Proficiency (speaking/listening)
R: English Reading Proficiency
W: English Writing Proficiency
SLA: Stage of Second Language Acquisition

Cognitive

How does the student **process information** (e.g., solve a math problem, complete a science experiment, summarize a story)?

What **learning style** preferences should be taken into account for this student?

Academic

What **prior academic experiences**/exposure does the student have to promote content learning and transfer of knowledge?

In what **grouping** configuration is the student most comfortable (i.e., total group, partner, small group, or independent)?

Adapted from Herrera (2007), pp. 17–18. Used with permission of KCAT/TLC, Kansas State University.

FIGURE 5.5
CLD Student Biography Card: Back

Sociocultural Dimension
Home + Community + School =
Background
Knowledge

_____
_____
_____
_____
_____
_____

Linguistic Dimension
Valuing L1 & L2

_____
_____
_____
_____
_____

Cognitive Dimension
Implications for Practice

_____
_____
_____
_____
_____
_____

Academic Dimension
+   State of Mind   –

_____
_____
_____
_____
_____
_____
_____

Biography-Situated

Sociocultural
Consider insights gleaned from conversations and interactions with students, parents, and colleagues (in both academic and non-academic settings) about what brings the student **life**, **laughter**, and **love**.

Linguistic
Consider aspects of **comprehension**, **communication**, and **expression** in both the student's first language and second language.

Cognitive
Consider ways the student's culture might influence how he or she **knows**, **thinks**, and **applies** new learning.

Academic
Consider factors that are helping or hindering the student's **access** to equitable educational opportunities, **engagement** in instruction, and **hope** for success in the learning community and in the future.

Adapted from Herrera (2007), pp. 17–18. Used with permission of KCAT/TLC, Kansas State University.

of my writing skills, my ideas were always good and I could always look for editors. Today I'm grateful to Ms. Porter for filling my life with hope. I still use an editor, grammar check, and any other resource I can to support my becoming a better writer, because I have discovered that writing is a lifelong process.

This idea of seeing the future as a time when what we now are working toward will potentially be a reality is a perspective on learning that CLD students crave as they sit in classrooms today.

As learners, we all want to:

- Experience a sense of hope about what we can accomplish
- Have a place where relationships of support and encouragement are part of daily interactions
- Actively participate in learning situations that are low risk and accepting of current abilities and understandings, yet always challenging us to higher levels of understanding
- Have discussions in which our thoughts and perspectives are valued
- Experience a sense of accomplishment with regard to content and language development
- Have opportunities to be evaluated in ways that reflect the meaningful work we have produced in classroom endeavors

It is this validation from both peers and the teacher that gives students a sense that they are valuable members of the learning community. In this way, hope can become a source of student motivation that is greater than any learning strategy or instructional technique that we can bring to a lesson. According to Kuhrt (2007), hope "is the factor that allows even the poorest most destitute individual to succeed" (section 7.3.4). As teachers, our goal is to use our interactions and orchestration of learning to set conditions that give our students, regardless of sociocultural, linguistic, cognitive, or academic background, the hope they need to become motivated and engaged learners in our classroom.

In these times of adverse political agendas, we must be very clear about where we stand in our beliefs about teaching and learning. Do standardized tests, grades, and cumulative folders close the door to the hidden potential of our CLD students? Or do we intentionally design our classroom and instruction to encourage students' sharing and use of their talents and background knowledge to accomplish the academic goals we have set? Our attitude and approach to instruction with diverse learners will set the stage for interactions among all learners and the potential for hope in our classroom.

Using strategies at the beginning of the lesson that activate the knowledge (words) students have related to the topic or target vocabulary increases the likelihood that students will use what they know to scaffold their own learning.

—Christy Lee, High School, Kansas

CLD Student Biography Cards

Our ability to respond to students' needs and to validate students' assets requires that we first *know* our students. As the National Research Council and the Institute of Medicine (2004) note:

> Instruction that is appropriately challenging for all students requires considerable knowledge of each student's understanding and skills. Instructional decisions about tasks and next steps also need to be informed by data on student learning. Standardized testing done annually does not provide useful information for these purposes. (p. 214)

Rather, we teachers must find ways to explore each dimension of our students' biographies. Creating a CLD Student Biography Card for each diverse learner in our classroom can be an especially helpful first step for getting to know our students and beginning to plan instruction with the student biography in mind. Although biography cards can be tailored to each teacher's specific classroom needs, consideration should be given to each of the four dimensions—sociocultural, linguistic, cognitive, and academic. Figures 5.4 and 5.5 (see pages 64 and 65) provide an annotated sample of a CLD Student Biography Card that can be used with students of all ages. A card such as this enables teachers to document both school-situated and biography-situated information. Figure 5.6 shows an example of a completed card. A template of the CLD Student Biography Card for classroom use can be found in Appendix B.

FIGURE 5.6

Example of a Completed CLD Student Biography Card

School-Situated side:

Name:

Age: 11

Grade: 5th

Country of Origin: Saudi Arabia

Time in USA:

L1:
R: Reads Quran (Arabic) prof.
W: Writes some vocab. in English

L2 Proficiency
(LAS/IPT/Other): KELPA
O: 4
R: 3
W: 2
SLA: overall : 3

Student Processing:

Learning Style:
Is a very visual learner primarily likes highlighted text.

Prior Academic Experiences:
Has studied in Saudi Arabia. Did half-day in Arabic half-day in English. Is good at Math.

Preferred Grouping:
Small / pairs. Prefers to work with girls.

School-Situated

Biography-Situated side:

Sociocultural Dimension
Home + Community + School =
♡ **Background Knowledge**

There is a very active Arabic community here so the family is always associated with them. Students also attend an Arabic school on Sunday.

Linguistic Dimension
Valuing L1 & L2

Family is very focused on readings from Quran. They are always making associations with Arabic.

Cognitive Dimension
Implications for Practice

Prefers to see material visually and is good at making associations with vocabulary.

Academic Dimension
+   State of Mind   –
←————————→

She is usually a very motivated young girl. As teachers we have to be careful during the month of Ramadan.

Biography-Situated

Although CLD students will be able to share with us many of the most basic aspects of each dimension through informal conversations, surveys, and so forth (at times along with the help of a parent, sibling, peer, or translator), we as teachers also need to incorporate opportunities for students to share connections and ways of thinking in each of our lessons. It is by capitalizing on these student insights, connections, and associations that are directly linked to the content that we are able to provide students with pedagogy that is culturally responsive and biography-driven.

Reflections on the Academic Dimension

Perhaps the most important finding of Thomas and Collier's (1995) research is the emergent understanding that *the four components of the prism model are interdependent.* Recognition of this interdependence reminds us of the importance of providing a socioculturally supportive school environment that nourishes natural language growth, cognitive development, and academic progress in both the native and second language. Teachers who place an inordinate focus on CLD students' learning English and postpone the students' exposure to core content knowledge actually increase the time that it takes for students to close the academic achievement gap in English. Second language learners need simultaneous linguistic, cognitive, and academic development.

We can promote such development for CLD students when we proactively find ways to ensure their access to the grade-level curriculum. Students need opportunities to build their content and language proficiencies in ways that first value what they already know. By considering students' backgrounds and states of mind in our planning and implementation of instruction, we can more effectively ignite student motivation and increase their engagement in our classrooms. Furthermore, as we continue to encourage, support, and build on students' current progress and success, we demonstrate the care and respect that provide students with hope for their own achievement.

CHAPTER 6

Biography-Driven Planning, Teaching, and Assessing

THE FOUR PRECEDING CHAPTERS focused heavily on the complex and multidimensional aspects of the CLD student biography. The prism model provided a point of departure for exploration of the sociocultural, linguistic, cognitive, and academic dimensions of the student from two perspectives—the school-situated perspective and the culturally responsive perspective. Both perspectives have an important role to play in teachers' planning, delivery, and evaluation of instructional practice.

This chapter takes us further on our journey beyond "business as usual" in schools, moving toward an understanding of what culturally responsive pedagogy looks like in practice by providing an *overlay* that can be used in the classroom. I have chosen the term "overlay," rather than "guide" or "steps," because I have found in my work in schools that most teachers are already using school-prescribed lesson plans or curricula that outline both the scope and the sequence of the material to be taught. In architecture, overlay refers to a set of beneficial adaptations that can be made to an existing blueprint or building as it is being constructed or remodeled. This chapter provides a culturally responsive, classroom-based overlay that teachers can apply to their existing programs and curricula. In addition, the chapter discusses processes and factors that can either inhibit or increase student learning. It also explores the role of the teacher as participant observer within the learning community.

Contextual and Situational Processes

The classroom is a place of constant change that demands continual reflection as we negotiate the processes of teaching and learning on a daily basis. As educators, we are the "masters of our domain." We are clearly in charge of setting the tone and conditions for learning within our classrooms. It is true that the learners in our classrooms help create the atmosphere, but we have the power to arrange and rearrange the "ecology" and the "actors" within that

ecology to remove limitations on the learner. We can all relate to learning situations in the past that either created an opportunity or denied us the access we felt necessary to our success. As adults, we can usually circumvent a problematic situation (or take advantage of an opportunity) and access what we need to make "it" happen. CLD students, however, depend on the *teacher* to establish and manipulate contextual and situational classroom conditions to maximize their learning.

Contextual Processes: Classroom Ecology

Contextual processes in teaching are the things we do with the physical setting in which we teach, the curriculum, and the community of learners in our classroom. Together, these factors constitute the *context* in which learning takes place. Talk among educators often focuses on creating a friendly, culturally inclusive environment—a place where students feel welcome and see their culture and language represented within the classroom. In most cases, we teachers work hard to have books that represent the cultures and languages of our students and to build classroom word walls that use the native language to facilitate transfer of information. These and numerous other efforts help to create places that are representative of our students. However, we may be limiting our focus to the physical *environment* and not considering the overall *ecology* of our classroom.

In considering the distinction between ecology and environment, we can begin to reflect on the complex dynamics that take place in classrooms, that is, the role of classroom relationships and their interdependence with teaching and learning. Classroom *ecology* encompasses the structures, arrangements, and events that influence student and teacher action in the classroom. In nature and in the classroom, an environment is "physical" in character, while ecology specifically involves the inherent interconnectedness of the multiple agents and aspects at play. Outdoors, ecology describes the complex interactions of various forms of plant and animal life within a particular physical environment, be it a marsh, a tallgrass prairie, or a mountain range. In the classroom, ecology emphasizes the human element in the context of the particular environment determined by the curriculum and physical space. Both the environment and the larger ecology of our classrooms—including the way we design our classrooms, select materials, plan instruction, and build the classroom community—should reflect our valuing of students and their needs.

Contextual processes in classroom practice are shaped by the ethnic and cultural identities of both the teacher and the learner. The teacher is aware of, and asks questions related to, everyday classroom dynamics. According to Allen and Butler (1996), attention to both the contextual conditions for learning and the prior and background experiences of the learner can lead to greater engagement in learning and academic achievement. Reflect on the following questions:

- How do I currently set the stage for a climate of trust and respect of diverse cultures and languages?
- In what ways do I tap into the home and community experiences and knowledge of the students I teach?
- How do I use observations of students' experiences to hook onto and bridge to what students bring to each lesson?
- In what ways do I check my habits of teaching and actions based on the culture of the school, curriculum, or previously held expectations for CLD students?

This is an example of a cultural quilt (Herrera et al., 2007), in which students record important biographical events and turning points that reflect cultural and family values. By using the cultural quilt with her students, the teacher was able to gain valuable insights about each of her students that she was then able to use for developing a classroom community that values and builds upon students' diverse backgrounds.

To create basic contextual conditions that will optimize learning, we as educators must understand our power to conceptualize and create an ecology in which every student feels safe to share his or her cultural identity without fear of ridicule. Teachers who are conscious of contextual factors and bear them in mind when setting up their classrooms increase the chances that students will be engaged and motivated to learn. For each lesson—and overall—contextual factors that must be considered include the following:

- Biographies of the students
- Content and language objectives
- Grouping configurations/structures
- Applicability of lessons to the real world
- Standard(s) to be addressed during lessons
- Physical aspects of the classroom that support learning
- Curriculum and applicability to students' frames of reference

Explicit attention to the context in which each lesson will take place prepares us to move forward with more confidence, knowing that classroom conditions for learning have been designed with the sociocultural, linguistic, cognitive, and academic assets and needs of the students in mind.

Situational Processes: Teaching in the Moment

Situational processes are the means through which teachers orchestrate teaching and learning dynamics "in the moment." This concept applies to each and every student and teacher action and reaction in classroom practice. Think about the dynamics at play during any given lesson; there are many "contingencies" during instruction that could not have been anticipated. Every task we ask students to perform is subject to contextual factors and is interpreted uniquely by each individual student. Each action and reaction must be "mediated" by the teacher, who continuously navigates and negotiates the sociocultural, linguistic, cognitive, and academic biography of the student, as well as the objectives of the lesson.

Situational processes enable us to guide students to achieve the goals we have for their social and academic development, and to take students a step beyond the lesson as it was originally planned. We must be attuned to students throughout the lesson, monitoring the learning experiences CLD students are having as they participate. Situational factors that we as teachers should consider include the following:

- Students' states of mind
- Language demands on students
- Levels of student interest during the lesson
- Opportunities for, and students' comfort with, native language use
- Development of student responsibility and autonomy
- Adequacy of "think time" being provided to students
- Feedback and validation of student connections

If our goal is to have a climate where trust, respect, engagement, and academic achievement are part of the ongoing dynamic of the lesson, we must commit to an ongoing consideration of situational factors such as these.

Attending to situational factors requires us to manipulate the context of the lesson as it develops, to create conditions in which students can be socially and academically successful. Such decisions require planning as well as on-the-fly reflection and problem solving. For example, we may need to reflect on contextual factors that might be hindering student learning, in which case we will have to identify possible solutions in the form of contextual changes and modifications. Therefore, the situational conditions for learning might change throughout the course of the lesson, and such changes are in direct response to what is happening with the dynamics of student learning. Reflecting on current classroom practice, we can all think of some examples of how we have modified a planned lesson in progress to better suit the situation as it occurred in real time. By challenging ourselves to attend explicitly to the situational factors relevant to CLD students, we can greatly improve their chances for social and academic success.

Contextual and Situational Teaching

In the simplest terms, as stated by Gay (2000), "Teaching is a contextual and situational process" (p. 21). Optimally, contextual and situational teaching takes into account each student's biography and aligns teaching and learning to respect the prior experiences, community settings, cultural backgrounds, and identities of every individual in the class-

In this 8th-grade classroom, Ms. Frank has students from four different countries. She creates an effective learning ecology by attending to both contextual and situational factors. At this point in the math lesson on graphing, Ms. Frank has students work in pairs seated throughout the room so students are able to share their diverse perspectives about the terms and concepts and she is able to listen to their conversations and observe their learning. This allows Ms. Frank to support students in making meaningful connections and to re-teach and re-route as necessary.

—Julie Frank, Middle School, Kansas

room (Gay). Educators that continually monitor contextual and situational processes set up a community of trust and respect where students carve out their own place in the community. Students fully understand and believe they are contributing members of the classroom in both social and academic ways. Figure 6.1 lists some considerations related to contextual and situational factors that contribute to community building and learning.

Knowing how best to design our ecology, plan for teaching, and make adjustments during instruction requires that we understand students' social, cultural, linguistic, and cognitive responses during the lesson. As discussed in previous chapters, understanding the biography of each student provides the teacher with a guide for consideration of the factors that might be threats to student learning. Honest, critical reflection on our own beliefs and assumptions is key to this process. According to Gay (2000), students often are "taught from the middle class, Eurocentric frameworks that shape school practices" (p. 21). Regularly assessing our perspectives helps ensure that our teaching practices actually reflect the ideals we have for CLD students' learning. Teachers can proactively reflect by doing the following:

- Considering the culture and sociopolitical climate of the school
- Exploring the visible environment and asking questions about what is invisible

FIGURE 6.1
Contextual and Situational Factors/Decisions

Contextual Factors	Situational Factors
• Initially group CLD students for reading instruction based on stage of second language acquisition (SLA). • Create a word wall to help CLD students learn key content words. • Create opportunities at the beginning of the lesson to activate students' prior knowledge about the new topic. • Develop and share with CLD students your objectives for the lesson. • Formulate authentic postinstructional assessments.	• Adjust group membership during the lesson, based on emergent language development among students. • Add to the word wall during instruction, based on words illustrated or discussed. • As CLD students discuss and work to make sense of the new content, help them draw connections between their prior knowledge and the curricular material. • Add to or adapt your lesson objectives, based on students' familiarity with the topic and associated academic language. • Develop/modify postinstructional assessments, based on students' life experiences shared during lesson delivery.

• Viewing curriculum from a "student biography" perspective versus a "prescriptive response to learning" perspective

• Becoming informed about the myths and misconceptions that may have negatively influenced their expectations of CLD students

• Examining pedagogical perspectives for any indications of a deficit perspective (i.e., one that does not maximize learning by building on students' assets and documented potential)

• Noting whether (or to what degree) social interactions among students in the classroom are based on a mutual respect of student biographies, which results when each student understands that knowledge and learning are uniquely shaped by the multiple languages and cultures represented in the classroom

Such reflection is the catalyst for aligning ecology, curriculum, student biography, teacher biography, and learning with a "what is possible" mind-set, rather than dwelling on challenges to be overcome. A classroom ecology that exemplifies what we would like to see in society is one in which there is clear evidence that learners and teachers trust each other and respect what each brings to the classroom community. When educators actively create classroom environments of trust and respect, the chance for motivation, engagement, and hope in the learner is exponentially increased.

Community Climate

Classrooms are small universes. In those universes, we learn to accept and appreciate one another's variances—or we learn to resent and be suspicious of differences. We learn to celebrate one another's victories and support one another's efforts—or we learn to compete in ways that undermine rather than dignify those with whom we share time and space.

—*Tomlinson and McTighe (2006, p. 45)*

Given recent and ongoing demographic shifts, as discussed in Chapter 1, many of our classrooms have become rich tapestries of culture, language, religion, socioeconomic status, and ways of perceiving that are difficult to understand unless we make it a priority to create a climate where being part of a diverse ecology is cause for celebration. According to Charney (2002), being in a community means having "the capacity to care for oneself, for others, and for the world" (p. 15). In creating a community, we educators must hold ourselves accountable for strategically planning ways to bring students together to share their knowledge before, during, and after each lesson. Learners must become aware of the diversity of perspectives that exist within the social and learning classroom space.

Walqui (2000) asserts that in a community of learners, "teachers and students together construct a culture that values the strengths of all participants and respects their interests, abilities, languages, and dialects. Students and teachers shift among the roles of expert, researcher, learner, and teacher, supporting themselves and each other" (Principle #1). If we believe this to be true, how do we set up classrooms that are not solely concerned with the academic dimension of learning? Ask yourself the following questions:

• The last time I taught, what activity did I plan/use that allowed for all students to share a little of themselves—their knowledge or understanding of the new vocabulary words or the concept to be introduced, or their perspective on the issue to be discussed?

- Did I take time to absorb what was shared or reflect on the essence of what the student was trying to share?
- Did I incorporate partner or small team talk that allowed CLD students an opportunity to use their language of choice to share their knowledge, questions, or interpretations with a peer?
- What did I do with the information I gathered? Did I use it to fill the empty spaces that often create separateness in the classroom?
- How might I use the information and knowledge I gained to guide my thoughts and actions in the future?

Answers to these questions help us become more aware that the opportunities we create for validating and affirming every student can set us on the path to increased student engagement and learning.

In classrooms that constitute a true community of learners, teachers are less likely to have difficulty with classroom management. According to Freeman and Freeman (2002), community-oriented classrooms unify learners through shared experiences. Affirmation and validation of experiences, or academic insights shared during the lesson, bring to life the contributions of all learners. By making sure the classroom represents a safe environment and by creating situations that provide opportunities for each student to actively participate during the lesson, educators create the conditions for all members of the learning community to discover the many gifts and assets that each possesses.

Following are a few suggestions for fostering a climate that supports social and academic community in practice:

- Model social and academic talk for students.
- Remind students that no one person has all the answers.
- Share personal stories of your own difficulty with learning and how you overcame such challenges.
- Create a climate where every answer can be reevaluated and changed to arrive at the destination.
- Set up conditions and opportunities for members to build both personal and academic relationships.

Remember that it is relatively unimportant whether answers are right or wrong in the classroom; what matters is that learning is taking place. Keep in mind that we each have different strengths and talents. Not everyone is a great artist; otherwise, we wouldn't have paint by number, clip art, and stencils. Not everyone is great at math, or we wouldn't need accountants, calculators, and computerized spreadsheets. However, together we bring the multitude of talents needed to accomplish our goals—in life and in the classroom.

Classroom Community and the CLD Student

Earlier in this section, I discussed the importance of understanding contextual and situational processes and our power to create a community where the climate of teaching and learning serves to engage the learner. At some point while you were reading, the following thought may have crossed your mind: *If only this author knew my students or taught in my school!* Multiple factors are at play within our classrooms. While some are beyond a teacher's control, there are many others we can try to influence in positive ways. The climate of a classroom community can be affected by factors such as the following.

- Organization of classroom structures
- Social relationships among the students
- Teacher beliefs related to ability grouping
- Social relationships between CLD students and the teacher
- Psychological states of mind of the students and the teacher

The psychological state of mind of the CLD student has a large impact on his or her engagement and motivation in the classroom. The teacher cannot control what happens in a student's life outside the school setting. However, the teacher's understanding of what is happening has profound implications for decisions about contextual and situational processes in classroom practice.

Common sense suggests, and research clearly shows, that the climate we create greatly influences the cognitive and affective learning outcomes of our CLD students (Clandinin & Connelly, 1995; Conant, n.d.; Cummins, 1996; Lackney, 1998; Straits, 2007). As Jensen (2008) notes, "There is no such thing as an unmotivated learner. There are, however, temporary unmotivated states in which learners are either reinforced and supported or neglected and labeled" (p. 119). Educators can consider the questions below, which apply to each of their students, but are particularly important for exploring specific situations and supporting the learning of struggling and CLD students. A teacher can use the resulting information and ideas to make decisions about daily practice.

- What is happening outside the classroom that is impacting the student during instruction? What can be done to help the student feel more comfortable about the situation?
- What is happening inside the classroom that is impacting the student during instruction? What can be done to alter those conditions?
- If anxiety related to classroom climate is keeping the student from engaging in the lesson, what strategies can be employed to lessen the anxiety the student is feeling?

As Krashen (1982) points out, the student's negative emotions, including anxiety, self-consciousness, boredom, annoyance, alienation, and so forth, constitute an *affective filter* that can greatly "interfere with the reception and processing of comprehensible input" (p. 468).

We all have had experiences with the reality of the affective filter in our own lives. For example, if you have ever taken a course in which the professor came in and said, "By the end of this semester, only a few of you will be left in the course," you have probably experienced anxiety and fear accompanying the thought that you might fail to achieve your goal, as well as resentment that a teacher would express such indifference to your personal success or failure. As an adult learner, you use the many skills you have gained over the years to lower that anxiety and to turn anger into motivation. You might:

- Use a social strategy, such as self-talk, to calm your nerves.
- Think about the people you know who may have taken the course or find someone in the class with whom you can study throughout the semester.
- Consider taking notes during class and comparing them with your text or someone else's notes.

These are but a few of the skills you have gained over the years.

As educators addressing the needs of CLD students, we must provide learning conditions that minimize anxiety and maximize learning while at the same time helping students develop the kinds of strategies that support adults in monitoring (and lowering as necessary) their levels of stress and anxiety. Each CLD student in the class will demonstrate his or her reality and needs in different ways at different times. We must be ready to respond and keep students moving forward in their personal development and academic endeavors. By remaining active in our role as a "negotiating agent," we can better respond to students' needs as they transition into the culture, language, and community of our classrooms.

When creating risk-free and low-anxiety learning conditions, educators can do the following:

- Incorporate the language of the student into all aspects of classroom life.
- Value and use the CLD student's culture as a bridge to understanding the curriculum.
- Observe for the CLD student's feelings, attitudes, self-concept, and interaction preferences during all phases of lesson delivery.
- Provide varied opportunities for interaction among *all* students in the classroom, regardless of linguistic or academic ability.

In addition, lessons that provide *each student* in the classroom with a chance to be heard from his or her own point of view will be more likely to lower the student's affective filter and lead to greater participation. Such opportunities to be heard promote students' social adjustment processes, positive attitude toward school, and academic success.

Biography-Driven Instruction: An Action Model

In our professional practice, we need to reflect continually on the contextual and situational processes of teaching, keeping in mind the ever-changing dynamics of our learning community and ensuring that student biographies are central to all our decisions. Classrooms where students feel safe to take risks, learn, and contribute are classrooms where learning is optimized for all students. Figure 6.2 illustrates the interrelatedness of the many facets of biography-driven instruction that are discussed in depth throughout this text. The diagram is intended to serve as a tool for understanding how the CLD student biography provides the foundation for all instructional decisions related to developing a classroom ecology, drawing on students' background knowledge, and supporting students' linguistic and academic development. These factors play out in different ways during each phase of the teaching and learning process.

Observe, Facilitate, Affirm

Research has long documented the importance of valuing what every child brings to each act of learning (González, et al., 2005; Keefe & Padilla, 1987; Moll & Greenberg, 1990; Vélez-Ibáñez & Greenberg, 1992). As discussed in Chapter 1, many instructional models and frameworks exist to

Brief, one-on-one conversations with students are a great way to gather additional information about the strengths and knowledge that individual students bring to the lesson.

—*Socorro Herrera, Elementary, Kansas*

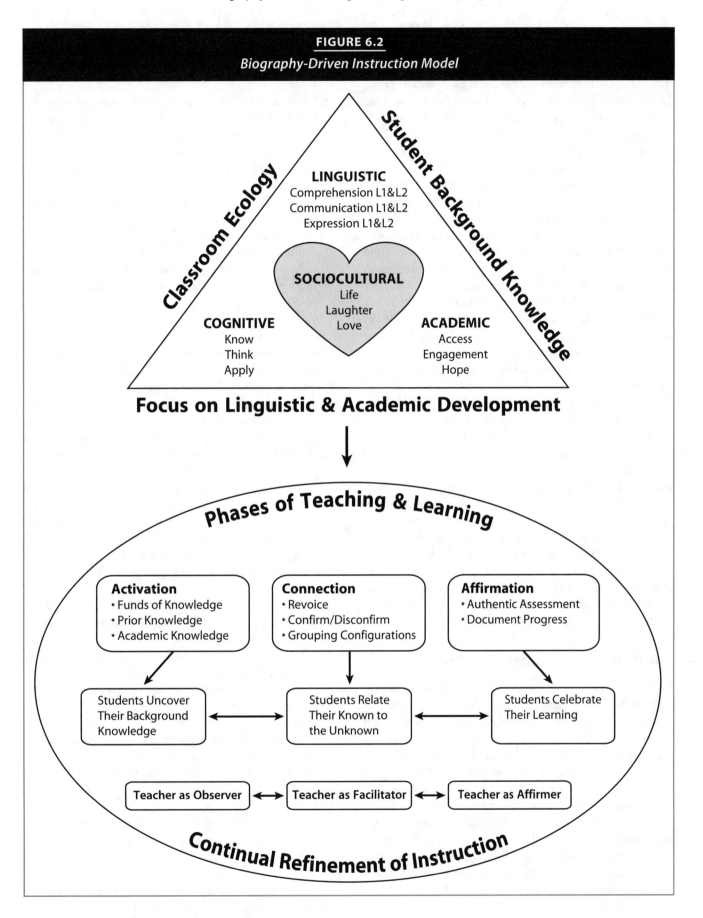

FIGURE 6.2
Biography-Driven Instruction Model

support teachers in planning, delivering, and assessing the lesson. However, often lacking is explicit guidance on how to take these models and frameworks into practice in ways that clarify the multidimensional assets CLD learners bring. Understanding students' existing knowledge and various strengths enables teachers to move away from remediation and toward *acceleration of learning*.

If we are to begin at our CLD students' current levels of competence, we must first assess that level from a perspective that looks for assets rather than deficiencies; that is, we must assume that every student we teach has something to contribute to every lesson. If we use only school-situated data and assessments to inform ourselves about a CLD student's linguistic and academic abilities, we discount the truly dynamic and intricate nature of each individual's second language acquisition and learning process. In Chapters 1 and 3, I discussed the importance of Krashen's (1982) i+1 theory of language development and Vygotsky's (1978) construct of learning. Understanding and using these two "ideals" as we plan for teaching requires us to move beyond a superficial, school-situated knowledge of students' assets and into the role of active observer and facilitator of learning. Those who challenge themselves to do so will likely be rewarded by the sight of their CLD students, as well as all their other students, beaming with delight at reaching deeper levels of understanding.

We must become observers and listeners within our own community. Our students have much to share when we provide a risk-free space—a space where CLD students know that if rerouting is necessary, the teacher and his or her peers will make it happen without penalty. In such spaces, appropriate strategies and scaffolds help learners connect their background knowledge to the topic of the lesson or the vocabulary being taught. As discussed throughout the remainder of this text, the teacher takes on a responsibility to observe, facilitate, and affirm.

The Teacher as Participant Observer

In this section, I more specifically discuss how to implement culturally relevant pedagogy within the context of a lesson. You are probably wondering, *How exactly do I plan for instruction that is contextualized and situated with specific considerations for the CLD student biography?* In beginning to answer this question, I ask that you first imagine that you are an ethnographer—a researcher—within your own classroom. Focus your thoughts on what you know about the biographies of your CLD students. What knowledge and understanding does each student bring from his or her previous academic and life experiences (no matter how distant that knowledge may appear from the "standard" you are about to teach)? Now, take a few moments to do the following:

- Think about what you already know from the school-situated biographies you were handed at the beginning of the year, or from what you have collected since your students' arrival.
- Think about what you are going to teach and what you can do to learn more about students' knowledge, as it relates to the topic or vocabulary.
- Pose some questions about the learning community and the new chapter, novel, vocabulary, or concept to be taught.
- Think: What can I gather? What questions can I pose to students before I teach so I can get insights into what they already know?
- Think about how you can delve into what often remains "invisible" because it may initially appear that there is nothing the student brings that can be uncovered or discovered.

Your aim is to keep an open mind about the "participants" in your classroom—to take what you can learn from reflecting on the biographies of your students and prepare to "ignite" and make public what CLD students know. Doing so will invigorate your practice, bringing added meaning to your teaching and to their learning, and to the learning of every student in your classroom. Figure 6.3 illustrates how one teacher gained insights about her students.

Every step of the way you will strive to consider what you already know, reflect upon what you are hearing, and observe within the social and academic context of your learning community for even the tiniest detail that will inform you about the thinking of even the most difficult student. You will begin to ask questions such as:

- How can I best make accommodations throughout this lesson for the levels of language acquisition represented in my classroom?
- Which students have strong academic biographies related to this topic?
- Which students have knowledge of this topic as a result of experiences in their home and/or community?
- What group configurations will be most beneficial given the objectives of this lesson?
- What activity will be most useful for introducing the topic and target vocabulary at the beginning of this lesson?
- Have I made clear my objectives and expectations for this lesson, as well as the directions for specific tasks?

According to Massey (1998), this type of reflection forces us to ask ourselves the difficult questions, the ques-

FIGURE 6.3
Mind Map and Explanation

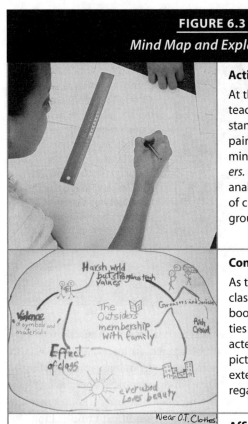

Activation

At the beginning of the lesson the teacher activated students' understanding by dividing the class into pairs and having the pairs do a mind map of the book *The Outsiders*. In pairs, students performed analyses focusing on the two sets of characters (i.e., the two rival groups) depicted in the book.

Connection

As the lesson proceeded and the class continued to talk about the book, students found commonalities between the two sets of characters. The students used both pictures and words to share their extensions of the mind maps regarding the characters.

Affirmation

At the end of the lesson, the students were asked to share their mind maps with the whole group. During this time, the teacher used a rubric to gauge students' understanding of the topic.

—*Lisa Muldoon, Middle School, Kansas*

facts as a means to understanding what is happening at the time. Becoming a participant observer requires the teacher to become totally immersed and involved in the situation. As Ladson-Billings (1998) explains, "Teachers develop an informed empathy, rather than a patronizing sympathy" (p. 300) by *feeling with*, instead of *feeling for*, students as they share what they bring to the lesson. The teacher gathers information about what students know, how they interpret what is to be studied, or gaps that exist in background knowledge, becoming better able to truly differentiate the instruction to meet the needs of every student.

The information and knowledge collected and documented by the teacher then can facilitate "instructional bridging and contextualizing," that is, the *scaffolding* of instruction at Krashen's i+1 level of language comprehension and production or Vygotsky's zone of proximal development for student learning (see Chapter 1 for discussion of these concepts). Just as a building under construction is less likely to collapse if it is scaffolded by a supporting structure, a student's emergent understanding of a concept is more quickly and effectively built when the teacher takes care to surround it with a framework of existing knowledge. Examples of Howe's (1984) and Ormrod's (1995) *principles of learning*, summarized by Gay (2000), reaffirm the importance of this scaffolding.

tions that count, and to be open to learning about those who inhabit our classrooms. Rather than jumping to conclusions about what a CLD student is or is not capable of doing alone or with support, we wait until the data have been collected to proceed on our journey. With the insights we have gained, we are able to route and reroute students as necessary to make sure everyone has a chance to achieve the goals of the lesson and arrive at the academic success we want for all our students.

Although we are not technically ethnographers, we can learn from the ideals and methodology of being a *participant observer* and apply these new understandings to our role within the classroom culture we are trying to learn more about. Alexander (2003) describes participant observation as a way of observing the setting, learning about the participants (students), and analyzing documents and arti-

- *Principle of similarity:* Students' existing knowledge is the best starting point for the introduction of new knowledge.
- *Principle of efficacy:* Prior success breeds subsequent effort and success.
- *Principle of congruity:* New knowledge is learned more easily and retained longer when it is connected to prior knowledge, frames of reference, or cognitive schemas.
- *Principle of familiarity:* Reducing the "strangeness" of new knowledge and the concomitant "threat of the unfamiliar" increases students' engagement with and mastery of learning tasks.
- *Principle of cognitive mapping:* Understanding how students' knowledge is organized and interrelated—their cognitive structures—is essential to maximizing their classroom learning. (p. 149)

Our observation before beginning a lesson is crucial to our ability to capitalize on not only *what* students know but also *how* they have come to know about the vocabulary, concept, or topic. Gay (2000) states: "It is not enough for teachers to know 'what the learner knows about individual facts and concepts' (Howe, 1984, p. 68). They also need to understand how students come to know or to learn so that they can convey new knowledge to them through their own learning systems" (p. 149). Understanding how students derived the information they know gives teachers a link that is stronger than any explanation, visual, or hands-on activity they might have originally planned to use to teach the given concept.

Education has a long history of using terms such as "prior knowledge" and "background knowledge" interchangeably. For many educators, this can be frustrating and confusing, if not misleading. For example, Stevens (1980) defines background knowledge quite simply as "what one already knows about a subject" (p. 151). The definition that Biemans and Simons (1996) provide is slightly more complex: "[prior/background knowledge is] all knowledge learners have when entering a learning environment that is potentially relevant for acquiring new knowledge" (p. 158). The language of these definitions may limit what teachers do in classroom practice, because teachers may assume they already are optimally using students' previously acquired knowledge. Teachers sometimes make comments such as, "This student has very little background knowledge." Yet they may be unable to explain exactly what they mean by such a statement.

Here, I will attempt to respectfully elaborate on the three "roots" of student experience and learning—*funds of knowledge* (home assets), *prior knowledge* (community assets), and *academic knowledge* (school assets)—to clarify the often subtle but important distinctions between the multiple sources of students' previously acquired, or "background," knowledge. These distinctions are drawn to support teachers' observations before, during, and after the lesson. Understanding and differentiating between the types of knowledge students bring to our classrooms supports our efforts to provide students with culturally relevant pedagogy.

Funds of Knowledge

Teachers frequently comment on how little they know about the home lives of their students or how students' home lives do not support what is being taught at school.

In Hindu households, a brother is supposed to protect his sister and uphold her honor. In this photo, a mother is tying a Rakhi (a thread) around her son's wrist, with his sister looking on. The Rakhi symbolizes the bond of protection that exists between brother and sister. Families also celebrate the bond between siblings by sharing traditional sweets.

—*Pooja Agarwal, New Delhi, India*

However, many teachers have discovered the value of home visits and what can be gained from learning about the resources that students acquire from being part of a family, with its unique makeup and dynamics. These assets have been referred to as the *funds of knowledge* that families and students possess, and they have significant implications for classroom practice.

As a theoretical construct, the concept of "funds of knowledge" (Moll et al., 1992) has been guiding educators' thought and practice for more than a decade. The term "funds of knowledge" focuses on the wealth of knowledge and assets a student has accumulated from his or her life at home. A student's primary socialization occurs within a group of people who bend, shape, and mold his or her language and ways of thinking and being in the world. The literature defines funds of knowledge as those historically developed and accumulated strategies or bodies of knowledge that are essential to the function and well-being of a household (Moll et al., 1992; Vélez-Ibáñez & Greenberg, 1992). Certain events and experiences occur in the home of any given student that are uniquely tied to his or her understanding of the world, as reflected in native language, primary discourse patterns, traditions, actions, and individual roles.

Discourse, or communicative exchange, is explicitly connected to the "bodies of knowledge" that develop within a student's immediate household and that are unique, and often "secret" or "hidden," from the community or the school. This knowledge is transmitted from generation to generation, understood through a shared lens, and passed on in daily activity. Such knowledge includes, but is not limited to, the cultural features described in Chapter 2. The strategies understood and employed by the student thus represent the historical ways of being and participating within a "cultural unit," that is, the family.

I often say to educators that these ways of being in the world are passed on by osmosis without having to be explicitly explained to the members of the family. We all can think of a family saying, practice, joke, rule, or guiding assumption that makes automatic sense to us in the context of our family but would be difficult to explain to an outsider. These personal examples are microcosms of the larger bodies of knowledge that may differ radically among cultural groups. Consider the following scenario:

I have a very close friend who has a daughter in high school. This young woman is beautiful, intelligent, outgoing, and fully grounded in her cultural identity. As I have watched her grow, I have been fascinated with the ease with which she has learned to live within her cultural reality and the reality of being a teenager in the United States. She fully understands how two worlds may look the same and yet be incredibly different. Her own "culturally prescribed" ways of participating are very different from those of her cheerleading peers. Her parents attend all functions, are very involved in her life, and prohibit dating; she is expected to participate in family life beyond what most teenagers would think is "cool." On a recent 2-hour trip together, we talked about her experiences as a cheerleader and the expectations her mother and father have of her. I asked how she managed to live in both worlds, especially with regard to dating. I found her response something to smile about. She shared that when someone asks about "the ways of doing" within her family unit, she says, "I won't be able to do that." When asked why, she simply responds, "It's very complicated, you see. You'd have to live there to understand."

Funds of knowledge, especially those that relate to culture, are not always capitalized on in the classroom. It is our responsibility, as educators, to set up contextual and situational conditions that provide students with an opportunity to share these often hidden ways of doing that are evident only to those who share a long history with individual students or interact with them on a daily basis. Understanding the dynamics that create the richness of what every family—poor or wealthy—possesses sets the stage for moving beyond surface levels of using students' backgrounds and cultures during instruction. As González et al. (2005) note:

Using the concept of funds of knowledge as a heuristic device provides teachers with a pragmatic avenue to engage with their students' lives. It allows the possibility of seeing beyond the classroom and glimpsing the circulating discourses and shifting fields of power that shape students' lives. (p. 44)

When we create opportunities for families and students to share what is happening in their homes and lives, the resulting insights become resources—*authentic* information we can use to make connections between what the student brings and what is being taught.

The concept of funds of knowledge provides a lens for understanding the primary socialization of students who come from homes where the culture and the language of their environment are different from those of the school. When appropriate observations are made in the classroom, educators are provided with a rich tapestry of CLD student assets that are available for knowledge construction processes for the entire learning community. With this in mind, we can begin to look for strategies that will make public what the student knows about vocabulary, topics, and so forth that may support what is going to be taught. Consider the following scenario and reflect on what the teacher learned by using a strategy that provided space for this student's funds of knowledge to be made public in the classroom.

Mrs. Nowakowski, a 2nd-grade teacher, showed her students the cover of the book and said, "One of our objectives for today is to use the DOTS Chart to prepare for reading our story of the week, *The Piñata Maker*, by George Ancona." The previous year, Mrs. Nowakowski had learned the DOTS Chart strategy in a graduate level course in ESL methods. (See Appendix C for a full description of the DOTS Chart and a template for classroom use.)

Mrs. Nowakowski then asked the students to reach deep into their memories and "splash" onto their DOTS Chart (see Figure 6.4) the words or pictures that came to mind. She said they could write in the language(s) of their choice and/or draw pictures. As she walked around the room observing and noting what students were writing, she noticed that one of the students had written the word "rheumatism," not a typical word for a 2nd-grade student with a limited English vocabulary. She stopped and asked about this "big" word. The student shared that her *abuelita* (grandmother) used to make piñatas in Mexico before coming to live with them. However, she no longer made piñatas because she had rheumatism.

This information was one of those little disclosures that provided Mrs. Nowakowski with a window into her student's immediate connections to the story

FIGURE 6.4
DOTS Chart: Determine, Observe, Talk, Summarize

Name: _____

DOTS Chart
(<u>D</u>etermine, <u>O</u>bserve, <u>T</u>alk, <u>S</u>ummarize)

Topic: _____

A–B	C–D	E–F
ball ★brown	carets colors cone	fomous
G–H	**I–J**	**K–L**
glue How to make a Pintata.		
M–N	**O–P**	**Q–R**
Make years Newspaper Neck	Pintata orang Paper Paste	★ rheumatism
S–T	**U–V–W**	**X–Y–Z**
Jamdraw Swap twine		years

and the lesson. By providing the students in the class with the opportunity to voice what they were thinking, seeing, or feeling, she was able to listen and observe for student associations that could be used later in the lesson to build trust, community, and academic knowledge.

We must always be aware that long before we come into students' lives, they are living and breathing the history of their innermost circle. The languages they speak, their values, and their beliefs already have been communicated in verbal and nonverbal ways. These have been passed on from one generation to the next through parenting practices that teach social and communicative behaviors. According to Vygotsky (1986), we first understand our identity through the hearts and minds of those who have socialized us to see and feel the world in a certain way.

To understand what our students know and how they communicate that knowledge, we must first understand the cultural constructs that shaped them *before* they arrived in our classrooms. These constructs cannot be understood unless we make a conscious effort to observe our students throughout the lesson as they make sense of what we teach. If we consider what educators and researchers have discussed in relation to a funds-of-knowledge perspective, we then can begin to conceptualize contexts and situations that will allow students to voice in our classrooms their individual biographical roots.

According to Cremin (1976), the school and classroom are not the only place where students learn. Instead, he says, learning takes place in the family, community, and school. Each source of learning has its own goals and objectives and contributes to what the student knows and believes (Delgado-Gaitan, 1987; Mehan, Hubbard, & Villanueva, 1994; Phelan, Davidson, & Yu, 1998). None, however, has as long-lasting effects as the family, in which the student has been primarily socialized. As Cremin (1976) notes, "every family has a curriculum which it teaches quite deliberately and systematically over time" (p. 22).

Prior Knowledge

Considering students' *prior knowledge* has long been part of the lesson planning process. Prior knowledge relates to the understandings and knowledge a student has gained as a result of being part of a community. Prior knowledge is anchored in the student's primary socialization in the home and is wedged between what happens at home and what happens in school (Gay, 2000). Current and past economic and social trends (e.g., employment opportunities, political threats) have forced many CLD students to be very mobile, moving from community to community and continually

A community of learners is solidified through continual opportunities for interaction and sharing. In this photo, Ms. Johnson, a 2nd-grade teacher, is creating conditions in the classroom that can help her learners connect to their prior knowledge. In this lesson, the students were getting ready to focus on the topic *rain forest*. Before the students actually got into the content of the lesson, the teacher activated their prior knowledge by having them first write their individual thoughts about the rain forest on paper and then talk to one another about what they knew. This made the lesson less threatening for the students, gave everyone a chance to share, and provided Ms. Johnson with insights into student knowledge that she could use to make connections to the content. Although this example is from a 2nd-grade class, the process described is effective with learners of all ages, including adults.

—Denise Johnson, 2nd Grade, Kansas

adjusting to new people and new surroundings. Although this does not hold true for all CLD students, for some it redefines our common understanding of the "community" in which a student has been socialized. Therefore, it often holds true that what is learned in the community will be based on where the CLD student and his or her family find themselves at any point in time socially, economically, and linguistically. When the community has resources available to support the family, the student's role(s) often will be different from the role(s) he or she might play in a community where few resources are available to support the family. Students bring the cumulative prior knowledge they have gained from each of the communities in which they have interacted.

In preparing to tap into a student's prior knowledge, the teacher once again takes on the responsibility of becoming a participant observer of the student and family, to understand the literacy and other assets the student has gained from being an active participant in his or her community context(s). A student's prior knowledge is closely tied to the following:

- The social climate of the community
- The role(s) the student has within the family unit
- The status and acceptance of the student's particular group
- The political climate of the community, region, and nation
- Community resources the student and family can access
- The types of experiences and opportunities available in the community

One of the most relevant and yet often overlooked assets that many CLD students bring to the classroom is derived from lived experience of being the only English speaker in their family. Take, for example, the previously discussed scenario in which the teacher's use of the DOTS Chart yielded a student sharing the word "rheumatism" during the activation phase of the lesson. From a funds-of-knowledge perspective, we learned that the student's grandmother had rheumatism. The teacher subsequently asked the student where she had learned how to spell the word, and she shared that she was the only one in the family who spoke English. Therefore, she translated when her grandmother went to the doctor and helped to give her the necessary medicine. The word was written on both her prescription container and the reading materials that were given during doctor visits. *Language brokering*, in which an individual (often a CLD student) serves to "interpret and translate between culturally and linguistically different people and mediate interactions in a variety of situations" (Tse, 1996, p. 226), is just one experience that many students in our classrooms have had in their respective communities.

Experiences in the community enable students to develop prior knowledge that then can be used as a resource when performing different tasks in school. For instance, when students use literacy for purposes related to life circumstances (e.g., filling out job applications, completing lease agreements, applying for services), such experiences contribute to students' literacy development. Though we generally assume that only adults perform such activities, CLD students often undertake them to assist their families. The resulting skills and knowledge can be capitalized on during reading and writing lessons. Some students have worked side by side with community members participating in activities that require real-life application of math, science, social studies, and other content areas. Students' prior knowledge about a particular, even unexpected, topic might therefore be quite extensive.

We teachers must consider, however, the effects that the acculturation process can have on students. CLD students often experience the acculturation process in different ways

In Ms. Metz's 6th-grade classroom, all the students are exposed to same content, but the route that each student takes in understanding the content is different. In this photo, students are working in a small group as they delve into social studies. The students are looking at the pictures that have been taken from their social studies textbook and drawing or writing about what they see in each picture. This activity provided Ms. Metz an opportunity to have students express their background knowledge by using a visual taken directly from the text. As the lesson progressed, students compared their learning with their initial thoughts.

—*Kendra Metz, 6th Grade, Kansas*

than adults, frequently learning English before their parents. Yet the discrimination they may experience in society can lead to their perception that knowledge and learning can only be gained in school. This perspective, in turn, can lead students to discount their own knowledge. It is up to us first to design opportunities for students to bring their prior knowledge to the surface, and then to validate that knowledge.

Distinguishing between student knowledge acquired inside the home and knowledge gained through participation in the community provides educators with different types of "anchors" for understanding each student. To best accelerate learning, educators need to understand how knowledge gained from the family and community can be used as a bridge to new learning. Connections made to both types of lived experiences are much more relevant and can do more to promote students' cognitive connections during the lesson than teacher explanations or descriptions of topics, concepts, or new vocabulary. By selecting and implementing strategies that allow students to share from their funds of knowledge and prior knowledge, actively observing for such insights, and using the information gained during the lesson, we set the stage for students to discover how their knowledge connects to the content.

In teaching, many of us have at least once looked at the curriculum we had to follow and become frustrated with the idea of teaching students whose related knowledge appeared so limited that we had little hope they would be successful in the classroom. We may have moved toward providing impersonal experiences for students by taking them on field trips and bringing in "concrete objects" in an attempt to provide students with experiences we perceived to be relevant to their becoming better prepared to learn within a prescribed content area. This mode of thinking views learning as the process of accumulating information or experience (Knowles, 1970). To make the best possible use of students' funds of knowledge and prior knowledge, our perspective on learning needs to shift. When we begin to view learning as "conceptual change" (Strike & Posner, 1985; West & Pines, 1985) from the unknown to the known, it becomes more natural to automatically search for existing knowledge to which we can tie new information.

Learning about the knowledge accumulated from students' socialization in the home and the community, and using it during instruction, helps our teaching to be culturally and linguistically relevant to the student. It demonstrates to students that we care about their lived experiences outside of the school. When we use students' funds of knowledge and prior knowledge, we learn about what is important to them. When we approach instruction with this new perspective, our use of field trips and the virtual reality experiences made possible by technology are more likely to achieve our goals for reaching and teaching CLD students.

Read the following stories, which summarize the experiences of two girls, Thuy and Sonya. Consider the academic value of each student's experiences.

Thuy's Story

Prior to immigrating to the United States from Vietnam, Thuy found herself waiting to hear that her father had earned enough money from working in U.S. beef packing plants to send for the family. During this time, it became the responsibility of the rest of the family to support themselves at home. Thuy's work consisted of selling candy her mother had made the previous evening. During her long hours on the street, she found herself calculating the number of candies she must sell that day to meet the family's needs. At the end of the month, she had to know how much money the family had spent on food in order to determine the amount of candy her mother would still need to make (including considerations for the days/hours of work were left) to pay the rent. When Thuy immigrated to the United States and started school, her teacher never realized that Thuy possessed this kind of experiential mathematical knowledge. Although Thuy excelled in math, she struggled in other areas. Years later, as she sat and recounted her story for a scholarship committee, she expressed her desire to teach math by using student experiences as the basis for what would be taught in school. She clearly had, on her own, realized what had made her successful.

Sonya's Story

When Sonya was a little girl she was fascinated with numbers. Seeing her learn to count to ten by the time she was one, her parents quickly recognized that she had a gift that needed to be developed. They made sure they bought her toys that supported her love of math, played games with her, and continually pointed out how the world in which she lived was surrounded with mathematical concepts. When she started school, she was immediately tested and provided an opportunity to continue growing. By the time she was a junior in high school, she was taking classes at the local university. She told the scholarship committee that throughout her school years she had been mentored, and that mentoring had helped her to get where she was today. Her goal was to make sure that students who were "gifted" in math would get opportunities to shine in school.

If schools do not consider additional sources of background knowledge, a student's background with formal schooling can create great advantages for some students and great disadvantages for others. As educators, our challenge is to look for ways to create multiple opportunities for CLD students to voice and make public the knowledge they bring from the home and community as well as from previous schooling experiences. Most CLD students do not have problems with processing and storing information; however, if they are not provided with opportunities to be part of the learning conversation, we discount the knowledge they bring and leave them at a disadvantage.

Academic Knowledge

In the previous two sections, an attempt was made to distinguish between what we have come to understand as "funds of knowledge" and "prior knowledge." In this section, I explore "academic knowledge" as part of the conversation on understanding and utilizing CLD student biographies in planning, teaching, and assessing. *Academic knowledge* refers to knowledge that students have acquired in formal educational settings. Academic knowledge reflects the kinds of understandings and skills that traditionally have been highly valued by schools and teachers.

When we make decisions about curriculum and instruction for a given student, we must avoid relying solely on the academic information with which we are provided at the beginning of the year or upon a student's arrival (e.g., enrollment form data, English language proficiency test scores, standardized content-area test scores). Consider the following scenario:

> A few years ago, I was asked by an ESL high school teacher to come and model a lesson in her classroom. I accepted the invitation and had a great time interacting with her students. It was evident from the first half of the class that these students had very different biographies and aspirations for the future. Shortly after class, a student came up and asked if I had any connections in the school. I smiled and asked what he meant by "connections." He told me that he recently had moved to the area and wanted to be placed in the AP math courses in the school. He had already taken the highest level of math before moving to the United States from Mexico. He had looked at the books and assignments of the AP courses down the hall and was confident that he could do the work. He said, "They have never asked what I know. What do they have to lose? If I fail because I don't speak English, they can put me back here all day." When I left the classroom, I visited with the counselor, who informed me that until students had reached a certain level of English proficiency, they were not "eligible" for any other class except ESL sheltered instruction.

When we consider a student's academic knowledge, we must remember to take into account not only the experiences the individual has had in the United States but also those in any other country in which he or she was schooled. By reflecting on our current efforts to learn about the academic biographies of our students *beyond traditional assessments*, we become aware of new possibilities for gaining insight into the knowledge our students bring to the classroom.

Knowledge Systems and Background Knowledge

Thinking about *knowledge* from the three perspectives I have discussed in this chapter reframes "what counts" in school and widens our lens to include more in our teaching. Understanding and differentiating among funds of knowledge, prior knowledge, and academic knowledge helps us better understand that *every* student brings something to the lesson that we can connect to as we teach new vocabulary and academic concepts. Knowing what students bring from all three types of knowledge sources informs us in plotting the best path for ensuring their academic success.

At the same time, we must remember that funds of knowledge, prior knowledge, and academic knowledge overlap and are intertwined in students' schema. Taken together, these *knowledge systems* represent a student's background knowledge. According to Lewis (2006), "a system is a collection of parts that interact with each other to function as a whole" (p. 458). Our students begin their life in a family that is full of language, culture, love, and much more, long before they begin to understand and interact with the community. Depending on where their life leads them and the dynamics within their family, they soon begin to interact with a given community in ways that help to mold their understanding of what happens outside the home as well as the implications that the larger society has for their family. This secondary socialization (Cushner, McClelland, & Safford, 2006) can happen as early as the preschool years and continues into young adulthood. Within these two knowledge systems (funds of knowledge and prior knowledge), educators can find untapped resources to affirm students' language, culture, and life and to promote their linguistic and academic development. Ultimately, these two systems come into contact with formal schooling.

The way we think about these knowledge systems influences our contextual view of teaching and learning, and informs our decisions regarding situational processes during the act of teaching. Figure 6.5 provides a brief review of the defining features of these knowledge systems and illustrates their interrelated nature. To capitalize on these types of background knowledge in the classroom, we must ignite students' associations with the topic at hand, observe as they share these associations, and elaborate on students' connections to make learning meaningful. As we incorporate these processes into our daily instruction, we begin to think in terms of *biography-driven instruction*.

Reflections on Valuing the Student in Teaching

In some respects, every classroom is a world unto itself—a community that has been created by the teacher in the image of the kind of learning ecology that the teacher believes will best meet his or her goals. In this educational space, conditional and situational processes either enhance or inhibit CLD students' learning. In this chapter, we have learned that teachers who strive to provide biography-driven instruction become participant observers of the assets that each member of the community possesses. By

FIGURE 6.5
Knowledge Systems

Background Knowledge

Funds of Knowledge	Prior Knowledge	Academic Knowledge
Home Assets	**Community Assets**	**School Assets**
• Traditions • Native Language • Home Literacy Practices • Family Dynamics	• Language Brokering • Community Environment • Family Employment • Community Support Systems	• Previous Content Knowledge • School Literacy Practices • School-Based Cooperation & Collaboration Skills • Formal School Dynamics

← Activate, Connect, Affirm →

Background knowledge becomes the catalyst for accelerating the academic success of students from culturally and linguistically diverse backgrounds. Educators must capture the knowledge that students bring from their homes, communities, and other life experiences. Funds of knowledge, prior knowledge, and academic knowledge cannot be considered as completely separate sources of knowledge because they are interrelated and each informs the others in multiple ways. Rough boundaries have been drawn to make it easier to ensure that each area is addressed before, during, and after the lesson. Often home and community assets are left on the periphery of teaching, yet when considered and used in practice they become powerful tools for increasing academic achievement.

becoming aware of and using student knowledge as a catalyst for new learning, teachers increase the likelihood of all students achieving academically.

One common myth among educators is related to the presumed lack of knowledge that CLD students have about academic content. The prevalence of this myth calls us to reflect on the value we place on different types of knowledge. If we claim, for example, to value our student's mathematical knowledge gained through the mechanical experience of setting the timing belt in a car, we must find ways to validate and use that knowledge in the learning processes of the classroom. If our thinking is focused exclusively on classroom learning that employs "school valued" knowledge rather than on what we can do with students' existing knowledge, we limit the possibilities for CLD students' success in school.

Teachers often say, "No two days are ever the same, and that's what makes education such a wonderful profession." As we daily provide opportunities for our students to share their thoughts and experiences, we come to a greater understanding of the background knowledge (i.e., funds of knowledge, prior knowledge, and academic knowledge) that each possesses from their life history and from attending school. Yet students will only be willing to make their knowledge public to the degree that we teachers have created spaces where human relationships are valued and learning is built on trust and respect. Motivation, engagement, emotion, and cognition are interrelated, and never exist in isolation when students are learning. Therefore, we must continually navigate our students' states of mind and attend to situational processes throughout the lesson.

Chapter 7 provides additional tools for discovering what each student brings. The strategies that are introduced will solidify what you have learned in this chapter. By listening and observing for glimpses into what students think and know, we allow students to teach us and to provide us with links to their lives that will make our content more relevant and comprehensible.

CHAPTER 7

A Canvas of Opportunity

IN PREVIOUS CHAPTERS, I focused extensively on the importance, even urgency, of understanding our students in terms of the rich and complex tapestry of their lives. Making deliberate use of what we learn both from traditional assessment tools, as well as from listening and observing students' actions and reactions to what we are teaching, will enhance our efforts to ensure academic success for every student. Only by closely attending to and using the assets that the learner brings to our lesson are we able to differentiate instruction for CLD students. Differentiation of instruction that places the biography of each student at the center of pedagogy has the potential to lead to better classroom management, student engagement, and motivation to learn. As Cummins (1996) reminds us, "Human relationships are at the heart of schooling" (p. 1). Unless we are continually learning about our students and the potential they bring to each lesson, it will be difficult to reach the destination we have set for our lesson.

A Social Constructivist Approach

According to Palincsar (1998), educators who use *social constructivist* approaches create conditions and situational contexts wherein the student drives the discussion and the teacher assumes the role of facilitator, or guide, alongside the learner. Any form of instruction that takes a constructivist approach strives to implement the ideal of "teacher as facilitator" in the classroom. However, what is often missing in constructivist classrooms is facilitation guided by what the learner brings, both culturally and linguistically, to the learning environment. The *social* constructivist classroom, on the other hand, is one in which the teacher uses what he or she has learned from the student in order to provide more opportunities for all students to fully participate in brainstorming, questioning, and directing student learning in the classroom.

According to O'Dwyer (2006), we must move away from strict adherence to the old pedagogical ideal that placed the teacher in charge of "transmitting knowledge" to students. Although transmitting information about the particulars of a content area is one important aspect of teaching, educators also should become facilitators of student learning. For example, the teacher not only teaches students the meaning of a new vocabulary word but also guides students along the path to where the applicable concept has meaning for their lives. Social constructivist pedagogy involves the facilitation of activities that are communicative, democratic, and student-centered. To become a truly effective facilitator of learning for all students, the teacher must value the CLD learner's experience and knowledge, gained both in and out of the classroom. The teacher's facilitation process begins with learning about and using CLD student knowledge as the "anchor" or "point of departure" for instruction.

In classrooms where the goal is to use the biographies of the students to bridge and connect to new learning, the teacher no longer follows the standard pattern of asking questions designed to obtain the correct answer from a student, and then evaluating whether the answer provided is correct, as determined by his or her expectations. Rather, the teacher connects student talk in ways that route and reroute learning to arrive at the targeted destination. Here, the teacher facilitates all levels of academic talk in ways that celebrate contributions by all learners.

In beginning to address the biographies of the students in our classrooms, we consider instructional factors that:

- Help to ensure that all students have opportunities to share what they know
- Enable teachers to capitalize on student assets and create conditions and situations that encourage students to become active participants in learning
- Support students in reaching their full potential, with the aid of our facilitation

The following tactics are fundamental to the social constructivist teaching strategy:

- Educators make "transparent," or explicit, to students what is going to be taught and how they will be supported in their learning.
- Teachers begin the cycle of making decisions that are situational in nature, based on their gathered information about students' needs and assets.
- Teachers provide all students with an opportunity to disclose the knowledge they bring from their backgrounds.
- Educators make clear to students that there are no right or wrong answers at the beginning of the lesson; there is only activation of each student's existing frame of reference, or schema, so that together the class can begin its journey toward learning.
- Teachers create a low-risk environment in which the learners of the community feel safe and respected and trust that their educated guesses and contributions, in whatever language(s) they decide to use for disclosure, will be accepted as part of the learning process.
- Educators take part in the "activation" process by observing for insights into students' systems of knowledge (i.e., funds of knowledge, prior knowledge, and academic knowledge) and reflecting on ways such background knowledge of students can be taken into the formal part of the lesson.

These tactics encourage the teacher to go beyond merely setting objectives, telling students what they are to learn, and then proceeding to teach and evaluate student learning. Instead, the teacher facilitates learning through biography-driven instruction, in which he or she brings all the resources of the learning community to the forefront of the learning process. Accordingly, the teacher strives to make public CLD students' knowledge and supports students in making their thinking processes explicit.

Transparency in Teaching

As discussed in Chapter 6, fostering a supportive classroom ecology means much more than creating an environment that values culture and language in superficial ways, such as posters with inventors from diverse backgrounds or labels for classroom objects in the various languages spoken by students. While these are important, ecology involves even greater consideration of the individual students in the class, the curriculum, and the teacher in charge. In our classrooms, we educators set in motion and orchestrate *everything* that happens. We model expectations, respect, and effective com-

Before students entered the formal part of the lesson about leaves, the teacher had the students record and then share in their small groups what they already knew about leaves. The teacher wanted the students to include as much information as they could regarding their ideas about where leaves come from, how they feel, what they look like, how they change, and what they are used for. The teacher then collected the drawings and words to support her explanations of the vocabulary words for the lesson.

—*Kendra Herrera, 3rd Grade, Texas*

munication even as we make decisions about what, why, when, and how the curriculum will be navigated.

Attention to ecological factors requires that teachers make a concerted effort to make their teaching transparent to students. Consider the following scenario:

After 13 years of teaching, Ms. Sanchez had given up on ordering many books on strategies and getting excited about every make-and-take workshop she attended. She found that once back in the classroom she just didn't have time to figure out where a given strategy fit into her curriculum. She also found that if she used one of the strategies, it took so much energy to explain it, model it, and practice it that it hardly seemed worthwhile. Over time she had begun to see little value in all the strategy "fads" that passed her way.

Yet one day, everything clicked for Ms. Sanchez. After presenting a session at a conference, I was delighted to have Ms. Sanchez come up to me and share, "I never thought about all the things you talked about and how my community of learners is made up of so many dynamic, complex, and interrelated variables. Simply finding an exciting strategy to shove into my existing 'agenda' does little to change much of *what* or *how* I teach. Rather, multiple things have to be considered and changed before I can say that my practice is both culturally responsive and relevant. Simply learning a new strategy and using it may or may not lead to learning. Instead, I have to choose my activities based on multiple variables and what is happening in my classroom. The activities I choose to use eventually will become strategies for my students as I make them a part of our classroom routine. Students will need opportunities to practice and apply the strategies multiple times through multiple lessons in order for the strategies to become part of the classroom rhythm. That makes so much sense! If I choose the strategies that work for *my* community, given *my* standards and curriculum and *my* style, and then I let my students know why it works, it just might move my ELL students forward to success."

Later I received an e-mail in which Ms. Sanchez told me that she now strategically selects her strategies based on what is going to be taught and how she envisions students will be participating in the learning process. She also takes the time to let the learners in her classroom know the destination!

When planning our instruction for maximum relevance to all students, we first align our standards, curriculum, student biographies, and learning strategy. We then explicitly state to students the learning tasks that will be accomplished by using the particular strategy, sharing with them the destination and the stops that will be made along the way. As Kulesz (2007) simply states, "Pedagogy is about making what we teach transparent" (p. 5). Just as knowing our destination and what landmarks to look for helps us feel comfortable as we travel to a new place, by making our instructional intentions transparent, we increase the likelihood that all students will engage in learning. Students will understand the purpose behind the lesson's activities and tasks rather than assuming that some (or all!) are merely included as "busy work." Furthermore, by using students' biographies to connect to the content, it becomes easier to model strategies and discuss how CLD students' background knowledge will contribute to what is to be learned. Making our students aware of what we teachers often keep secret gives them an open invitation to be a full participant in the community and its activities. Figure 7.1 summarizes key ways to make the teaching and learning process transparent for the learners in your classroom.

Ideally, transparency in teaching is like retelling an important experience to someone and not wanting to leave out a single detail. You want the other person to feel as though he or she was there with you every step of the way—living the same experience. The same kind of energy,

FIGURE 7.1
Transparency in Teaching

1. **Know your standards, content, and curriculum.**
   - Have your "stuff" together.
2. **Know your community of learners.**
   - Plan for instruction and management that aligns with your conditional and situational processes for learning.
   - Find ways to communicate respect and set high expectations for all students, regardless of cultural or linguistic background.
   - Create opportunities to draw out and learn about the assets that each student possesses.
3. **Understand pedagogy from a "biography" perspective.**
   - Use your biography cards, which capture a snapshot of each of your students, to inform your instructional decisions.
   - Select strategies that facilitate language use, allow for multiple perspectives to be shared, and encourage different ways of completing academic tasks.
   - Modify and adapt your curriculum as necessary to provide all students with opportunities to contribute in constructive ways.
   - Configure small groups to meet the lesson's objectives as well as facilitate students' development of language skills, conceptual knowledge, and cross-cultural understanding.
4. **Announce to your students the destination and what will happen along the way.**
   - Create academic routines that enhance student participation.
   - Model respectful ways to have students remind one another of the routines that lead to learning.
   - Remind students that the overarching mission of the classroom community is to ensure that all members learn and support one another in learning.
   - Remind students that, as teacher, you will serve as an observer and facilitator of learning.
   - Inform students of your learning expectations through the use of language and content objectives.

excitement, and attention to detail will help each student to "experience" the content with us. One of the most effective ways to enable transparency in teaching and to ensure that CLD students become active participants in learning is to plan instruction that is guided by clear content and language objectives.

Content and Language Objectives

Content and language objectives have been discussed in the literature for over two decades as tools for ensuring transparency regarding (a) the concepts to be taught and (b) the ways the content will be practiced and applied during the lesson and then assessed. However, our development of content and language objectives should be guided by both *who* we are teaching and *what* we are teaching.

Content Objectives

According to Mager (1962), clearly identified content objectives serve to empower students by letting them know what is to be learned during the lesson. For the teacher, defining content objectives sets the stage for his or her selection of content, instructional strategies, and materials (Kim, 2007). Content objectives also provide educators with a basis for assessment at the end of the lesson. As Gronlund (2004) explains, "If the intended learning outcomes are clearly stated, there is no problem in constructing a valid test. Just match the test item to the learning outcome to be measured" (p. 35).

Bear in mind these guidelines when writing content objectives:

- Select the overarching standard to be addressed during the lesson from the national, state, or grade-level standards (Echevarría, Vogt, & Short, 2004).
- Write your content objectives, aligning them with the national, state, or grade-level standards (Echevarría et al., 2004).
- Align content objectives with the key grade-level content concepts to be covered in the lesson.
- Scaffold the language used to explicitly share with the class *what* (content objective) is going to be taught (Herrera & Murry, 2005).

Content objectives often come as second nature to educators, given the time they have spent learning about and writing these types of objectives from the beginning of

This is an example of a content objective that a middle school teacher used to relay the expected learning outcomes for the lesson (**T**he **C**lass **W**ill . . .). As the teacher listed content objectives such as this for the students, she also explicitly shared with them what she meant by solving the linear equations.

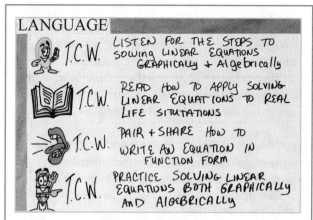

The teacher has taken the content objectives and translated them into steps and activities that will occur during the lesson. This supports CLD students' learning by letting them know the sequence of teaching that will guide them through what they are expected to accomplish during the lesson.

their teacher preparation program and beyond. What often is more difficult and time-consuming is conceptualizing and writing language objectives, that is, letting students know *how* the content is going to be learned.

Language Objectives

I like to think of language objectives as the ways we "bring to life" what we plan to teach our students during the lesson. Language objectives make it necessary for the teacher to take notice of the context and foresee some of the situational processes that may occur during the lesson, given the biographies of the members of the learning community. It takes time to make decisions regarding language objectives that will address the language demands prompted by both the content and academic needs of our CLD students.

According to Numelin (1998) and Snow, Met, and Genesee (1989), we can think of language objectives as relating to one of two language categories: *content-obligatory* and *content-compatible*. Content-obligatory language is that which must be understood in order to understand the concept (Kim, 2007); content-compatible language supports the lesson but is not critical to concept learning. For example, in a science lesson on the three fundamental types of rock, *igneous, metamorphic,* and *sedimentary* would be content-obligatory words. Content-compatible words for the same lesson might include *magma, crust,* and *settle.* Content-compatible language can increase CLD students' academic language skills when it is embedded during instruction in community interaction, strategy use, and other classroom activities. With this distinction in mind, suggestions for writing language objectives include:

- Consider the biographies of the students (e.g., stages of SLA) when making decisions about language objectives, that is, decisions about *how* or *by what means* the content objectives will be taught and learned.
- Develop language objectives that reflect the academic language students need to fully participate during the lesson and reach the highest level of learning (Met, 1991).
- Write language objectives that vary between cognitively undemanding and cognitively demanding tasks in order to maximize language development and conceptual understanding during the lesson (Cummins, 2000; Verplaetse, 2002).
- Make decisions about the *language functions* (e.g., compare, summarize), *skills* (e.g., scan text, draft an essay), and *structures* (e.g., questioning patterns, future or past tense verbs) that will be needed to complete the assigned tasks (Echevarría et al., 2008).
- Translate the content objectives into concrete activities that involve listening, speaking, reading, and writing.
- Consider the particular language functions, skills, structures, and grammar that are essential to your content area.
- Write language objectives with an *activity/strategy* in mind that will address both the content and the language needs of your students.
- Think about language objectives as providing students with a concrete link to the lesson.

Content and Language Objectives Are for Everyone

A few questions that may be going through your mind at this point are, "Given that language objectives flow from the content objectives, aren't content objectives enough? Will 'giving away' so much of what is going to happen in the lesson make my lesson less exciting to students? Will older students think content and language objectives are 'beneath' them?" These are valid questions. The following scenario provides some insight regarding the answers to such questions.

For the courses delivered through our center, at both the undergraduate *and* graduate levels, we write, post, and discuss content objectives as well as language objectives. At the end of one semester, I had a young lady from Korea stop to discuss her experience in the course. She was a doctoral student whose proficiency in English was quite advanced. I was surprised to have her tell me that the most rewarding experience for her throughout the course was our posting of the language and content objectives. She said, "Although I can speak English well, there

were times during class that the terms and pace were overwhelming for me. But I always knew that I could pause and wait until we moved on to the next objective! What was important for me, as a student, was always knowing where we were going to end up that day and what was expected of me at the end of the lesson."

In this scenario we see an educated, graduate-level student benefiting from the posting and discussion of content and language objectives. The benefits to CLD students in K–12 classrooms in which I have observed are even more profound. Content and language objectives promote a sense of *hope* and *expectation* for engagement that is of inestimable worth, especially given the sociopolitical climate of schools today. This fact is reflected in academic research: language objectives recently have received a heavier focus, as educators have begun to recognize the need for integrating content and language instruction when meeting the needs of CLD students.

Together, content and language objectives serve as a road map for our instruction. At the beginning of the lesson when they are both posted and orally shared, they let everyone know where the class is going. During the lesson, they provide us with landmarks along the way as we implement strategies and create opportunities for student interaction throughout the learning process. At the end of the trip, they announce that we have arrived at our destination as we restate the objectives. Figure 7.2 provides a guide that can assist you in writing both content and language objectives.

Using Content and Language Objectives to Guide Lesson Preparation

As Echevarría et al. (2008) remind us, "An objective is not a by-product of an activity, but the foundation of one" (p. 27). Strategic and systematic planning is supported by our making decisions about which activity, or strategy, would best guide students to achieve the content and language objectives of the lesson.

When preparing and conducting a lesson, attention should be given to:

- Selecting a particular strategy as a tool for moving CLD students from the known to the unknown. The strategy should provide students with a "through line," connecting the lesson's various activities and tasks, which are employed as a multifaceted effort to promote students' development of conceptual understanding, vocabulary knowledge, and proficiency in all four language domains: listening, speaking, reading, and writing.

FIGURE 7.2

Five Steps for Writing Content and Language Objectives

Step 1

Identify the state **standard**, benchmark, indicator, etc.

Step 2

Identify the **key vocabulary** within the overarching standard.

Step 3

Identify the **content** (or concept within the content) you wish to teach. This is the "**WHAT**" of what you want to teach.

> *Example:* The students will identify the *elements of a short story* within a given text.

Step 4

Once you have identified the "**WHAT**" of the concept, it is time to decide the "**HOW**" of teaching it. This is where you will consider:

- Strategy to be used throughout the lesson
- Language functions to be targeted
- Grouping configurations throughout the lesson
- The four domains of *listening*, *speaking*, *reading*, and *writing*

Step 5

Revisit the content objectives and language objectives as they align with the state standard, and then align the course texts and materials with these objectives.

Available for free download and printing from www.tcpress.com

---

- Focusing on activities that promote engagement of *all* students throughout the lesson.
- Making preliminary decisions about which *grouping configurations* will meet both the language and the content objectives and in what ways the configurations will be used during strategy implementation.
- Making *all* expectations transparent before, during, and after the lesson to ensure more students arrive at the destination.
- Planning for both linguistic and academic assessment throughout the lesson.
- Making explicit for students the target language functions and content-specific academic language, as well as ways that listening, speaking, reading, and writing will be part of the lesson.
- Observing, as the lesson unfolds, how the grouping configurations are working to enhance the learning opportunities and engagement of all students. The grouping configurations should be designed—and

adjusted mid-course, if necessary—to provide CLD students with multiple opportunities and language models for practicing and applying language (both social and academic vocabulary) and content in varied and meaningful ways.

The graphic organizer depicted in Figure 7.3 can be used to simplify thinking about biography-driven instruction that uses activities and strategies to attend to the lesson's content and language objectives before, during, and after instruction.

How Vocabulary Fits into the Picture

Vocabulary is touted as the one essential ingredient for comprehension of text (Tompkins, 2004; Vaughn & Linan-Thompson, 2004). Many frameworks and models exist for selecting and teaching vocabulary to grade-level and CLD students, including those of Marzano (2004), Beck, McKeown, and Kucan (2002), and Calderón (2007). (The work of Beck et al. and Calderón will be discussed in detail in the sections that follow.) Yet in many classrooms that I visit, educators continue to lament how difficult it is to move students forward when they come to school with such "limited vocabulary." The teachers say there is not enough time in the day to fill in all the gaps necessary to meet the many vocabulary demands of the curriculum. They note that some students seem to lack linguistic ability in their native language as well as in English. "How will I ever meet these students' academic needs?" teachers often ask with distress in their voices.

What frequently prompts some of these types of concerns is a perspective on vocabulary that views language as a set of words that must be part of the linguistic makeup of each student. This perspective leads teachers to devote the majority of their time and attention to detecting "deficiencies" in students' word knowledge and then scrambling to help them "catch up." A perspective that leads to more productive efforts involves recognizing that *all* students bring large vocabularies. The difference in vocabulary knowledge that exists among our students often lies in the *kinds* of words they know. According to Schifini (1994), we each have words that make us who we are—words that help us express who we are and what we know. These same words can be used to teach academic concepts and related academic words.

Biography-driven instruction provides us with a guide for setting the context and observing situational processes in order to determine CLD students' current linguistic resources. Students have gained their vocabulary knowledge from language use in the home and community, prior schooling, and other linguistic interactions. Once we know the words students *do bring* to our classrooms, we can better create opportunities for introducing new academic

Available for free download and printing from www.tcpress.com

FIGURE 7.3
Content and Language Objectives

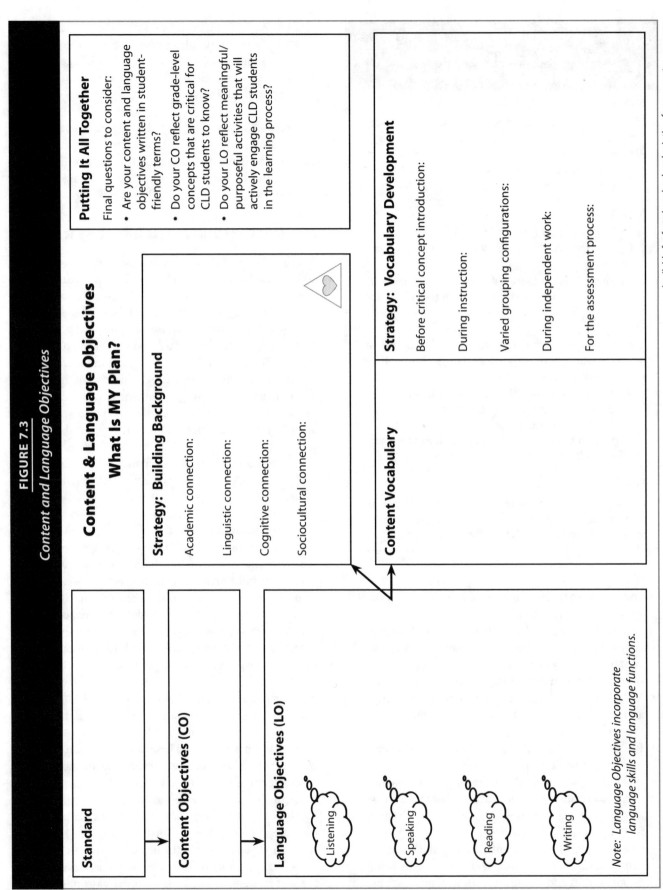

Content & Language Objectives

What Is MY Plan?

Strategy: Building Background

Academic connection:

Linguistic connection:

Cognitive connection:

Sociocultural connection:

Putting It All Together

Final questions to consider:

- Are your content and language objectives written in student-friendly terms?
- Do your CO reflect grade-level concepts that are critical for CLD students to know?
- Do your LO reflect meaningful/ purposeful activities that will actively engage CLD students in the learning process?

Content Vocabulary

Strategy: Vocabulary Development

Before critical concept introduction:

During instruction:

Varied grouping configurations:

During independent work:

For the assessment process:

Standard

Content Objectives (CO)

Language Objectives (LO)

Listening

Speaking

Reading

Writing

Note: Language Objectives incorporate language skills and language functions.

One high school teacher used the linking language strategy (see Figure 7.5) to activate students' background knowledge related to a geography lesson. Students were asked to do a "silent quick write" related to each of the visual representations that were placed on four different tables. Upon completing the "silent quick write," students discussed with their small groups what they had written and why. The teacher took this information to support explanation of the topic and vocabulary for the lesson. These conversations became sources of connections throughout the lesson.

dents generally know prior to entering school. Tier 2 words are words with which students are already conceptually familiar (e.g., *temperature, front, moisture*). That is, native English speakers would be able to explain Tier 2 words using words that they already know, but they might not possess the exact academic term necessary to refer specifically to the concept. These Tier 2 words are important to the development of mature language users. Beck et al. (p. 19) introduce the following considerations for identifying Tier 2 words:

- *Importance and utility:* Words that are characteristic of mature language users and appear frequently across a variety of domains.
- *Instructional potential:* Words that can be worked with in a variety of ways so that students can build rich representations of them and of their connections to other words and concepts.
- *Conceptual understanding:* Words for which students understand the general concept but provide precision and specificity in describing the concept.

Finally, Tier 3 words have a low frequency of use and are often limited to specific content areas (e.g., *barometric, nimbus, meteorology*).

When selecting words to teach, the question becomes "Why would I want my students to understand *these* words as opposed to others?" Beck et al. (2002) suggest that Tier 2 and Tier 3 words are the ones that educators must emphasize over basic Tier 1 words. Tier 2 words, according to these authors, are those that can be applied across texts of varying content areas and also are heard in the spoken vocabulary of mature language users. Additionally, Beck et al. emphasize the need for students to develop a heightened awareness regarding the words that surround them. These authors further note that students need to use words repeatedly if the words are ever to become "their own."

Calderón (2007) applies the tiered vocabulary concept of Beck and colleagues within the arena of second language learning, providing a three-tiered vocabulary framework with guidelines as to how the principles can be applied to CLD students who are still in the process of acquiring English. Calderón reminds educators not to make assumptions about which words CLD students might already possess in their new language. Although in most cases it is safe to assume that native English-speaking students will be

words during instruction. Effective vocabulary instruction, delivered in the course of teaching our curriculum's content-area concepts, requires that we educators study and explore words in order to make the best decisions about which words to teach, how to teach them, and ways we can build on what lies within CLD students' schemata to make links to conceptual and vocabulary knowledge.

Not All Words Are Created Equal

Beck et al. (2002), in their work on vocabulary development with native English-speaking students, present vocabulary words by classifying them into three tiers, which are used to explain the varying levels of difficulty among words. According to Beck and colleagues, Tier 1 words (e.g., *sun, rain, clouds*) for native English speakers do not require direct instruction because they are words that such stu-

familiar with most age-appropriate Tier 1 words, the same cannot be said for CLD students. CLD students might need explicit instruction if they are not familiar with these basic words in English. However, CLD students will most likely know these words in their native language. Therefore, Tier 1 words are relatively easy to teach to CLD students. Educators can show pictures of these words to impart meaning, or the words can be translated into the student's native language to make the meaning apparent.

Tier 2 words, according to Calderón (2007), frequently have cognates in Spanish. Therefore, Spanish speakers have an advantage in that they might already be familiar with the words and the concepts represented by the word in English. Tier 2 words include content-area words that are used across a variety of academic contexts as well as small words, such as *by, if,* and *so,* that are essential to CLD students' comprehension. Calderón maintains that Tier 2 words

> do not receive as much attention as Tier 1 and Tier 3 words because ESL teachers typically teach Tier 1, and mainstream teachers focus on Tier 3 (content key) words. It's our hypothesis that the lack of explicit instruction of Tier 2 words is what keeps ELLs from moving on to Tier 3 words and thus developing reading comprehension of content texts. (p. 31)

Tier 3 words comprise content-specific concepts that CLD students may or may not already be familiar with in their native language, depending on their level of literacy in the primary language. Once again, Spanish speakers have an advantage when learning Tier 3 words, because many

FIGURE 7.4
Spanish Cognates Across Vocabulary Tiers

Tier 1 Cognates

Many words that end with *-ción* in Spanish can have the same meaning in English. Keep in mind, Tier 1 words are usually concepts that CLD students will already possess in their native language, although they may not be familiar with the *word* in English.

> *information* ⇒ *información*
> *preparation* ⇒ *preparación*
> *contribution* ⇒ *contribución*

Tier 2 Cognates

Tier 2 words, according to Calderón, frequently have cognates in Spanish. Therefore, Spanish speakers have an advantage in that they might already be familiar with the words and the concepts represented by the word in English.

> *disaster* ⇒ *desastre*
> *determine* ⇒ *determinar*
> *object* ⇒ *objeto*

Tier 3 Cognates

According to Calderón, "Literate Spanish speakers have a great advantage over monolingual English speakers with Tier 3 words because many cognates are high frequency words in Spanish but low frequency words in English (e.g., *coincidence/coincidencia, absurd/absurdo, concentrate/concéntrate,* and *fortunate/afortunado*" (p. 33).

Source: Adapted from Calderón (2007).

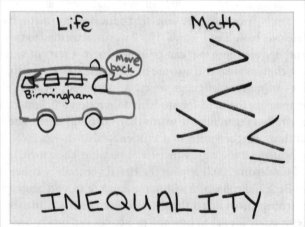

Providing students with an opportunity to define polysemous words using both linguistic and nonlinguistic representations can help scaffold their learning of these words. In this example, the teacher had the students relate the math vocabulary word *inequality* to their own background knowledge.

cognates exist between the two languages. Calderón (2007) suggests that these words/concepts be pre-taught to CLD students, using their native language whenever possible. Figure 7.4 elaborates on ways Spanish cognates can be used as resources for students' learning of vocabulary in each of the three tiers.

Calderón (2007) also discusses the importance of *polysemous words,* that is, words that can have different meanings depending on the context in which they occur. Some examples of polysemous words include "*power, cell, radical, right,* [and] *leg*" (p. 32). Tiers 1, 2, and 3 each can contain words that are polysemous. Teachers should explain to CLD students how the same word can have multiple meanings, depending on the context or content area.

Calderón (2007) emphasizes that "selecting words for the three tiers will also depend on the subject, grade level, and student background knowledge. *There are no lists for Tiers 1, 2, and 3.* Each classroom will be different" (p. 33).

Therefore, it is imperative that educators take into account not only their CLD students' academic needs, but also the sociocultural, cognitive, and linguistic dimensions of their biographies when deciding which words to teach.

Cognates for Conceptual and Linguistic Understanding

Cognates have long been touted as a port of entry for students' transfer of conceptual and vocabulary knowledge from the native language to English. August, Carlo, Dressler, and Snow (2005) call attention to the importance of using students' first language as a resource for their understanding of new vocabulary and academic content during the lesson. Cognates are defined by August et al. as words in two languages that are similar "orthographically and semantically" (p. 52). Cognates can be used to support word recognition and entry into academic words within all three levels of tiered vocabulary. When students are taught to be aware of how their language compares to the English language, they are more likely to view their language as an asset to learning. Students' native language can assist their understanding of many words that initially may appear to teachers to be too difficult for CLD learners.

Yet cognates are only an instructional asset when teachers guide CLD students in comparing and contrasting English with the language(s) they already know. This does not mean that teachers must become experts in every language represented in their classroom. However, teachers should encourage students to become "word detectives," and teachers themselves should be continually on the lookout for any language similarities that could be useful in helping students understand vocabulary and content.

Some educators comment on their hesitancy to use cognates in their practice because, as they do not speak the language of their students, they are unsure whether a word is a true cognate or a "false cognate"—that is, a word that sounds the same in two languages but has very different meanings in each language. Some examples of false cognates between English and Spanish are *embarrass* and *embarazada* (pregnant) and *exit* and *éxito* (success). Although we should be aware that false cognates exist, the use of cognates in teaching has proven to have many more benefits than drawbacks in inching CLD students toward greater comprehension. Figure 7.5 provides a list of English–Spanish cognates tied directly to content that have been collected from practicing teachers.

Biography-Driven Vocabulary Instruction

Research by Beck et al. (2002) and Calderón (2007) has helped to reinforce the importance of thinking about vocabulary in systematic and strategic ways. If we want students to have access to words that will accelerate their comprehension of academic content, then what we do with vocabulary during instruction matters. For many teachers, this involves a new way of thinking. Consider the insights of Ms. Lopez:

> For all the talk we have in schools on individualized and differentiated instruction, I had never thought that students would have different takes on the vocabulary I was teaching. I always had my list, based on what the book gave me, and that is what I taught. We talked about the words, read them in the book, looked in the dictionary, and finally drew a picture that would help the students remember them. Like robots, my students knew the drill. This year has been one of uncovering, discovering, and getting to know how my students think and what they know about the words. I've been amazed at how much I assumed and how wrong I was about their limited knowledge of English.

In differentiated instruction, educators strive to make adaptations to their teaching to meet the needs of the particular individuals in the classroom. What this looks like during vocabulary instruction often tends to be a shade of gray, because teachers frequently continue to use the same worksheet or technique to teach vocabulary to all students, regardless of biography.

When selecting target vocabulary, consideration of the type of vocabulary words being identified directly affects CLD students. Vocabulary words that are merely new labels for concepts that CLD students already understand are approached differently than words that represent new and potentially difficult concepts (Garcia, 2003). Ultimately, the question becomes "When my CLD students finish this lesson, will they be able to tell me the essence of the story or concept I have been teaching, given the words I have selected as the target vocabulary?" Often, teachers will comment that there are too many words to teach. What is important to remember is that some words are taught through "incidental" opportunities, whereas others must be taught "intentionally." Understanding this distinction relieves undue pressure while still ensuring that words needed for content tests and high-stakes tests are made accessible to all students.

Critical to this entire process of selecting and teaching vocabulary words is our knowing the biographies of our CLD students! It is essential that we teachers delve into our CLD students' funds of knowledge, prior knowledge, and academic knowledge. Knowing which concepts the student possesses in his or her native language will help us determine the type of instruction needed to teach key words. For example, if a student has already studied *fotosíntesis*

FIGURE 7.5
English–Spanish Cognates

Subject: ENGLISH

Abbreviation / Abreviación
Analogy / Analogía
Anecdote / Anécdota
Audience / Audiencia
Bibliography / Bibliografía
Biography / Biografía
Comprehension / Comprensión
Debate / Debate
Definition / Definición

Dialogue / Diálogo
Edit / Editar
Expression / Expresión
Novel / Novela
Allegory / Alegoría
Alliteration / Aliteración
Characterization / Caracterización
Chronological Order /
    Orden cronológico

Contrast / Contraste
Criticism / Criticismo
Description / Descripción
Descriptive language /
    Lenguaje descriptivo
Purpose / Propósito
Coherence / Coherencia
Cohesion / Cohesión
Exposition / Exposición

Subject: GENERAL HISTORY

Agriculture / Agricultura
Asia / Asia
Chronology / Cronología
Colonial government /
    Gobierno colonial
Colony / Colonia
Constitution / Constitución
Declaration of Independence /
    Declaración de independencia
Expansion / Expansión
Expedition / Expedición

Hemisphere / Hemisferio
History / Historia
Idea / Idea
Independence / Independencia
Justice / Justicia
Liberty / Libertad
Mayan calendar / Calendario maya
Middle class / Clase media
Minority / Minoría
Society / Sociedad
Civil rights / Derechos civiles

Cultural tradition /
    Tradición cultural
Cuneiform / Cuneiforme
Era / Era
Immigration / Inmigración
Pioneer / Pionero
Vote / Voto
Industrial revolution /
    Revolución industrial
Oral tradition / Tradición oral

Subject: MATH

Addition / Adición
Base / Base
Circle / Círculo
Circumference / Circunferencia
Classes of triangles /
    Clases de triángulos
Convert / Convertir
Decimal / Decimal
Diagram / Diagrama
Distance / Distancia
Division / División

Area / Area
Cardinal number / Número cardinal
Constant / Constante
Dispersion / Dispersión
Dividend / Dividendo
Equation / Ecuación
Perimeter / Perímetro
Prism / Prisma
Simplification / Simplificación
Absolute value / Valor absoluto
Equivalent fractions /
    Fracciones equivalentes

Experimental design /
    Diseño experimental
Geometric pattern /
    Patrón geométrico
Linear equation / Ecuación lineal
Logarithm / Logaritmo
Matrix / Matriz
Negative exponent /
    Exponente negativo
Subtraction algorithm /
    Substracción algorítmica

Subject: SCIENCE

Air / Aire
Conductor / Conductor
Ecosystem / Ecosistema
Formula / Fórmula
Gamma ray / Rayos gamma
Gas / Gas
Observation / Observación
Organism / Organismo
Science / Ciencia
Atom / Átomo

Balance / Balance
Cellular response / Respuesta celular
Condensation / Condensación
Digestive system / Sistema digestivo
Gravitational energy /
    Energía gravitacional
Photosynthesis / Fotosíntesis
Precipitation / Precipitación
Semiconductor / Semiconductor
Viscosity / Viscosidad

Asexual reproduction /
    Reproducción asexual
Atomic energy / Energía atómica
Experimental control /
    Control experimental
Hypothesis / Hipótesis
Meiosis / Meiosis
Protein / Proteína
Refraction / Refracción
Solubility / Solubilidad

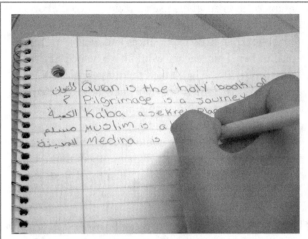

In this photo, a 6th-grade student is recording vocabulary words in her native language along with definitions of the words in English in a notebook. The student was given this opportunity in an attempt on the teacher's part to help the students make personal connections to the vocabulary of the lesson in a way that they could refer to throughout their learning.

(photosynthesis) in his or her native country, then a simple translation of the English term into Spanish may be all that is necessary to clarify the concept.

When educating CLD students, vocabulary instruction must be approached from the perspective that although a student may not be proficient in English, he or she is surrounded by English words, words in the native language, and lived experiences that may support the teaching of the academic words. Consider the following scenario:

Saul, a middle school student, had been referred for testing given his slow academic progress. As is customary when I am invited to assess an ELL learner using multiple district assessments in Spanish, I began by getting to know the student prior to formally beginning the testing. That day I asked Saul to share a little about the school and his teachers. I was amazed at how articulate he was regarding his perception about what was right and what was lacking in his education.

First, he told me that not all teachers wanted him to learn. That is, some of his teachers, although they did not speak Spanish, went to great lengths to teach him the academic content so he could be a good student. Some, he said, were not as eager, and he thought they saw him as a slow learner, given his background. Since Saul had not mentioned his ESL teacher, I asked, "What about your ESL teacher?" He responded, "Oh! Her. . . . Well, she must serve lots of

students at lots of schools, because she comes in here sweating everyday, pulls out some cards and starts to teach me all these words. We play bingo, memory games, and more games!" he responded. "What would you want to be different?" I asked. He said, "I want her to teach me the words that the mean teachers are not teaching me, the words I need so I can answer the questions. What she is teaching me I learn from my friends, watching TV, and just being here in the United States. I want her to teach me the words I need to be smart, the words to pass the classes so I can be a veterinarian when I grow up!"

Through this conversation, I realized that many of the words that teachers spend significant amounts of time on can be learned incidentally by CLD students—both through out-of-school experiences and through opportunities we provide for students to talk with one another and discuss as a class. Academic vocabulary, on the other hand, must be taught differently. Teachers must be intentional in their planning for explicit vocabulary instruction (Carlo et al., 2004).

Teachers who set contexts for explicit instruction to teach Tier 1, 2, and 3 vocabulary prior to formally beginning the lesson create ecologies where culture and language help connect vocabulary to the content they teach. Words are selected systematically, taking into account the biographies of the students in the learning community. The number of words selected is limited by the relevance of the words to the most critical information about the concept. To provide students with multiple exposures that are culturally, linguistically, and academically connected to the learners, potential selections of vocabulary words may be further narrowed given the planned contexts. Teachers provide opportunities before, during, and after the lesson for students to discuss and use new words in multiple settings with a diverse group of their peers.

Students who are provided with opportunities to use words in meaningful ways and in a variety of contexts are much more likely to improve their oral language development, feel safe in voicing their learning, and take ownership of the target vocabulary. Selecting activities and strategies that support students' construction of meaning with the new words, discussing the relationship between the new words and what students already know, and, ultimately, defining these words by making cultural and linguistic links have the potential to improve academic learning for CLD students.

As stated earlier in this chapter, no one single activity or strategy is sufficient for teaching academic vocabulary. As educators, we must be attentive observers of students' culture and language so that we can maximize connections during instruction. In broad and narrow brushstrokes, our teaching can create opportunities for both incidental word learning and intentional word teaching.

Creating Opportunities for Disclosure

After selecting academic vocabulary words to be taught, educators embark on the path to making decisions about what will happen with these words before, during, and after the lesson. There are many models for the teaching of vocabulary that include explicit steps for introducing students to the academic content vocabulary. These steps have in common the following characteristics:

- The teacher is in control of the word, as demonstrated by his or her saying it, explaining it, and contextualizing it.
- Students are asked to repeat the word after the teacher to personally experience the word.
- Students work with a partner or team to practice the word.
- Students draw a nonlinguistic representation of the word.
- Students write a definition of the word using their own words.

Models that exhibit these characteristics are more teacher-centered and tend to limit the potential for CLD students to make lasting personal connections to the words as well as fully develop their English language skills.

During observations of lessons, I often see teachers explaining words from their own frame of reference while their students listen as idle participants. Consider the following scenario:

As I sat in the library waiting for the principal to arrive and let me know where to set up for the session on vocabulary development, I was drawn into a 5th-grade language arts class. The topic being addressed was the importance of understanding "sequence" when writing a story. The teacher offered a group of 28 Latino students the following explanation: "I love to cook," she said, "Have you all ever watched a cooking show on television?" The students all nodded in agreement. She continued, "Well, in a recipe, it is very important for you to follow the sequence." All students agreed. "If you don't follow the sequence," she added, "whatever you are cooking will not turn out right." At that time the bell rang, and all the students shuffled out of the classroom.

I was left wondering how many of the students actually had ever watched a cooking show and how many of their mothers used a recipe to cook. For nearly 10 minutes, the teacher had discussed sequence from her own lived experiences and what was important to her. This teacher would have helped her students more if she had asked them to each think to themselves of something they knew how to do or had seen done, like cooking something, or washing, or solving a problem, that had to be done one part or step at a time. Then she could have asked them to write or draw those steps, write numbers to indicate which came first, then second, then third, and explained to students that that was a sequence.

This type of classroom dynamic can be observed across the country in classrooms where students' background knowledge is, though often unintentionally, discounted in the course of instruction. Often we might find ourselves thinking that certain students have not had any contact with the academic words or concepts we are introducing. Yet this question remains: *How will we really know what students know, if we don't give them an opportunity to share their experiences with the new words before we go into our "teacher explanation" of the vocabulary?*

A Canvas of Opportunity: Spaces and Places for the Known

What students already know about the content is one of the strongest indicators of how well they will learn new information relative to the content.

—*Marzano (2004), p. 1*

Every day teachers begin new lessons based on curriculum guides or prescriptive programs assigned by their school or district. Absent from many of these initial activities are avenues for investigating students' background knowledge and interest. Learning can be thought of as a search for meaning, using formal education and one's own experiences as the foundation for making sense of new information. As the brain interacts with input from the environment, it forms patterns of understanding, or schemata (Caine & Caine, 1991). When the brain encounters new information, it interprets the information using existing schemata. Because these patterns of understanding develop through personal experience, schemata reflect the cultures and experiences of the learner (Quinn & Holland, 1987).

What we do before the lesson is important to the engagement and motivation of CLD students throughout the lesson. Many educators, based on their knowledge of or assumptions about students' levels of English proficiency and academic readiness, exclude students from full participation in the learning process by providing limited opportunities for involvement from the beginning of the lesson. According to Rubie-Davies et al. (2006), expectations are evident to students in the opportunities that educators provide, "in the affective climate created and in the interactional content and context of the classroom" (p. 430).

When planning a lesson, it is important to consider what will be done to learn about students' background knowledge related to the topic or vocabulary to be introduced. Many current strategies that exist for "activating" student engagement are effective for students who are willing to raise their hand or who are called upon by the teacher to respond to the stimulus. Often absent, however, are opportunities that require *all* students to respond and that hold students accountable—from the beginning of the lesson—for their participation. I refer to teachers' incorporation of such opportunities as creating a "canvas of opportunity" for every student to respond to a teacher prompt through listening, speaking, reading, or writing. Teachers then have a chance to collect from *every* student what he or she might perceive related to what is going to be taught.

For example, once we have selected words for instruction, we must provide students with opportunities to share personal associations and insights related to the vocabulary that might be useful to our instruction of the words throughout the course of the lesson. According to Honig, Diamond, and Gutlohn (2008), a student's knowledge of a particular word can be described in one of the following ways:

- The student has never seen or heard the word.
- The student has seen or heard the word before but does not know what it means.
- The student vaguely knows the meaning of the word and can associate it with a concept or context.
- The student knows the word well and can explain it and use it.

By allocating a small portion of our time to providing opportunities for students to share their personal connections to the target words, we are more likely to be able to teach/explain vocabulary using CLD students' background knowledge to accelerate learning. This will also support the vocabulary development of native English speakers.

Creating an opportunity for all students to respond before formally getting into the lesson enables teachers to move away from abstract ways of using students' background knowledge and toward specific ways of linking students' culture, language, and experiences to the content and vocabulary. Consider the Linking Language strategy presented in Figure 7.6. This activity provides students with an opportunity to make meaning using their own background knowledge and to make their knowledge public for the

FIGURE 7.6
The Linking Language Strategy

Directions

- Select three or four pictures that illustrate key concepts from the lesson (pictures can be taken from the internet, clip art, or magazines, or the actual textbook pictures can be used).
- Tape each picture on the center of a large piece of chart paper (if using the textbook, place the textbook in the center of the chart paper).
- Divide the class into groups of four or five students.
- Instruct the students to write down everything they think of or feel when they look at the picture.
- Allow only 1–2 minutes for students in each group to write.
- Then have the whole group rotate to the next chart/picture.
- Continue until all groups have visited each picture.
- As students are working at each picture, rotate around the room and circle any words that come close to the target vocabulary or actually reflect the academic vocabulary for the day.
- At this time, you can work as a silent observer to reflect upon the knowledge that students bring to the learning community.

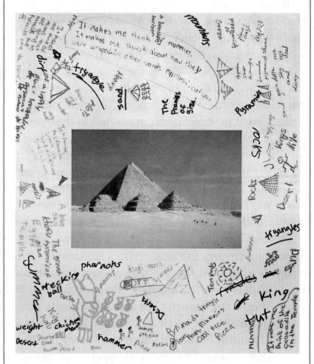

Source: Adapted from Herrera (2007), p. 32. Used with permission of KCAT/TLC, Kansas State University.

learning community. It is through CLD students' negotiation of what is known and what is being learned that they are able to make sense of new language, vocabulary, and content.

Brain-Compatible Teaching and Learning

According to contextual learning theory, learners are most likely to process what is taught when they can connect it to their own frames of reference and patterns of understanding—their own schemata. The brain naturally attempts to make meaning of what is presented. It will do this by looking for relationships that make sense based on the individual's background.

Current research on how the brain learns has provided a much-needed look at what happens to learners during instruction. These findings may help teachers understand the importance of "igniting" the brain and then using culturally responsive and relevant ways of fueling students' learning. Although the work of many researchers and authors (e.g., Bransford, Brown, & Cocking, 2000; Caine & Caine, 1991; Jensen, 2006, 2008; Willis, 2006) who focus on brain-based learning has informed my efforts, I draw most heavily on the work and writings of David Sousa (2006, for example) in explaining the process by which the brain makes sense of information. Figure 7.7 depicts Sousa's Information Processing Model and provides a simplified look at the overall process the brain goes through when making sense of new information.

According to Sousa (2006), the brain must first notice and perceive something before it can become engaged in responding to what it is experiencing. If in that split second of stimulation the brain does not connect to the input, the brain's attention will move on to other things. In the classroom context, the stimulus is the introduction of the vocabulary or topic through a strategy that involves active student participation through listening, speaking, reading, or writing. The stimulus is some aspect of the information that the teacher wants students to understand (e.g., visual, written word, spoken word), as perceived through one or more of the learner's five senses. When any aspect of a new concept is introduced, the principles of brain-based instruction and brain-based learning take effect. At this point, one of two things can happen. The new information can be either ignored or perceived by the student. If the new information is ignored or filtered out by the *sensory register,* no information is passed on and it disappears. On the other hand, if the student perceives (notices) this new information, it is passed on to the student's *sensory memory.* If the student perceives the new information through one of his or her five senses, it is stored in sensory memory only for a very short period (only seconds in length).

In this classroom, the teacher provided her students with an opportunity to work in small groups to look at pictures related to the topic and make instant connection to the content. These 2nd-grade students were able to record their immediate associations on paper and refer back to them during the learning process.

—*Christine Sloan, Elementary, Kansas*

To increase the likelihood that information from the environment will make it through the filtering process and farther into a student's memory (and eventually, we hope, into the long-term memory), teachers should first activate the student's background knowledge about the topic through the use of multisensory activities and strategies. It is through the activation of the student's long-term memory (the funds of knowledge, prior knowledge, and academic knowledge that he or she already possesses), and through multisensory stimulation, that new information is transferred into the sensory memory and, from there, into the *immediate memory.* At this point, teachers have a window of opportunity in which to help the student make and record as many connections as possible between the new information and the concepts, words, and ideas he or she already knows.

Immediate memory lasts only for approximately 30 seconds. During those 30 seconds we can imagine the brain placing images, emotions, words, sounds, and so forth on a "clipboard" of sorts. The pieces placed on the clipboard come from both the new information that was recently received from sensory memory as well as information related to the learner's past experiences that is stored in his or her permanent memory. Our goal is to have students capture these immediate associations for later discussion and use during the learning process. These sometimes fleeting schematic connections, if documented, can be maintained, built upon, and navigated to help students better remember and understand the new material.

Information that successfully passes from immediate memory to *working memory* is then consciously processed

FIGURE 7.7
Information Processing Model

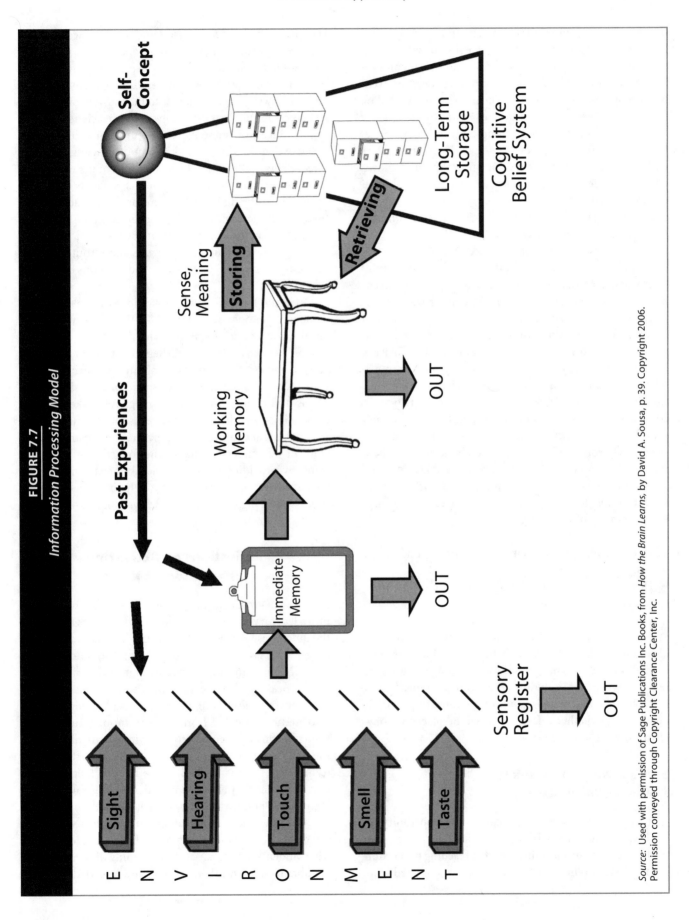

Source: Used with permission of Sage Publications Inc. Books, from *How the Brain Learns*, by David A. Sousa, p. 39. Copyright 2006. Permission conveyed through Copyright Clearance Center, Inc.

by the learner (processing of information in immediate memory can take place either subconsciously or consciously). According to Sousa (2006), working memory is where "we can build, take apart, or rework ideas for eventual storage elsewhere" (p. 45). The information placed on the "work table" of our mind can come from sensory/immediate memory as well as long-term memory. Therefore, repetition of the new material should take place within learning contexts that value the background knowledge the student already possesses. In other words, this kind of repetition does *not* involve students mindlessly repeating isolated facts. Beneficial repetition is *mindful* rather than mindless!

The various activities incorporated throughout the lesson reinforce (and further ignite) the brain's connections to the new material being held in working memory. The average time span during which the learner can intently focus on material before becoming mentally fatigued or bored is dependent on both the age of the learner and his or her motivation. In general, a preadolescent learner can focus on the material for approximately 5–10 minutes, whereas an adolescent or adult learner can focus intently for 10–20 minutes. As Sousa (2006) notes, "For focus to continue, there must be some change in the way the individual is dealing with the item. For example, the person may switch from thinking about it to physically using it, or making different connections to other learnings" (p. 47).

Whether the new material makes it from working memory into a student's long-term storage depends on the learner's assessment of two things:

- Does this make sense? Is it logically coherent in a way that I can understand?
- Does it have meaning? Can I connect it to my life in some significant way?

When the answer to either of these questions is "yes," the likelihood of the information being retained in long-term storage increases. The possibility of storage is greatest, however, when "yes" is the answer to both questions. Finally, between sense and meaning, *meaning* is more important in determining whether information will be placed in long-term storage (Sousa, 2006).

Student Words as a Link to Academic Vocabulary

As I have discussed, creating a canvas of opportunity for students to show their background knowledge provides the teacher with insights that have far-reaching effects during the lesson. When teachers take the accumulated word knowledge that students possess and use these words as the point of departure for explanations of academic words, the CLD student's culture and language is much more likely to be part of the classroom conversation. This dynamic, in which every student contributes to the learning of the classroom community, cannot happen if we teachers continue to introduce words and explain them from a limited perspective that puts us in charge without providing avenues for students to share their interpretations of the words. The beauty of opening doors through which students' voices can emerge is in the discoveries we make about students' cultures, languages, perspectives, and understandings of the world. During the lesson, we then have multiple opportunities to return to students' thoughts and reroute them, as necessary, to move them to accurate definitions of the academic words.

Often teachers will question the idea of providing students with an open forum in which they write whatever a given word reminds them of, saying, "Isn't that guessing?" I prefer to liken this part of the learning process to making educated guesses or hypotheses about the meaning of the word. After all, that is what we spend our life doing with words and concepts we are learning. We make tentative associations, test their appropriateness and accuracy given the context, and continue negotiating the meaning of the word or our understanding of the concept until we get it right. By providing these ecological contexts and guiding CLD students as they proceed through different situational processes, we highlight what students *do* know—knowledge that too often goes untapped.

Reflections on Activating What Students Know

When we begin using student assets as avenues for moving into a lesson, we increase the likelihood that we will achieve the objectives we have set for meeting the standards of the content and grade level we teach. By igniting student interest early and choosing strategies that ask all students to listen, speak, read, write, and think about what they have experienced or learned in the past, we set the stage for new information to move from sensory input (stimulus) to students' sensory memory, to their immediate memory, to their working memory, and eventually into their long-term memory. It is through our efforts to help students uncover what they already know that we are able to bring them to the point where they fully negotiate the meanings of words and their understanding of concepts within the safety of the classroom. When we listen and learn from what students have to say at the beginning of the lesson, we are able to draw on their background knowledge during the lesson, rather than using only our own cultural frames of reference to introduce and explain vocabulary and content concepts. Cummins (1996) says it best when he reminds us that

> When students' language, culture and experience are ignored or excluded in classroom interactions, students are immediately starting from a disadvantage. Everything they have learned about life and the world up to this point is being dismissed as irrelevant to school learning; there are few points of connection to curriculum materials or instruction and so students are expected to learn in an experiential vacuum. Students' silence and nonparticipation under these conditions have frequently been misinterpreted as lack of academic ability or effort, and teachers' interactions with students have reflected a pattern of low expectations that become self-fulfilling. (pp. 2–3)

In short, the context we create and the opportunities we provide in our classroom must make it clear that we respect and value the experiences and knowledge that each student brings to our learning community. Holding every student accountable for what he or she knows does much to increase student engagement and learning.

Chapter 8 will discuss how to work with target vocabulary during the lesson, using insights gained from observations made in the activation phase. It provides ideas about how we teachers can plan for:

- Using students' native language, experiences, and other assets as points of connection during the lesson
- Orchestrating meaningful student interaction based on student biographies
- Using vocabulary multiple times and in multiple contexts
- Using text to make connections and draw attention to important content-specific vocabulary and concepts

Lessons that are prescriptive in nature and preplanned based solely on the curriculum, without taking into account the learner, begin from a flawed point of departure. Every student in every classroom has something to share. It is up to the teacher to decide whether he or she will give students an opportunity to disclose their knowledge so that those assets can be used in the learning process.

CHAPTER 8

Navigating from the Known to the Unknown

THE PRECEDING CHAPTER examined the "before" phase of instruction and set the stage for going into the lesson armed with critical and relevant information about what the CLD student knows related to the vocabulary and content to be taught. Having observed for students' funds of knowledge, prior knowledge, and academic knowledge, the teacher must next make decisions about what to do with the student assets and identified "gaps" in background knowledge. This chapter explores the "during" phase of instruction, when the teacher employs culturally responsive pedagogy during the lesson as he or she uses the information gathered before the lesson. I discuss why such efforts during instruction are important and describe what this kind of pedagogy looks like in practice.

In hundreds of hours spent collaborating with teachers across the country on preparing and delivering lessons to increase CLD students' motivation, engagement, and academic achievement, I have often observed teachers plan and proceed into the lesson with wonderful strategies for differentiating instruction so that all their students can be successful. Often missing from their preparation, however, is a strategic plan for using students' biographies for making decisions about contextual and situational processes. During instruction, teachers may underestimate the importance of their own active listening as students work to make meaning of the new content. Active listening is essential to our ability to reroute students as the lesson progresses and respond in ways that lead to a greater level of student affirmation.

According to Tylee (1992), teachers should become the "intermediary" between the biography of the student outside of the classroom and what is taught during the lesson. Tylee (1999) states, "The function of being an intermediary means that the teacher has the role of facilitating student learning." This is accomplished by the teacher becoming part of the learning process during instruction.

Facilitation is the act of navigating student learning by continually connecting what we are teaching in school to what happens in the lives of students. Teaching focused on student knowledge has a much greater chance of being comprehensible to the learner, because it builds on what he or she already knows.

Comprehensible Input

According to Krashen (1985), providing *comprehensible input* means providing students with input that is appropriate for their level of language competence. This ensures that the input (i.e., the information being taught by the teacher) is accessible to the CLD student. Comprehensible input has long been one of the crucial ways educators have sought to accommodate the linguistic and academic needs of CLD students who are learning English as a second language. Efforts to provide learners with comprehensible input generally focus on four fundamental components: hands-on activities/manipulatives, cooperative learning, guarded vocabulary, and visuals. Each of these components is detailed in Figure 8.1.

Teachers who have CLD students in their classrooms use these four components to guide their instructional planning and to monitor their delivery of that instruction. For example, teachers may try to control their rate of speech, avoid using idioms, and use supplemental materials to help make the content accessible to CLD students. Although these are great ways to begin meeting the needs of CLD students, traditional ways of providing comprehensible input are not sufficient for sparking student engagement and optimal learning. Many other factors (some previously discussed in this text) can inhibit learning. If the contextual and situational processes of the classroom have not been planned with specific consideration for the diverse members of the learning community, anxiety and fear may keep students from fully participating and taking risks

FIGURE 8.1
Components of Comprehensible Input

Hands-On Activities/Manipulatives

Definition: Cooperstein and Kocevar-Weidinger (2004), explain that through the use of hands-on activities and manipulatives "abstract concepts become meaningful, transferable, and retained because they are attached to performance of an activity" (p. 145)	• Can lead to increased student–student/student–teacher interactions • Create opportunities for students to interact with the subject matter being studied • Activate the sense of touch and thereby increase the likelihood that students will attach meaning to the content they are learning • Provide CLD students at any level of English language proficiency with an outlet for demonstrating their learnings (Echevarría et al., 2008)

Cooperative Learning

Definition: "Cooperative learning is the instructional use of small groups through which students work together to maximize their own and each other's learning" (Johnson, Johnson, & Holubec, 1994)	• Emphasizes reliance on positive interdependence among learners; the success of each group member is dependent upon that of his or her cooperating peers—one cannot succeed without the others • Encourages students to work together in order to complete specific tasks while simultaneously fostering important social skills • "Cooperative learning is a helpful way to discuss other cultural groups' perspectives, and such groups allow ELLs to feel comfortable speaking while they are developing English fluency" (Lacina, New Levine, & Sowa, 2006, p. 140)

Guarded Vocabulary

Definition: Guarded vocabulary involves efforts to reduce the linguistic load in order to increase comprehensibility of material for CLD students (Herrera & Murry, 2005, p. 255)	• Using speech that is appropriate for CLD students at their specific stage of English language acquisition (Echevarría et al., 2008) • Simplifying sentence structure—using subject, verb, object order versus passive or more complex sentence structures (Echevarría et al., 2008) • Avoiding idioms such as "It's a piece of cake" (Echevarría et al., 2008) • Calling attention to cognates (e.g., information = información) (Echevarría et al., 2008)

Visuals

Definition: "The use of photos, media, computers, drawings, charts, tables, diagrams, and more to illustrate concepts and processes in classroom instruction" (Herrera & Murry, 2005, p. 254)	• Activate CLD students' background knowledge, in their native language or in English, thereby leading to increased reading and listening comprehension (Tang, 1993) • Support comprehension of text; such visuals include graphic organizers, charts, diagrams, and webs that can help CLD students organize their thoughts in a way that is meaningful for them (Echevarría & Graves, 2003) • Supplemental materials, including visuals, can be employed to increase CLD students' comprehension of content-area material (Echevarría et al., 2008)

in learning. Krashen (1985) finds that language acquisition can occur only when comprehensible input passes through a student's affective filter. In classrooms where "teacher lecture" is the norm, CLD students may demonstrate low levels of "risk taking" and, at the end of the day, less learning.

Comprehensible input from a biography-driven perspective takes on additional meaning in that the background knowledge of the student, rather than solely the level of language acquisition, becomes the focus. Learners are able to comprehend content material because measures have been taken to ensure that their sociocultural, linguistic, cognitive, and academic needs are met and that connections are made between the new information and what they already know. For instance, merely showing a picture associated with a vocabulary word does not guarantee that the student will make a connection. Rather, an opportunity must be provided that allows the student to voice, or make public, how he or she is interpreting the visual. We must learn about our students' background knowledge and use comprehensible input techniques in *meaningful* ways during the lesson. Meaningful experiences and connections are essential because students cannot learn new material unless they are able to understand the input and connect it to their background knowledge (Wessels, 2008).

Effective educators focus their efforts, regardless of students' linguistic or academic levels, on the attainment of meaning. They do this by actively engaging students in the learning environment and by implementing strategies that use the words and concepts students *do* know in explaining and elaborating the target vocabulary and content. As students learn from and about the English language through content embedded in a rich context, they develop their English language skills and reach high levels of academic success. When teachers select and implement strategies that position all students as capable contributors to the learning process, students begin to see the activities the teacher has planned as true opportunities for engagement.

Activities Versus Strategies

In recent years, there has been a great deal of discussion about the importance of teachers both recognizing the implications of brain research for education and adjusting their instruction to capitalize on the way the brain processes information (e.g., Jensen, 2006; Sousa, 2006; Willis, 2006). Information that is currently available calls attention to the educational realities of CLD students and the types of experiences and interactions they have in the classroom. At every moment in the classroom, students learning a second language experience "input" within two processing spheres, the linguistic and the academic. The more that is done to plan for what I call "broad and narrow brush-strokes of teaching and learning," that is, bold, large-scale actions and fine, detailed words and behaviors that focus on moving students from the known to the unknown, the more we ensure that students have pathways for reaching a thorough understanding—a clear picture—of the content.

Activities are teacher-generated opportunities for students to interact with the curriculum. Activities are initiated and facilitated by the teacher to provide students with a hook to connect to the lesson and to move the lesson forward. We teachers use activities to (a) provide a canvas of opportunity for students to share with us what they know from their prior experiences, (b) support students in making connections between what they know and the new material, and (c) provide opportunities for students to demonstrate what they know. Targeted and systematic modeling of activities eventually enables students to use

Providing students with a canvas for sharing what they know about a word makes public for the teacher how the student is interpreting what he or she is seeing, hearing, and reading. This then becomes a source of information the teacher can use for bridging the student's knowledge to the content concepts. In this example, one of Ms. Apodaca's 1st-grade students heard the word "moth" instead of "moss," which was the target vocabulary word. Ms. Apodaca was then able to work with the student to pronounce and read the word, supporting the student by rerouting her understanding of the word before the lesson.

—*Marisol Apodaca, 1st Grade, Kansas*

these activities in more independent ways to take responsibility for their own learning.

Strategies that students have adopted gain effectiveness and become student-owned learning strategies through continued, consistent use. In this context, the definition of a strategy according to Afflerbach, Pearson, and Paris (2008) is "a systematic plan, consciously adapted and monitored, to improve one's performance in learning" (p. 365). As educators, one of our intents is to provide students with skills that support their learning beyond their time in our classrooms. This happens when teachers select activities that have potential beyond scaffolding of student learning. Eventually, these activities become student-owned strategies that facilitate comprehension and allow students to take responsibility for their own learning.

Figure 8.2 shows how a teacher has used the foldable activity (Herrera, Kavimandan, & Holmes, in press) as a tool for guided note-taking during a lesson. He moved from teacher-directed, partner, and small-team components to students' individual completion of the task. It was exciting for this teacher when other teachers began to comment about students using the foldable as a study tool in their classrooms. This teacher's CLD students also have commented on how the foldable has helped them earn higher scores in their other classes. Selecting teacher activities and tools that, with practice and application, have the potential to be adopted by the students as their own learning strategies should be one of the central goals of our teaching.

Students can apply a wide range of strategies to comprehend, interpret, and evaluate their learning. They draw on their prior experience, interactions with peers, knowledge of word meaning, and other strategies they have learned to make sense of talk and text. Teachers can move beyond traditional ways of thinking about student learning strategies when we use strategies that both support students' content understanding and teach students to utilize their language and cultural experiences. Such practices connect the biography of the learner to cognitive, metacognitive, and social/affective learning strategies that have proven effective in increasing academic achievement for CLD students.

When I think of learning strategies, I think of the ways many parents coach their children to "work through" difficult times they might have in school. Often I have told my own children to close their eyes and "visualize" what they have been studying in order to remember information when taking a test. These and other little tricks help them to see ways they can recall information, get through giving a speech in front of the class, or call a friend when they do not remember how to solve a difficult equation. Some learning strategies start at home and later are elaborated upon in school. Teachers can explicitly model, practice, and apply the three types of learning strategies detailed in the academic literature: cognitive strategies, metacognitive strategies, and social/affective strategies (see Figure 4.6 for Chamot & O'Malley's [1994] examples of such strategies). When consistently implemented across lessons and content topics, these strategies can lead CLD students to better take responsibility for and control of their own learning.

FIGURE 8.2
From Teacher Activities to Student Learning Strategies

Select teacher activities that have the potential to become cognitive, metacognitive, or social affective strategies for students in the future. In this example, the teacher uses a foldable to guide the students in taking notes in sequence as he presents vocabulary and concepts.

—*James Sparks, High School, Kansas*

Students are given opportunities to practice using the foldable by comparing what they have written with peers in the classroom. The teacher reminds students to add additional information from the textbook.

—*James Sparks, High School, Kansas*

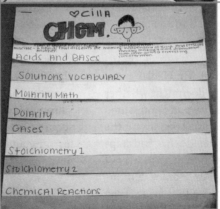

After observation, the teacher makes the decision to have students work independently. The students are encouraged to make sense of the information as it relates to their own lives and their own learning needs.

—*James Sparks, High School, Kansas*

The foldable ultimately becomes a tool to be used to study for a test, to synthesize the information learned, or as a scaffold for responding to questions after the lesson. The tool has become a learning strategy for the student when he or she uses it to support his or her own learning across content areas.

Cognitive Strategies: Tools in My Hands

Cognitive learning strategies are those tools that students can use to learn through the rehearsal, organization, or elaboration of material. Consider the following scenario and ask yourself: How has this teacher used the mind map as a strategy for guiding student thought from the known to the unknown?

> Mr. Hanley was getting ready to start a lesson with his 7th-grade social studies class on what changes a person's character. His objective was to connect students' responses to a novel the class was getting ready to read. He gave each student a piece of blank paper and had them create a basic mind map in which they drew and wrote life events they had experienced that had changed the way they behaved or thought about the world. Examples of such events included becoming the oldest child in the home after an older sibling moved out, moving to a new location, or changing schools and trying to fit into the new school. Students also indicated whether the events and circumstances transformed their character in positive or negative ways.
>
> After they had finished this activation phase of the lesson, Mr. Hanley told his class that one of the objectives of the reading for the next week was to add the main characters of the novel to their own mind maps as they read. Using a pen of a different color, the students were to incorporate the individuals in the story and what was happening to them in the novel that was causing them to change the way they behaved and looked at the world (their personal character). Mr. Hanley reminded the students to use both pictures and words to document what was happening in the novel. He also asked them to draw and make notations about any connections between their own lives and the lives or feelings of the characters in the novel.

> At the end of their study of the novel, Mr. Hanley's students used yet another color of pen to document whether the changes in the characters in the story had contributed to how things had turned out in the end. Then, using the mind map as a tool, students summarized what had happened in the novel and connected it to their own lives—past, present, and future. In this way, Mr. Hanley demonstrated how a mind map can be used as a tool for keeping notes and making sense of what one is reading. He reminded students that when they are preparing for a test, they can follow five easy steps:

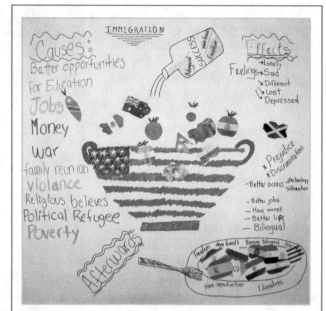

Cognitive strategies support students as they rehearse and retrieve information. In this example, students worked cooperatively to write and draw what they remembered as a group about the concept of "immigration."

—*Julieta Zuluaga, Middle School, Kentucky*

- Jot down everything you can remember about the topic. Write or draw what you remember.
- Look at the study guide you have been provided and determine which questions you would be able to answer, given what you remember.
- Go back to your notes and your text and then add to your mind map what you left out, using pictures and words.
- Use the mind map to study by aligning the questions with the words and pictures you jotted down.
- Create a visual representation of the mind map in your memory.

By using the mind map as a strategy, Mr. Hanley was able to first activate students' permanent memory to gain access to their background knowledge related to the topic. Throughout the remainder of the lesson (and during subsequent lessons), he was then able to facilitate students' learning and explicitly model how the mind map can be a tool for:

- Elaborating on prior knowledge
- Taking notes
- Organizing information
- Summarizing

Metacognitive Strategies: Tools in My Head

Metacognitive strategies include those strategies that lead students to monitor their own learning and the success of their in-progress efforts to understand new material. In essence, metacognitive strategies are ways of paying conscious attention to what and how we are thinking. Metacognitive strategies have great potential to enhance CLD students' comprehension during and after the lesson. When teachers ask students to think about the connections they make as they read, they are better able to actively listen to their teachers and peers and make links to the content and language objectives of the lesson. Metacognitive strategies help to demystify the learning process and to lower CLD students' anxiety, which is often provoked by being in a linguistically demanding learning environment. Consider the following scenario:

Using her story bag strategy, Ms. Kavimandan asked her students to predict which 8 of the 12 words that were listed on the board were going to be in the story. She read the title of the book and showed several of the pictures. She then asked students to write the words they had selected on 3 × 5 cards (one word per card). After writing the words, they were told to write or draw why they thought the selected word was going to be in the story and whether they had heard, seen, or could define the word. Students were encouraged to make an educated guess and write what they thought the word *might* mean.

Ms. Kavimandan then asked the students to place their series of selected words in front of them because they were going to be listening for the words as she read. Their task was to use a strategy that involved using their "selective attention" to listen for these very important words they had identified. She told them that she would be stopping at different points in the lesson to give them an opportunity to discuss what they had heard about the words and, as a team, they would begin to define the words in context.

Ms. Kavimandan was very explicit about having students understand that when they were learning new vocabulary, the ability to read and know why you are reading is important. She also told them that having questions about what we are reading sometimes helps us not to become overwhelmed with very difficult reading. She proceeded to explain that there are multiple ways to confirm answers to the questions we have. One way is through reading, and another is through listening attentively to what the

teacher has to say about a word or topic. Ms. Kavimandan let students know that through the use of metacognitive strategies, they can plan for their learning and continually self-monitor their understanding of what is being read or taught during the lesson.

Explicit instruction on metacognitive strategies supports CLD students in performing metacognitive activities such as the following (Brown, 1980):

- Clarifying the purposes of reading and the demands inherent to the task
- Identifying significant aspects of a message
- Allocating attention
- Monitoring ongoing activities
- Engaging in review and self-questioning with regard to attainment of goals
- Taking corrective action when necessary
- Recovering from distractions and disruptions

Metacognitive strategies are especially useful for helping all students understand how they can become more efficient readers. Through advance organization, students become *prepared* readers. Through selective attention, students become *aware* readers. By monitoring their comprehension, students become *strategic* readers. Finally, by monitoring their production, students become *reflective* readers (Swartz & Perkins, 1987).

Social/Affective Strategies: People Tools

Remember how important it was to call a friend when you didn't understand the dense reading that was assigned in your English class? How, for hours, between socializing, you would try to figure out what the author was really saying about the topic? From my work in schools, I have found that *social/affective learning strategies* are the type of strategy most often absent from the classroom. Citing a lack of time, the need to have control over the classroom, and students' inability to help one another given differing language proficiencies and academic abilities, teachers frequently comment that it is difficult to model, practice, and apply social/affective strategies. Yet these strategies are some of the most effective for creating learning communities in which differences in students' cultures and languages are valued as assets and used to help all learners develop a more thorough understanding of the content as well as a more global perspective.

A risk-free, inquiry-based environment in which students frequently have opportunities to interact with their peers encourages all students to meet our high expectations for learning. What the teacher does to prepare students to work in cooperation with one another, to learn how to ask questions when something is beyond their grasp, and to learn to risk without fear of being ridiculed is of utmost importance. Students should understand that when facing challenging concepts and tasks, they should feel comfortable with coming together for problem solving. After all, this is how most adults determine how to solve problems when the answer is not evident.

Consider this scenario and reflect on how the teacher is creating spaces for students to learn social/affective strategies:

> Mr. Davila always reminds his students that no one in the classroom possesses all the answers, all the time. He continually tells students that one of the greatest gifts that comes from different students using different strategies to arrive at the same answer is that the class always has more than one way of looking at a problem. To prove the point, he selected multiple excerpts from the novel he was introducing, read them to the class, and had the students sketch and label each selection he had read. The students then compared their thoughts and ideas, first with a partner and then within small groups. In this way, each student's cultural and linguistic thoughts were made public.

> In the groups, the students next worked together to sketch and label what they predicted the novel was going to be about. Mr. Davila then asked them to discuss within their groups the following questions:

- What were the commonalities in what was heard, sketched, and labeled?
- Were these commonalities derived from personal experiences or school knowledge?
- What were the differences?
- What were the sources of these differences?
- What was the group's prediction, and how were group members able to come to agreement?

This type of activity allows students to value the input of each student as well as clarify and elaborate on concepts. Merely having students turn and talk to a partner at some point in the lesson does not achieve the same results as the planned use of social/affective strategies to promote higher order thinking and relationship-building. Social/affective strategies, when planned with a definite purpose and out-

Pair work is one way of creating a learning community in a classroom that is low-risk and that emphasizes the importance of teamwork. As students worked in pairs on this strategy, they were encouraged to ask each other questions for clarification and work together to find answers as they moved forward with their learning task. This kind of interaction is important for the creation of a balanced learning community and for the development of social/affective skills.

—Denise Albertson,
Middle School, Colorado

come in mind, can enhance learning and lead to relationships that reach beyond classroom walls.

Social/affective strategies can support CLD students as they generate questions about the content, relate ideas and questions to their own lives, and risk using language (if grouping configurations are strategically planned based on sociocultural, linguistic, academic, and cognitive factors). Students are more likely to engage with the curriculum if they perceive that they have a support system to use during and after the lesson. In short, cognitive, metacognitive, and social/affective strategies enable teachers to gradually release ownership of and responsibility for learning to the learners themselves.

Navigating States of Mind

CLD students, like all students, are eager to become members of the community of learners. However, many CLD students have feelings of failure that stem from perceptions (on their part or on the part of their teachers or peers) of incompetence or inability to fully participate due to language or cultural background. Some students will say, "Why try? I usually fail." In these instances, we can choose either to ignore the student's concern or to think about the context and situational processes we create, making sure that everyone in the classroom experiences success.

For many of our CLD students, the individual's behavior often can be connected to his or her current state of mind. Sometimes we may be seeing the results of fear, anxiety, boredom, apathy, frustration, or confusion. At other times we may sense students' anticipation, excitement, and curiosity. As discussed in Chapter 6, states of mind vary given what is happening in the classroom. Have you ever watched students begin to slump in their chairs after an especially difficult lesson? What do you choose to do when this happens? Tsai, Kunter, Lüdtke, Trautwein, and Ryan (2008) write about the importance of the learner's psychological state. A learner's state is affected by both external and situational stimuli. Such stimuli have a stronger impact on creating a positive (or negative) state of mind than do individual learner variables.

The best way to promote positive states of mind for CLD learners throughout a lesson is to do the following:

- Select activities that create situational interest.
- Move into the lesson using strategies that change the general context and situation often enough to support autonomy, facilitate memory processes, and create positive learning interactions.
- Use the native language when needed.
- Provide positive performance feedback.

Figure 8.3 summarizes considerations for the successful navigation of students' states of mind.

From Interest to Practice and Application

Teachers who understand the importance of interest and motivation to the learning process are cognizant of the "rhythm" and "duration" of tasks and interactions during a lesson. Given the biographies of our learners, we must plan lessons to ensure that practice and application are "chunked" into time frames that provide students with time to process what they have been learning. In so doing, we make it possible for students to "work smarter, not harder" and increase the chances that what we have taught will be retained. According to Sousa (2006), if information is going in faster than it can be sorted and placed, it becomes a big pile that may clutter the brain and lead to reduced learning. If the student cannot make sense of or find meaning in what is being taught, little retention will occur. However, by planning lessons that provide students with multiple opportunities for interacting with multiple people along the way as they grapple with new concepts and vocabulary, we increase the likelihood that students' states of mind will remain positively slanted toward learning.

Jensen (2008) advises that if educators want students to learn what they are teaching, they must be aware of their students' states of mind, and navigate them. In addition, we must actively monitor our own state of mind. One of the most easily managed aspects of our situational processes is our ability to configure and reconfigure the context in which

> **FIGURE 8.3**
> *Tips for Navigating Students' States of Mind*
>
> - Understand that there are thousands of states of mind, both positive and negative.
> - Know that states of mind can be changed, because they exist at individual points in time.
> - Realize that being aware of what our CLD students are feeling, thinking, and learning helps us tap into their states of mind.
> - Remember that when we change negative states of mind to positive ones, we enhance student learning!
> - Keep CLD students' affective filters low to promote positive states of mind.
> - Provide comprehensible input through varying degrees of linguistically and cognitively demanding tasks.
> - Vary group configurations (e.g., total group, pairs, small groups, individual).
> - Support the native language.
>
> Adapted from Herrera (2008), p. 31. Used with permission of KCAT/TLC, Kansas State University.

we teach, based on our learners' social, emotional, linguistic, and academic needs.

From Individualism, Competition, and Cooperation to Biography-Driven Grouping Configurations

Cooperative learning has been a topic of great interest to educational and sociological researchers for many years. In fact, in 1989 Johnson and Johnson noted that nearly 900 studies had been carried out on the subject of cooperative learning, and this number has continued to grow. Overwhelming evidence clearly illustrates the benefits that cooperative learning has for all group members, when compared with more individualistic or competitive experiences (Deutsch, 1949; Johnson & Johnson, 1989; Johnson, Johnson, & Maruyama, 1983; Lewin, 1935; Pepitone, 1980; Triplett, 1898). Among these benefits are increases in student productivity, achievement, use of higher order thinking skills, idea generation, and transfer of learning from one context to another (Johnson & Johnson, 1994).

Johnson and Johnson (1994) attest:

> Our research and the research of many others dating back to the late 1800s has established that having students work together cooperatively is a powerful way for them to learn and has positive effects on the

classroom and school climate. This has been verified by teachers in classrooms from preschool through graduate school. However, the importance of emphasizing cooperative learning in classrooms goes beyond just achievement, positive relationships, and psychological health. (p. 43)

These authors extend their findings to encompass the overall well-being of society, stating that most day-to-day situations require a person to understand and get along with others. Therefore, lessons learned during school-based cooperative learning carry over to situations in the workplace as well as to personal relationships with others. *While competition benefits few, cooperation has the potential to benefit all!*

Biography-Driven Grouping Configurations

It is the office [responsibility] of the school environment to . . . see to it that each individual gets an opportunity to escape from the limitations of the social group in which he was born, and to come into living contact with a broader environment.
—*John Dewey (2007/1916, p. 23)*

Long ago, John Dewey eloquently wrote about the conditional and situational processes that existed for students who came from cultural environments that were different from those of the school setting. He reminded readers that coming into contact with others from diverse backgrounds was essential to the broader development of all students. Today, when we educators are working with learning communities that mirror the diverse society in which we live, we must use a variety of grouping configurations in order to create space for all of our students to come together in learning. By providing students with opportunities to cooperatively learn with and from others whose biographies are different from their own, we provide the learners in our classroom the opportunity to see the world through a different sociocultural, linguistic, cognitive, and academic lens.

One of the most effective ways to ensure this kind of learning is to design groups based both on the task and on the biographies of the students. Group configurations that support the teaching of content as well as engage and motivate students require high levels of interaction among all students, regardless of language or academic level. These groups do not form without thought and action on the part of the teacher. They must be planned strategically and aligned with the dynamics of human and ecological factors at play during instruction. Configurations that are designed merely for classroom management, or simply to ensure that the class is "doing" cooperative learning, are less likely

In this setting, Mr. Pride separated his class into small groups so that students could discuss the new content with one another. Over the course of the 50-minute science lesson, the students were organized into several different grouping configurations. They began the activation process individually. Next, they moved into pairs, and then transitioned to small groups. During small-group discussion, each group was assigned a topic and group members were asked to become experts on it with help from the other members of their learning community. As the groups worked, Mr. Pride and a paraprofessional rotated around the room to listen to students' conversations.

—*Jeremy Pride, Middle School, Kansas*

to promote an ecology where learners' states of mind are anticipated and navigated to create positive cooperative learning results.

Planning for biography-driven grouping configurations involves thinking about the following:

- Insights gained during the first phase of the lesson regarding the assets and needs of the CLD learner and the community. These insights inform decisions about the kinds of grouping configurations that will best meet learners' needs for this lesson.
- Biographies of the individual CLD students
- Skills necessary to complete the task, including academic knowledge and vocabulary
- Time available for employing multiple configurations, each with a specific purpose
- Complexity and demands of the curriculum. The more complex and decontextualized the information, the more critical is the students' need for scaffolding and comprehensible input.
- Insights gained during the lesson about students' states of mind

We must always remember to think of engagement and motivation as responses to our willingness to vary instruction, challenge all students, and allow the cultural and linguistic resources of CLD students to be used while they are mastering academic content. In addition, Brock and Raphael (2005) urge educators to recognize the importance of supporting students' learning by using a variety of educational contexts and interaction patterns. These contexts and interaction patterns should be designed to promote both academic and social relationships (Urdan & Schoenfelder, 2006).

Consider the following scenario and ask yourself, "What does this scenario tell us about the power of relationships in academic success?"

After a professional development session involving a group of CLD students and their teachers, a young lady came up to me and shared the following story:

I came to the United States when I was in the 4th grade. I hated going to school every day. I felt so out of place, and everything moved so fast. In Mexico I had been a very smart student; here I felt like a failure. The only thing that saved me was my friend Sophie. I remember my teacher would always move us around a lot to work with different students in the class. My eyes were always full of tears because I thought no one liked me because I was different. I was poor, didn't speak English, and my family was not like everyone else. As we were placed in groups to work, I remember how Sophie always found a way to sit next to me in our groups. She also seemed to want to be my partner. Her smile and voice when she would say, "Don't cry, I'll help you," helped me get through many days. In a few months I will be graduating from high school, and Sophie and I help each other out in lots of ways. I have learned so much from her, and today I can say she is passing her AP Spanish class because she has learned from me. So thank you for telling teachers to use teams/groups in their classes. For people like me, it's a matter of survival!

That day I learned from this young lady that grouping configurations are not only about language and academics. They are about the community and climate that are essential for engagement, motivation, and academic success. At one level they create environments that teach, and at another they develop spaces were students can establish mentoring relationships and friendships, built on trust and respect.

Collaboration with teachers has further solidified my understanding of the power of interaction in the learning environment. When making decisions about which grouping configurations would be best, given the content and language objectives of the lesson as well as the students' biographies, I like to remember the following five steps:

- Start by igniting and documenting what students bring from their background.
- Based on this information, consider the pairs and groups that likely will move each student forward linguistically and academically during the lesson.
- Consider each student's emotional needs and his or her current state of mind.
- Remember the accountability measures you have selected for the end of the lesson, and consider ways you will want to document the linguistic and academic growth of students during the lesson.
- Remember that you are not grouping solely for student cooperation (i.e., students should not be working only with their self-selected friends). To make the most effective use of your instructional time, you are strategically configuring "teams" of learners that will support one another in their linguistic, academic, and social development.

Figure 8.4 presents a brief overview of cooperative learning, both from more traditional perspectives and from the perspective of biography-driven instruction.

In culturally responsive pedagogy, the goal is to move from the biography of each student to instruction, and then to have the lesson culminate with the student's awareness of how much he or she has learned linguistically and academically. Meeting this goal requires the use of grouping configurations that keep *all* students engaged and motivated to learn. Our team of researchers refers to this conceptualization of the role of grouping configurations in the teaching/learning process as the *i+tpsI model*. What then does *i+tpsI* (pronounced "I plus tipsy") represent?

- **i** (individual student) = The "i" refers to the opportunities the teacher provides to CLD students in the "before" phase of the lesson to activate their background knowledge and share that knowledge with the rest of the learning community.
- **t** (total group) = Armed with a new understanding of students' background knowledge that can be used for the explanation of new vocabulary, introduction of new concepts, or adaptation of curriculum or lesson delivery, the teacher enters the "during" phase of the lesson. What the teacher has learned from the "i" has implications for how he or she will help students move from the known to the unknown. Ultimately, the "t" refers to the teacher-directed aspects of the lesson in which the educator teaches the whole, or total, group.
- **p** (pairs/partners) = The teacher considers various opportunities for pairs or partners that will accelerate students' learning of language and content concepts.
- **s** (small groups) = The teacher makes decisions about small groups, in which CLD students will have

---

FIGURE 8.4
Overview of Cooperative Learning

Cooperative Learning

- Concept of **positive interdependence** predominates, that is, the notion that *without you* and all that *you* have to offer, the task cannot be completed
- Importance of **interdependence** among collaborating students
- **Face-to-face interaction** among participants
- Holding both the **individual and the group accountable** for the outcomes
- Teaching of interpersonal skills and skills needed to work in small groups
- Self-reflection and discussion among group members regarding the effectiveness of group processes

Source: Johnson, Johnson, and Holubec (1994).

Kagan Structures

- **Definition:** "A Kagan structure is a **content-free, repeatable sequence of steps** designed to structure the interaction of students with each other and/or the curriculum in ways which align with basic principles and efficiently realize specific learning outcomes" (Kagan, 2000)
- Structures are based on cooperative learning philosophy
- Structures, as discussed by Kagan, are based upon four main principles:
  - Positive interdependence
  - Individual accountability
  - Equal participation
  - Simultaneous interaction

Biography-Driven Cooperative Learning

- **Cognitive:** Fostering cooperative learning opportunities for CLD students that cognitively stretch them to their $i+1$ level. Are students thinking critically about the material or just repeating information?
- **Academic:** Using grouping structures that support CLD students' attainment of the learning objectives. Does the composition of the grouping structures promote CLD students' content understanding and language proficiencies?
- **Sociocultural:** Purposefully arranging conditions that support sharing, cooperation, and collaboration among all students. Are students' funds of knowledge, prior knowledge, and academic knowledge used in the cooperative construction of meaning?
- **Linguistic:** Building upon student knowledge gained through the native language as well as through English. Are students allowed to make contributions to cooperative learning endeavors using both their L1 and L2?

---

extended opportunities to observe and listen to more proficient language models. Small groups are designed to ensure that all students, including CLD learners, have opportunities to teach and to model for peers.

- **I** (individual accountability) = In the "after" phase of the lesson (to be discussed in detail in Chapter 9), students should feel more empowered as learners and should possess a greater level of linguistic and academic knowledge. The teacher assesses individual growth, with students being held accountable for what they learned in relation to where they started.

This mnemonic reminds teachers that learning is an interactive process that moves from student knowledge, to curriculum learning, and back to the student. This interaction happens through different contexts, conditions, and situations. Such learning and teaching processes make social and academic talk public for the benefit of the entire learning community. Using strategic grouping configurations during the lesson increases the chance that each student will share something of significance to the lesson that can then be used as a springboard for meeting the lesson's objectives. Figure 8.5 provides a checklist for reflecting on the ways we can maximize $i + tpsI$ grouping configurations in our classrooms.

"i" as the Anchor to Learning

I like to think of every student in every classroom as having something in their background that anchors them to their own learning. Sometimes the link is a stretch, but as breathing and thinking individuals, we are always trying to make sense of the world around us. I spent many years as a second language learner wishing there were just split seconds during instruction when I could say to someone: "I know. . . . I remember when. . . . I know something that looks like that. . . ." Yet most teachers seemed to be in a hurry to teach me something. I often observe the same urgency in the classrooms I visit: "Get your books out. . . . Let's get started. . . . Soon we will be out of time." Sometimes there is a brief "Here it is—make a connection" and then the lesson moves on. When I hear and see this, I wonder how many students in the classroom have something to say, or how many already know something about the vocabulary or topic being explained or introduced.

As discussed in Chapter 7, the activation and documentation of students' background knowledge is an important goal to strive for. As teachers, we first need to become keen observers to record or make a mental note related to what students know from both their experiential and their academic backgrounds. With this information as a resource, we have new tools in the form of pictures, words, or stories from the students that can be used to move the class toward

	FIGURE 8.5
	i + tpsl *Grouping Configurations Checklist*
Grouping	**What did you do to support your CLD students' sociocultural, linguistic, academic, and cognitive dimensions throughout the learning process?**
i = Individual student	☐ Student interest in the lesson was sparked through stimulation of one or more of the five senses. ☐ All students were provided with opportunities to document and share their initial connections between the topic and their background knowledge (i.e., funds of knowledge, prior knowledge, and academic knowledge).
t = Total group	☐ Whole-group modeling, discussion, and/or authentic application of learnings in practice occurred. ☐ Whole-group activities were structured to provide explicit opportunities for CLD students to interact with their peers. ☐ Whole-group activities were strategically configured to provide CLD students with English language modeling by the teacher and/or more proficient peers.
p = Pairs/partners	☐ CLD students worked with partners to support their comprehension of academic tasks through one-on-one discussion and authentic practice and application of content-based learnings. ☐ CLD students worked with a more proficient peer who could speak the native language and clarify information in the native language, if needed. ☐ Partners produced a product that demonstrated their understanding of a critical concept or vocabulary term.
s = Small groups	☐ Students worked in small groups so that they could hear multiple perspectives and elaborate on their own schemas. ☐ Teams were purposely structured so that CLD students were able to see and hear language modeled by more proficient peers. ☐ Small teams were held accountable to demonstrate their learnings informally or formally.
l = Individual accountability	☐ Students independently practiced and applied their learnings. ☐ Individual activities allowed students to demonstrate what they had learned. ☐ Authentic assessments were implemented that enabled CLD students at multiple language proficiency levels to successfully demonstrate their learnings.

a greater understanding of the vocabulary and content concepts to be taught.

A professor of mine continually reminded us that "from small words come bigger and bigger words." All writing and learning begins with a single picture, word, or story. As future teachers, we had to think about how we would "dig" for the knowledge that students would bring to our lessons. What would we do with student assets we discovered? We had to reflect on how we could use student assets during the lesson to benefit our learners. If we simply left students' background knowledge behind, we limited the potential for academic achievement by our CLD learners. Somehow, we needed not only to uncover experiential and academic knowledge but also to use the information in positive ways.

I learned never to discount what my learners brought to the lesson, knowing that if I did, I was discounting their culture, language, and life. This was as true for the students I taught in public schools as it was for the students incarcerated in the youth facilities in which I worked. Becoming familiar with the types of knowledge that our CLD students already have is the first step in being able to address their learning needs. Once familiar with the funds of knowledge, prior knowledge, and academic knowledge they possess, we can use this information to address state standards and the curriculum at hand. In reflecting on ways to encourage students to make connections between what they know and the new information we are teaching, consider the following scenario:

A few years ago I was co-teaching a lesson in a 5th-grade classroom, where the story was on Thurgood Marshall. The other teacher, Ms. Melton, and I had agreed that we would use the Vocabulary Quilt strategy (see Appendix E) as the activation activity for the lesson. She passed out all the quilts for the students to work in groups of 4. She had strategically placed the students in their groups based on what she knew about their home and school biographies and the objectives of the lesson. We wanted to learn how many of the target vocabulary words, which included terms such as *judge, courthouse, justice,* and *Supreme Court,* the students could relate to past experiences in or out of school.

Ms. Melton asked the students to go to the quilt and then quickly and silently write what was in their brains related to each of the terms. Ms. Melton was visibly excited about what was happening. It seemed that each of the groups had written several words that were directly associated with six of the eight vocabulary words on the quilt. Given what she was hearing and seeing, she asked each of the groups to write a statement related to their life experiences using the target vocabulary words on 3 × 5 cards. That day Ms. Melton not only learned about what this group of students knew about the topic but she also got a glimpse into their daily lives, which included friends, family, or themselves having first-hand immigration and other experiences within the legal system. She learned that there were two terms she would have to focus on during the lesson: *Supreme Court* and *justice.* It also was evident that, together, these students had many life experiences that would be useful for their understanding of the new material.

As the class read the story about Thurgood Marshall during the lesson, Ms. Melton returned several times to the stories students had shared and the words they had written. By the end of the lesson, they knew what *justice* meant in their world. They also understood why the Supreme Court is of such importance to our society.

As teachers, we must remind ourselves that students are not passive recipients but rather active participants in learning. The activation of background knowledge encourages students to be "connection makers" during the lesson, continually making links between new material and their own background knowledge. These connections are more likely to happen when we intentionally consider the CLD student biography so that the sociocultural, linguistic, cognitive, and academic needs of our CLD students are taken into account throughout the lesson. We make decisions about how to group students and adapt the curriculum at two levels. We make initial decisions going into the first part of the lesson based on what we know about our students' biographies. Later, as we enter the "during" phase of the lesson, our decisions are informed by what we have learned as silent observers of our students.

"i" + "tpsI": *Multiple Meaningful Exposures Using the Same Biographical Anchor*

During the lesson, the teacher serves as a facilitator by making connections to the background information he or she gained from students in the activation phase. Connections are made to the objectives of the lesson, the vocabulary, the key concepts, and the overall content. According to Sousa (2006),

> To convince a learner's brain to persist with [a given] objective, teachers need to be more mindful of helping students establish *meaning*. . . . Past experiences always influence new learning. . . . If we expect students to find meaning, we need to be certain that today's curriculum contains connections to *their* past experiences, not just ours. (p. 50)

Going from the "*i*" into "*tpsI*" requires teachers to consider the kinds of total group, pairing/partnering, and small-group work that will provide the best avenues for students' continued associations, interaction, clarification, and elaboration of the new material. As you read the following scenario, consider how the teacher first encourages every individual in the learning community to share what he or she knows and then uses resulting insights in the construction of knowledge.

> A few years ago I was observing a social studies teacher as he taught a lesson. He very effectively stated his content and language objectives and put out the materials needed for implementing the vocabulary quilt strategy (see Appendix E) to activate students' knowledge related to the vocabulary words for the chapter. He proceeded to give students the directions and form student groups, placing students according to where he thought they might be able to learn from one another's culture and language.
>
> Soon after the students had started working on the quilt, he moved over to one of his "intermediate" ELL students and pointed to the word *efficient*. This was one of the eight words that were part of the lesson. As I, too, moved over, I noticed that the student had

drawn a building with many windows. When the teacher smiled and asked about the drawing, the student shared with him that this was where she lived. He asked why she had drawn it for the word *efficient*. The student responded that she lived in an efficiency apartment. The teacher then asked if she knew why it was called an efficiency apartment, and she replied, "No." I wondered what he would do with this exchange as he moved on to other students and noted what they had written. The teacher then returned to the front of the room and jotted on the board some of the words, along with his sketch of the building.

Next, he asked his students to take out their textbooks. This week the focus was on efficient machinery, and he told the students that they were going to further explore the target vocabulary as they read the chapter and as he helped explain the words. The lesson proceeded with some partner reading, with portions of the text being read aloud by the teacher. He stopped at different points and went over to the board to talk about the students' words and their relation to the concepts. I observed that he had yet to point out the building or ask the student to explain her rationale for having drawn a building.

As the lesson began to come to closure, the teacher went over to the student and said, "Today the prize goes to Delia. She drew an efficiency apartment during our Vocabulary Quilt at the beginning of the lesson. Turn and talk to a partner. How is an efficiency apartment like an efficient machine?" After allowing a brief time for partners to share, the teacher then walked over to Delia again and asked her the question. Beaming, she said, "An efficiency apartment uses very little gas and electricity and does not take long to clean, so it's like a machine that does not use too much energy."

"You are a very bright student," he said, "Now, everyone return to your quilt and associate what you wrote at the beginning of the lesson with what you learned. You can use others' ideas since we have been discussing everyone's words during the lesson. Make sure to cross out the words or pictures that do not fit with what we have studied. You have 10 minutes to think and talk in your groups, and then I will ask you to work alone." As the students headed toward their groups, the teacher and I both smiled.

In observations of this teacher and others like him, I have listened to and learned from their use of traditional techniques of scaffolding to support learning in ways that are both culturally relevant *and responsive* to the CLD students in their classrooms.

Scaffolding from Student Words/Thoughts to New Learning

We never really cognitively understand something until we can create a model or metaphor that is derived from our unique personal world.
—*Eric Jensen (2008, p. 168)*

New ways of orchestrating comprehensible input, as discussed earlier in this chapter, lead to new perspectives on ways teachers can scaffold classroom practice to achieve a higher level of CLD student engagement, motivation, and learning. The biographies of our students affect what they bring to a given lesson, and this background knowledge, in turn, determines how we will use visuals, grouping configurations, meaningful activities, and student language to scaffold our teaching and guard our own language use during instruction. The key is to think of scaffolding as guided by students' biographies. CLD learners will use scaffolds at different times for different purposes. Understanding students' needs and assets informs our decisions about which types of scaffolds will be most effective.

According to Dickson, Chard, and Simmons (1993), scaffolding of instruction relates to how the teacher provides support for learners through the selection and use of materials, types of tasks, and interactions among students and between students and the teacher. Larkin (2002) notes, "scaffolding is a process in which students are given support until they can apply new skills and strategies independently." Instructional scaffolding has roots in Vygotsky's (1978) notion of the learner initially needing support in the learning process. As learning progresses, the support systems that have been employed during the practice and application part of the lesson are gradually removed, allowing the student to take responsibility for independently demonstrating what he or she has learned.

In culturally responsive pedagogy, providing instructional scaffolding goes beyond simply deploying superficial "safety nets" for the learner. Instead, the teacher must be strategic about the types of student support he or she uses during each phase of the lesson. Such supports include:

- Language and content objectives
- Activities that activate students' background knowledge about a topic and allow for use of pictorial representations as well as the native language and English
- Associations made throughout the lesson to students' documented background knowledge
- Grouping configurations that reflect insights gained from both the students' biographies and information shared by students throughout the course of the lesson

- Constructive and positive feedback throughout the lesson designed to increase students' motivation, reduce their anxiety, and route/reroute their thinking

Mediated Scaffolding

Difficult and complex tasks are made reachable or attainable through lessons in which students have multiple opportunities to think and rehearse what they are learning in multiple ways. One of the most effective ways to navigate learning for CLD students is to provide them with nonthreatening opportunities to voice what they are thinking.

Mediated scaffolding involves the teacher's systematic use of Bloom's taxonomy to vary his or her questioning techniques and then allow students to grapple with questions for minutes at a time. At this point, the teacher walks around the classroom actively listening to students negotiate the correct answers to the questions based on the readings, lecture, or other learning. By allowing peers to work together in an effort to respond to the questions, the teacher sends the message that there can be more than one correct answer to a question (or at least more than one perspective on how to arrive at the correct answer).

Remember, everyone processes information differently and arrives at the answer at a different time. Releasing questions to students allows more opportunities for students to all get back on the same page before the lesson continues. What an opportunity this provides for us teachers to make an informed assessment of the connections or interpretations all students are making about the content! Ask yourself: "How many questions do I ask? How often during the lesson do I provide risk-free opportunities for students to make public their thought processes?" Figure 8.6 provides some ideas for thinking about the "academic talk" that is part of the ongoing public conversation of the classroom.

Revoicing for Clarification and Elaboration

Have you ever stopped to listen—*really* listen—to student responses when you ask a question or talk to groups of students? What are they saying? What cultural and linguistic resources are they using to make sense of the content? Only when we actively listen to the hidden messages of student talk can we guide learners to interact with the content within their zone of proximal development. Great teachers often use the technique of *revoicing* to reroute, elaborate upon, and validate student responses.

A teacher revoices when he or she listens to what students have to say and re-utters their understanding through repetition, expansion, rephrasing, summarizing, and reporting what was shared (Forman, Larreamendy-Joerns, Stein, & Brown, 1998; Krussel, Springer, & Edwards, 2004; Kwon,

After students have been provided with the opportunity to make public the associations they made with the target vocabulary, Ms. Apodaca begins to have them think about the words in relation to the story that will be read that week. The scaffolding begins as she explains the words in context, begins to define them, and reroutes students' thinking toward the correct meaning of each word.

—*Marisol Apodaca, 1st Grade, Kansas*

Ju, Rasmussen, Park, & Cho, 2008). Revoicing is a technique found in the math literature and, as noted by Park et al. (2007), is a "discursive move that teachers use to facilitate students' learning" (p. 4). Other discursive moves used by teachers include telling (e.g., hinting, directing), requesting clarification, and questioning (e.g., challenging, probing) (Krussel et al., 2004). Our revoicing of CLD students' experiential and academic talk can only occur after we have actively observed their language and thought. Therefore, as noted by O'Connor and Michaels (1996), the teacher must be skillful in the orchestration of classroom discussion.

Teacher revoicing provides CLD students with an opportunity to hear the teacher use their words and thoughts to clarify or elaborate on what was shared and to make connections with the content. Revoicing therefore allows the teacher to connect student knowledge with content concepts and vocabulary and to model language and reroute student thinking as necessary. O'Connor and Michaels (1996) maintain that revoicing of students' language and thought may lead students to more fully see themselves as part of the learning community and participate in making, analyzing, and evaluating predictions. O'Connor and Michaels (1993) state that revoicing "affords the teacher the tools to coordinate the academic task structure and social participation structure, while simultaneously bringing students into the process of intellectual socialization" (p. 319).

Read the following exchange as the teacher revoices student thinking related to the target vocabulary. Think about how this teacher uses "connected talk" after students have

FIGURE 8.6

Capitalizing on Questions to Promote Student Learning

The right kinds of questions can take CLD students beyond factual question/answer responses to *i*+1 responses. By stretching students to *i*+1 responses, the teacher can access the deeper dimensions of the CLD student biography and enable students to elaborate on their learning.

For Questions That . . .	Important Considerations for the Questioner
Build upon CLD Students' Sociocultural Knowledge	• Do questions increase CLD students' connections between prior experiential/academic knowledge and new learning? • Are questions structured in such a way that they enable CLD students to draw upon their own culture/language to make meaningful links to new content? • Do the interactive grouping configurations used within the classroom promote discussion and questioning that encourages CLD students to share sociocultural knowledge?
Scaffold Student Learning	• Are questions posed in a manner that enables the teacher to determine what students are learning? • Can information gained from student responses help guide instruction and inform the educator as to where instruction might need to be revisited? • Do questions inform the teacher about areas in which CLD students might need additional support?
Promote Student Dialogue	• Does questioning engage students in rich dialogue that enhances thinking and learning? • Is questioning structured to promote small group/partner discussions that foster problem solving? • Are students strategically grouped based on their CLD biographies (sociocultural, linguistic, academic, and cognitive) in order to promote rich discussion and extended learning?
Build Critical-Thinking Skills	• Are questions posed that engage students in exploring deeper issues related to the topic? • Do questions push students to think "outside the box" and critically reflect on the implications of their learning? • Are questions posed in such a manner that they promote understanding of the concept rather than regurgitation of "facts"?
Promote Cognitive Links	• Does questioning promote higher order thinking skills? • Are questions posed in such a way that they take students to *i*+1 by having them *explain the process* they used to solve a problem?
Promote Self-Assessment	• Are students encouraged to monitor their own understanding of critical concepts by documenting questions about the content before, during, and after the lesson? • Are students guided to ask questions of themselves so that they can monitor their own understanding/learning?

Source: Herrera (2008), p. 120. Used with permission of KCAT/TLC, Kansas State University.

shared their thoughts with peers. Notice the numerous times the teacher revisits the word *justice* and tries to route/reroute students' responses.

Teacher: As the groups talked about "justice," I heard several takes on the word. Let's do a connected talk and see if we can connect our thoughts and come up with how justice fits in with what we have been studying.

John (*with no raising of hands, John starts speaking*): Ahh . . . justice . . . it's umm . . .

Teacher: It's hard to explain.

John: Yeah.

Teacher: You can do it!

John: Justice is a part of what you believe and stuff.

Teacher: Okay, it is a belief. You're on the right track. Can anybody add to what he said about justice?

Sophia: Kinda getting your rights back.

Teacher: Okay.

Sophia: Being . . . oh, it's hard to explain. When you get free or something, it's like you have your own beliefs. You can be under your own power. You're not under somebody else's . . .

Teacher (nods head in agreement): Let's see if somebody else can connect to what you're saying. *(points to Natalie)*

Natalie: Umm . . . sorta like . . . when people get what they deserve. Sorta like if someone died . . . umm . . .

Teacher: You can use it . . . Use "justice" with the Holocaust . . . *(nods head in encouragement)*

Natalie: Like the family would want justice from the Nazis. They would want the Nazis to get what they deserved. And the family . . . because, like, relatives died during the Holocaust. They want justice.

Teacher (points to Sophia): Does that thinking connect to where your group was going?

According to Forman et al. (1998), revoicing makes ideas public for the rest of the classroom. It gives the community an opportunity to hear explanations of words and concepts, negotiate text from multiple perspectives, reposition their own thoughts, and make changes to their understandings as necessary. Revoicing allows CLD students to hear peers and the teacher discuss and interpret the content multiple times. According to Chapin, O'Connor, and Anderson (2003), this gives students "more thinking space and can help all students track what is going on" (p. 2). As teachers navigate what students are thinking and learning, they use curricular and biographical insights to chart the course of their revoicing efforts.

Through revoicing, repetition happens naturally during the lesson. Such repetition provides CLD students with more avenues for participating in the academic conversation. Although revoicing has many potential benefits, especially for students whose first language is not English (Forman et al., 1998), one of the greatest is the opportunity it provides for the teacher to engage with all learners in the classroom.

Confirming and Disconfirming

Often teachers ask me, "Isn't it counterproductive to give voice to what students think a word means?" Some say, "Most ELL students don't have enough English language experience or academic background to know the words I'm going to teach." My reply is, "How can we really know that our students don't know, unless they have been given the chance to fully participate in learning?"

We must continually release learning to the students. Second language learners often hear a word and have a difficult time getting past what they initially thought the word meant. That is why we must provide space for them to talk with one another and come to consensus about the meaning of words in context. As students make sense of the vocabulary and the content, one of the roles of the teacher is to confirm and disconfirm learning. The teacher must confirm or disconfirm students' interpretations of the vocabulary and content during small-group interaction, large-group discussion, and students' completion of tasks individually. Consider the following scenario:

A CLD student sits in a science class taking notes. While she takes notes, the teacher begins to explain a concept using a "litter box" as an example to bring the vocabulary and concept to life for the students. The CLD student hears "little box" every time the teacher uses the term "litter box." At the end of the lesson she scours the textbook for "little box." She looks at her notes everyplace "little box" appears and still has no clue. She finally works up the courage to go to the teacher and ask where in the book it talks about the "little box" he mentioned in the previous lesson. He looks puzzled and says, "I don't recall. Show me what I was talking about." She shares her notes and the teacher laughs, "I wasn't talking about a 'little box,' I was referring to a 'litter box.' Now, let me explain!"

When we allow students to share their thinking at numerous points throughout the lesson, we increase the likelihood that we will be able to clarify any confusion before it leads students astray and detracts from their learning.

Confirming student learning also legitimizes students' thoughts and understanding. By going back to the text, activity, or tools they have been using since the beginning of the lesson to revisit students' original thought, the class is able to see the learning that has taken place and the value that their background knowledge had for the meaning-making process. Consider the following teaching and learning scenario. In what ways is the student's early thinking confirmed and yet disconfirmed, given the new context for the word?

As Ms. Baker's class talked about the vocabulary words on the quilt, two students in one of the groups were having quite a discussion about the word *apprentice.* The conversation was between an ELL student and one of the students that had been identified as gifted. The teacher noticed the discussion and walked over. For the word *apprentice,* the ELL student had drawn a television, while the gifted student had written "someone who learns from someone else." They both stated their thoughts on the word while Ms. Baker listened attentively. Then she said, "I think both of you may be right. Let's think about it as we read and discuss the chapter."

During the lesson, Ms. Baker stopped at different points to discuss how words change over time. Very skillfully she revoiced what she had heard from both of the students at the beginning of the lesson. She discussed the television show called "The Apprentice" and how the textbook was defining the word and concept. Toward the end of the lesson, she returned to the two students and had them partner to write about the word *apprentice.* At the end of the lesson, the pair shared that an apprentice was a person who learned a skill from another person. The television show might be called "The Apprentice" because, in a way, the people who are on the show are learning from the lead person. Although the ELL student's original thoughts about the meaning of the word had been disconfirmed, given the context of the lesson, she left the lesson having confirmed two meanings/uses of the word *apprentice* and she now understood their differing contexts.

Using an activation strategy that allows students to make public their word associations before the lesson enables the teacher to revisit and revoice those connections during and after the lesson. When we provide an opportunity for students to share their "understanding" of a word, distant though that understanding might be from our curricular use of the word, we are better prepared to scaffold the students to a new understanding of the word in the content-area context.

Students Negotiate Meaning

Chapter 1 outlined the relevance and importance of brain research in educating CLD students. Multiple fields, such as sociology, psychology, anthropology, and others, have researched the importance that student biographies play in the academic achievement of students from diverse backgrounds. The current findings from brain research also support this connection. As previously noted, according to Sousa (2006), information is most likely to be stored if it makes sense and has meaning. Students are unlikely to transfer information from their working memory to their long-term memory unless it has meaning to them. Educators need to purposefully select the activities and strategies that they employ to activate students' background knowledge and support meaning-making for each learner.

During the lesson, teachers should provide learners with multiple avenues of exposure to the vocabulary and content, in their efforts to help move the information into students' long-term memory. Willis (2006) states that "the more ways the material to be learned is introduced to the brain and reviewed, the more dendritic pathways of access will be created. There will be more synaptic cell-to-cell bridges, and these pathways will be used more often, become stronger, and remain safe from pruning" (p. 4). Jensen (2006) concurs, saying that "the human brain is designed to interact with the world and make changes, depending on the quality of interaction. If the interactions are positive and sustained, you'll get one set of changes. If the interactions are negative and intense, you get a different set of changes" (p. 12).

Using multisensory strategies with students is essential. "Drill and kill" strategies and the teaching of isolated facts and skills will not lead to student learning. Instead, educators should focus on teaching students how to become thinkers. When students reflect on what they are learning, they delve into their long-term memory to make connections between previously learned information and the new information. These connections are crucial. From a learning perspective, there is no reward in students memorizing material for a test and then forgetting it immediately afterward. Aiding students in the transfer of knowledge from short-term memory (where information can be permanently lost) to long-term memory should be our primary focus. When students demonstrate that they have stored content-area material in their long-term memory, we should continue to refer back to, and make additional connections to, that material to help students keep the information "alive."

Figure 8.7 presents a glimpse of the IDEA strategy (Ignite, Discover, Extend, Affirm) and elaborates on how teachers can use this strategy first to activate students' background knowledge and then to navigate the content-area curriculum, given the insights they have gained into their students' lives (directions for employing the strategy are given in Appendix F). This strategy helps to guide students as they negotiate their understanding of the target vocabulary and key content concepts. Joann McRell, a middle school teacher, discusses the benefits of this strategy: "The IDEA strategy is actually [designed for] a higher level of learning of Bloom's taxonomy and requires application, synthesis, and evaluation of the words, contrary to a vocabulary quiz, which is usually rote memorization."

IGNITE

- **Select an activity/strategy that will activate students' funds of knowledge, prior knowledge, and academic knowledge.**

  In this case, IDEA is the selected strategy.

- **Create the space and opportunity for risk-taking—there are no right or wrong answers, only educated guesses taking place.**

  Use visuals to activate students' background knowledge about the academic vocabulary words associated with the topic. Then have students do a "quick and silent write" (or use an alternative method) to document their knowledge of each word. Create the conditions for trust and respect during the activity by reminding the group that there are no right or wrong answers during this phase of the lesson, only "educated guesses" that will be confirmed or disconfirmed during the lesson.

- **Become a participant observer of what students draw, write, or share with peers.**

  Skillfully move around the room "collecting" the thoughts and voices of the classroom learning community to have for future reference. Be perceptive about where to stop and listen, glance, smile, or ask a question. Brainstorm how you will use the information you are seeing and hearing to engage and connect students to the lesson.

DISCOVER

- **Take what you have learned into the lesson to support vocabulary explanation, cultural connections, schematic connections, and validation of individual students.**

  Take every opportunity to go back to the students' words while "in the lesson" to make sure you validate the knowledge and understandings students brought to the lesson. Support CLD students in connecting their background knowledge with the content. Encourage students to take ownership of the words. Revoice what you hear and interpret to be happening as students respond to the content.

- **Consider the types of grouping configurations that will be possible during the lesson as you teach, address student misconceptions or gaps in understanding, and use formative assessments to reroute your teaching as you navigate students' understanding.**

  Use multiple grouping configurations to promote students' thorough understanding of the topic and to provide opportunities to confirm or disconfirm learning. Structured pairs, for example, often work well during the lesson to contextualize vocabulary in text.

EXTEND

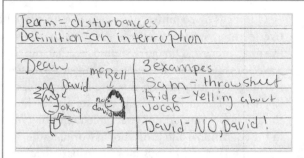

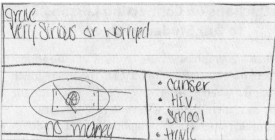

- **Provide multiple exposures to the words and text through listening, speaking, reading, and writing activities designed for students' practice and application of the new words and concepts.**

   Allow students to use both linguistic and nonlinguistic representations as they try to solidify their understanding of the vocabulary and concepts. Multisensory opportunities that emphasize peer discussion and collaboration support CLD students' higher order thinking.

AFFIRM

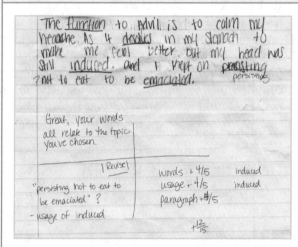

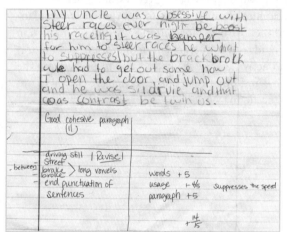

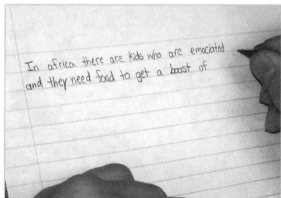

- **Provide opportunities for students to demonstrate individually their understanding of the vocabulary and concepts.**

   Remember to take each student's biography into consideration when designing options for student responses. Try to find a balance between promoting a student's linguistic development and ensuring that his or her response to the task will actually reflect his or her level of content knowledge.

- **Celebrate success!**

   Regardless of the degree to which improvement is still needed, take time to celebrate the progress and accomplishments of the learners in your classroom community. By recognizing the daily successes of your students, you increase their self-confidence as well as their willingness to take risks in making classroom contributions.

   —Joann McRell, Middle School, Kansas

See Appendix F for complete directions for employing the IDEA strategy.

Reflections on Connecting Lessons to Our Students' Lives

This chapter has emphasized the creation of educational spaces where *one size does not fit all*. Classrooms are much more dynamic when teachers become observers of the assets that each member of the learning community possesses culturally, linguistically, cognitively, and academically. By becoming aware of and using student knowledge as a catalyst to new learning, we increase the likelihood of all students finding both *sense* and *meaning* in the curriculum. In our efforts to help students negotiate meaning, we must find ways to make our instruction comprehensible to each one. To simplify this scaffolding process, we can use the CLD student biography as the foundation for our decisions regarding which techniques to use, for which students, and at which points in a given lesson. When we allow the biographies of our students to inform our lesson planning, and then we use information gained in the activation phase to guide our implementation of grouping configurations and activities, we are better able to orchestrate the conditional and situational processes that are critical to our students' academic success.

Our focus on cognitive, metacognitive, and social/affective learning strategies also is essential to our students' learning process. Our goal should be that our students leave our classrooms better able to manage their own future learning. The information they are learning will continue to change. The facts and skills that we are teaching them, though important, do not guarantee their ability to thrive in the educational and professional world. Rather, we must make the learning *process* more transparent for students, guiding them to see that their own background knowledge is pivotal to their understanding and retention of any new material. As we maximize students' interaction with the vocabulary and concepts we are teaching, we must be cognizant of, and responsive to, our students' (as well as our own) ever-changing states of mind.

Chapter 9 explores the role that review has in providing students with one more chance to make public what they have learned during a lesson. Authentic assessment is critical to our documentation of CLD students' linguistic and academic growth for each lesson, and it ultimately has implications for "the test." Throughout that chapter, critical considerations are provided for ways teachers can strategically employ the material used during the lesson to scaffold students to the end of the lesson.

CHAPTER 9

Gallery of Understanding and Knowledge
Assessing to Make Knowledge Transparent

THE PRECEDING TWO CHAPTERS focused in depth on how to activate students' background knowledge and scaffold instruction to support connections with their new learning before and during the lesson (see Figure 9.1 for a brief overview of critical concepts). In this chapter, I explore how assessment can be woven throughout the lesson, and discuss what final rehearsal and retrieval of vocabulary and conceptual knowledge might look like in the "after" phase of the lesson. Through strategic planning of how to assess students' linguistic and academic growth in all phases of the lesson, we as teachers can affirm student learning or reroute students in a respectful and caring way. Through continual consciousness of the needs of CLD students, we can increase the chance that their new academic understandings will be "linked and locked" into their permanent memory. Although there is no magic way of knowing that the information will be there forever, we can do our part to ensure that it is available for future use as CLD students continue to learn the English language and grade-level content.

Emotion, Cognition, and Assessment

How often do we see students who seem to understand what we are teaching only to have them fail the final test, leaving us wondering, "What happened?" Often, when we are in the last phase of teaching a lesson, we may neglect to replay in our mind how the student has performed throughout the lesson up to that point. These basic moments of reflection are key; they enable us to determine which activity or strategy will provide the most effective avenue for the student to "make public" for us the knowledge and understandings he or she has gleaned or constructed from the lesson. Although students must document their learning for our evaluation purposes, assessments for CLD students should be intentionally designed to lower the anxiety that many students experience when they are asked to recall or produce using traditional assessment tools.

Research has long documented how states of mind impact our ability to retrieve information. Stress, anxiety, and other negative states inhibit learning and have the potential to lock the brain into a nonproduction mode. For example, Sylwester (1998) states that stress can lead to impaired cognition, and fear can result in the physical deterioration of memory systems. CLD students' cognitive processes suffer in environments that do not provide multiple paths for demonstrating what they have learned. Vail (n.d.) says it best:

> The mere prospect of being asked to read aloud in class is enough to freeze some kids. Having to take a written test or exam, with its combined requirements for memory, reasoning, handwriting, planning and organization, can lock some kids' gears. The sight of a math word problem knocks some kids sideways. Scared kids perform poorly, and don't learn new information well. Anxiety is the enemy of memory. And, sadly, in many of today's classrooms, we see children whose intellectual energies and capacities are drained by negative emotional states. Emotion is the on/off switch for learning.

Given the volume of research on the role that emotions play in our ability to think and perform, I perceive assessment, as it exists today, as a form of pointing out to students all the things they are *not* capable of performing, rather than celebrating the learning they *have* accomplished during the lesson.

As teachers we are all fully aware of the assessment methods that are imposed upon us, both formal and informal. Figure 9.2 provides a glimpse into the types of assessments that provide point-in-time scores for documenting

FIGURE 9.1

Concepts Critical to Biography-Driven Instruction

Concept	Description
Culturally and linguistically diverse (CLD)	The preferred term to describe individuals whose culture or language differ from those of the dominant group.
CLD student biography	Refers to the four interrelated dimensions of a student—sociocultural, linguistic, cognitive, and academic—that influence his or her linguistic and academic development.
Classroom ecology	Encompasses the interconnected structures, arrangements, and events that influence student and teacher actions and relationships in the classroom.
Contextual processes	How teachers work with the physical setting, curriculum, and community of learners in a classroom to promote trust, respect, and engagement.
Activation phase	The teacher uses strategies to help all students make and document connections between their background knowledge and the key concepts and vocabulary of the lesson.
Background knowledge	Accumulated knowledge related to language and concepts derived from the student's funds of knowledge (home), prior knowledge (community), and academic knowledge (school).
Connection phase	The teacher uses what he or she learned from students before the lesson to make connections between what they know and the new information being presented.
Transparency in teaching and learning	Teachers explicitly inform students of the learning tasks that will be accomplished by a specific, planned strategy in a lesson, including the destination and the stops along the way. Students respond to the variety of opportunities provided to demonstrate through reading, writing, and speaking, their understanding of the concepts and language of the lesson.
Situational processes	How teachers coordinate teaching and learning dynamics throughout the lesson to increase engagement and guide students from the known to the unknown.
Revoicing	Observing students, listening to what they say, and repeating their understanding (through repetition, expansion, rephrasing, summarizing, or reporting) to validate, encourage elaboration, or reroute student understanding.
Affirmation phase	The teacher celebrates what students know and the progress they have made and uses both formative and summative assessments to inform subsequent instructional decisions.

CLD students' language development and content knowledge. Although such tools provide useful information, learning is much more complex than a paper-and-pencil test can reveal.

Jensen (2008) points out that the prevalent way of thinking about evaluation overlooks some of the most fundamental aspects of what we know about how the brain learns and the way the brain stores information in permanent memory. Relevant to the issue of assessment, Jensen (p. 226) posits the following considerations:

- Learning takes many forms that are not usually assessed (e.g., spatial, temporal, episodic, procedural).
- Memory is highly state- and context-dependent. The location of a test may not be where the information was learned or where the student will need to use the learning.
- Much of our explicit semantic learning requires tremendous repetition and meaning-making to become embedded for long-term retention. On top of that, most explicit learning is at risk for becoming outdated.

Office of Civil Rights (OCR)	Policy-Driven
• Home language survey • English language proficiency tests • Monitoring • Annual testing	• Focus on students' academic achievement • Standardized tests • Reading inventories • Content-based writing samples

Considerations Beyond OCR/Policy	
• Sociocultural • Academic	• Linguistic • Cognitive

• Nutrition and stress make scoring highly variable.
• The brain learns by making mistakes, not by memorizing correct answers.

Jensen (2006) reports that when we are teaching students and having them practice and apply information merely to memorize it and score well on a standardized test, we are limiting the learning that can take place when students learn through trial and error. When students are involved in making connections and experimenting with the information that is being taught, they are much more likely to become critical thinkers and use higher order thinking skills to learn the new information.

Jensen (2008) similarly states: "Smarter humans don't always get the answers first, and don't always get them right. But they do eliminate wrong answers better than their peers" (p. 175). This, he says, is not accomplished by having a teacher feed information to the learner. Rather, this goal is achieved through the process of the learner making educated guesses and then testing to see if they are correct. Thus, a teacher's job is to set the stage for assessment that both values the CLD student's efforts to make sense of the new information and provides meaningful feedback to accelerate his or her learning.

Throughout this volume you have been guided in preassessing what students know and deciding how to use the resulting insights to accelerate vocabulary and concept development. I have discussed the importance of selecting activities, asking questions that assess student understanding, and reflecting upon new ways to fill in gaps in student knowledge and understanding. Figure 9.3 sets the stage for moving through a continuum of assessment before, during, and after the lesson, culminating with a more accurate picture of student learning and performance that will develop right before our eyes.

Formative Assessment

From the first act of teaching performed as we embark on a new chapter, story, or concept, we as teachers begin using formative assessments as a guide in making decisions about instruction. Formative assessments are tools and strategies employed by the teacher before and during the lesson to determine what and how their students are learning so instruction can be modified accordingly while it is still in progress. In many ways, formative assessments can be thought of as a springboard for teaching. Their primary purpose is to increase student learning and engagement. Formative assessments are also pivotal tools for providing student feedback that is meaningful to the individual. The strategies, activities, and questioning techniques used during this time are critical for monitoring the sociocultural, linguistic, cognitive, and academic growth of the CLD student.

We can glean essential information by using preassessment and during-the-lesson strategies that provide natural opportunities for assessing how our students are processing and storing new content. This information becomes the catalyst for creating learning situations that meet students' unique needs. For example, general knowledge of a student's stage of second language acquisition, as described in Figure 9.4, combined with insights about the student's linguistic assets or challenges identified during a specific lesson, provides the teacher with the information he or she needs to make individual accommodations. Accommodations in types of activities used and questions posed are thus guided by what the student knows and is able to produce with scaffolding by the teacher and support from peers. Figure 9.5 (see page 130) elaborates on ways formative assessments enable us to link to students' biographies.

Using Preinstructional Assessment to Inform Our Teaching

In Chapter 7, I discussed how to provide a "canvas of opportunity" for CLD students to make public the knowledge they bring from their experiences in and out of school. In my work with teachers across the country, I have noticed that this seems to be the most difficult skill to develop. Much of the challenge lies with the perception that there is not enough time to "waste" on learning about the knowledge students already have on a topic or its associated vocabulary. After all, many teachers explain, most of their CLD students come from homes of low socioeconomic status and have limited sources of knowledge that would relate to the curriculum of the school. This way of thinking falls

FIGURE 9.3
Continuum of Assessment

Assessment should be thought of as a process that is ongoing throughout the lesson. Constantly reflect on what was learned at the beginning of the lesson to strengthen new learning during and after the lesson.

Before the Lesson: Formative in Nature

- What does the student bring from prior experiences in and out of school?
- What language is the student using to share what he or she knows?
- What connections to the lesson can be made from what the student has shared?

- Document the student's background knowledge.
- Reflect on ways you can use the information to explain new vocabulary or concepts, transition into the lesson, and reinforce what was learned.
- *This is an opportunity to "get into the student's heart and mind."*

During the Lesson: Formative in Nature

- Take every opportunity to connect the lesson to what you learned during preassessment of the student's knowledge.
- Observe for the student's academic connections and cognitive processing of information as the lesson is taught.
- Document growth in language and academic use of vocabulary as it relates to the lesson objectives and standards.

- Observe for links the student is making with his or her background knowledge. Take every opportunity to strengthen these connections and confirm, disconfirm, or reroute as necessary.
- Provide opportunities for the student to talk, read, and write about the content to give you multiple views of the learning that is taking place.
- *Document, document, document what you are observing!*

After the Lesson: Formative Becomes Summative in Nature

- Take what you have learned and begin to plan for one last review of the vocabulary and concepts to fill in any remaining gaps in the student's understanding.
- With all observations documented, reflect on how you will affirm what has been learned and not only what will need reteaching.

- Have the student practice with the content by reading, writing, and talking about it before you formally assess.
- Bring together all of the information (preassessment through summative assessment) to make decisions about the final grade.
- *Hold the student individually accountable.*

short in understanding just what a wealth of knowledge learners bring to our classrooms—knowledge that can be used to teach the content and accelerate student learning. When we show students that we care about what they know, they are more likely to care about what we are teaching and to perform at a higher level.

Preassessment informs the teacher about what the student brings from each dimension of his or her biography, as related to the vocabulary and topic of the lesson. This, in turn, provides the road map for making connections and for making decisions about where to stop during the lesson to fill in gaps that CLD students may have. Preassessment of knowledge makes it possible for us to truly work from the known to the unknown. Insights from preassessment guide our ongoing assessment throughout the lesson and frame the final assessment for determining what each stu-

dent has learned. Knowing where you are starting will increase the chances that you will be able to successfully navigate the curriculum and actually arrive at your final destination *with your students*! Preassessment before every lesson thus becomes the catalyst for CLD student motivation, engagement, and learning.

Using Formative Assessment During the Lesson

We teachers often become comfortable with our own rhythms of teaching and assessing as we go through a lesson. Bear in mind this word of caution, however: when we become comfortable, we easily can slip into using our comfortable "expectation" lens to assess learning without regard to what we learned during the preassessment phase. We

FIGURE 9.4
Assessment Using P-EP-S-I Ahh!

P-EP-S-I Ahh! is a teacher-friendly mnemonic device to help you recall Krashen's stages of second language acquisition. Knowing which stage your CLD student is in helps you to better plan/implement assessments.

Acronym/Student Behaviors	Teacher Tips
P **Preproduction** • Gain familiarity with sounds, rhythm, and patterns of English. • Rely more heavily on picture clues for understanding. • Respond nonverbally by pointing, gesturing, or drawing.	• **Preassessment:** Use authentic assessments that do not require speech (nonlinguistic), and tap into CLD students' sensory memory by making explicit connections to their previous experiences. • **During instruction:** Pair students with more proficient L1 peers who can translate to support comprehension and assess student understanding informally (e.g., with observation/monitoring of student work) throughout the lesson. • **Postassessment:** Check students' comprehension with performance-based assessments that do not require a lot of speaking or writing in English (e.g., create a visual representation of key vocabulary, act out key points).
E **Early** **P** **Production** • Use one-word type utterances; may verbally identify people, places, and objects. • Manipulate objects and ideas mentally. • Start using knowledge of letter–sound relationships. • Use routine expressions independently.	• **Preassessment:** Use visual cues to preassess CLD students' existing knowledge of key vocabulary terms/concepts. • **During instruction:** Have students work with a partner or small group to label or manipulate visuals and/or real objects that explicitly teach/model key vocabulary and concepts to assess their understanding of these terms in the context of the lesson (e.g., labeling visuals in English using key vocabulary). • **Postassessment:** Have students dictate or write sentences about the key vocabulary/critical concepts to assess their understanding. If the student is proficient in L1, you may have them write in L1 first and then work with someone to translate their sentences into English.
S **Speech Emergence** • Understand grade-level concepts. • Engages in much more independent reading as a result of increased oral language proficiency. • Apply and manipulate writing according to their needs.	• **Preassessment:** Use multiple strategies to assess CLD students' knowledge of key vocabulary/content before the lesson (e.g., visuals, graphic organizers, other hands-on activities). • **During instruction:** Monitor students' comprehension by having them explain, describe, compare, and retell information orally or in writing with a peer or small group (allow for grammatical errors or sporadic L1 usage to express meaning). • **Postassessment:** Provide assessments that focus on communication in meaningful contexts and expression in speech and short writing passages.
I **Intermediate Fluency** • Explore and utilize extensive vocabulary and concepts in content area. • Write and read a wider range of narrative genres and content texts with increased comprehension.	• **Preassessment:** Continue to preassess vocabulary knowledge with contextual/visual support. Students at this stage should also be able to write more about the key vocabulary terms in English. • **During instruction:** Use structured group discussions with concrete/documented outcomes to facilitate more advanced literature studies. • **Postassessment:** Incorporate more writing assessments with an emphasis on linking new learnings to past learnings/experiences.
Ahh! **Advanced Fluency** • Produce language with varied grammatical structures and vocabulary. • Construct multiple hypotheses and viewpoints.	• **Preassessment:** Continue to develop CLD students' academic knowledge by preassessing existing knowledge and building new academic vocabulary. • **During instruction:** Use interactive grouping configurations and multiple authentic assessments of students' work as they practice and apply new learnings. • **Postassessment:** Have students work in pairs/groups/independently to authentically demonstrate learnings via written or hands-on techniques.

Adapted from Herrera (2008), p. 69. Used with permission of KCAT/TLC, Kansas State University.

FIGURE 9.5

*Formative Assessments:
Linking to the CLD Student Biography*

Sociocultural Dimension

• Formative assessments affirm students' learning and give them hope that they can learn academic content with the proper support.

• Formative assessments can help make explicit links to the CLD students' families by involving them in the assessment process (e.g., a student might interview a family member about his or her immigration experience as part of a social studies unit on immigration).

• When multiple grouping configurations are used within formative assessment, all students have the opportunity to interact with peers from diverse cultural backgrounds and build links to new content.

Linguistic Dimension

• Formative assessments help CLD students see their growth in acquiring academic language.

• Formative assessments encourage CLD students to use English vocabulary in meaningful ways.

Cognitive Dimension

• Formative assessments allow CLD students to demonstrate learning in multiple authentic and contextually bound ways.

• Formative assessments enable CLD students to monitor their own learning and see what it is they "got right."

Academic Dimension

• Formative assessments allow for ongoing monitoring of CLD students' learning throughout the lesson.

• Formative assessments help teachers see where there might be gaps in student learning/knowledge that need to be filled.

• Formative assessments help students reach end goals.

Adapted from Herrera (2008), p. 116. Used with permission of KCAT/TLC, Kansas State University.

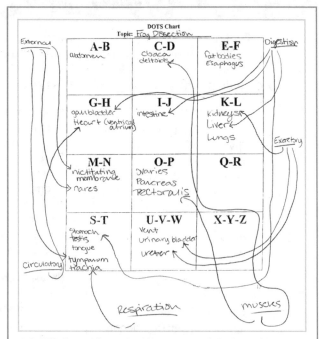

A DOTS chart (shown in Chapter 6 and explained in Appendix C) has been used as a preassessment tool for students and will be carried throughout the lesson as a strategy for learning about frog dissection. The teacher asked students first to come up with all the words they knew about the topic. As the students recorded words on their charts, they were also given an opportunity to discuss their known words with a peer. After this quick preassessment to see where students were in their understanding, the teacher proceeded with the strategy as a during-the-lesson tool with which students made connections to additional words they were learning. Finally, the teacher used the same tool for students' postassessment by asking them to write a summary of the topic using the words from their individual DOTS charts.

—*Brad Fabrizius, High School, Kansas*

often hear that no assessment is bias-free, and we tend to think about this in terms of the tests that have been developed by companies. However, bias can also exist based on the lens we wear while observing student learning.

Students' willingness and state of mind (as discussed in Chapters 6 and 8) and their level of acculturation have implications for the way they respond to assessment. At times, for example, CLD students may have feelings of anxiety, fear, or frustration resulting from one or more of the following:

• Amount of time the student has been in the country
• Type of ESL/bilingual programming the student is receiving
• Incongruity between U.S. assessment tasks and those used in the country of origin
• Level of linguistic ability in English
• Prior experiences with assessment in school settings
• History of success or failure in the academic subject
• Classroom climate

A CLD student's state of mind has implications for what he or she produces during the lesson. Therefore, we must assess students' motivation and engagement with an eye on their emotional state.

By creating a classroom climate that fosters positive thinking, acceptance, and respect, we better ensure that students

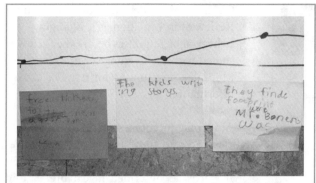

Comprehension of grade-level text is often difficult for second language learners. Having students work together and independently to make decisions about what is important in a text passage or chapter supports CLD students in taking more risks and deepening their understanding of the content. In this Relevance Scale strategy, students are asked to jot down with a partner the most important ideas from a text passage or chapter. Students' recorded details then are rated regarding how relevant they are to retelling the story/concept.

—*Leellyn Tuel, 2nd Grade, Kansas*

feel valued as members of the learning community. When we incorporate students' funds of knowledge, prior knowledge, and academic knowledge into the learning process, we build students' self-confidence and encourage them to see themselves as knowledgeable contributors to their own learning as well as that of their peers. And when we challenge students to think complexly in low-risk situations, we help develop learners who understand that wrong answers are part of the learning process and, therefore, are willing to take risks and share how they make sense of new material.

Interaction and Accommodation

The strategies we select to use throughout each phase of the lesson should set the stage for the progression of students' thinking, interaction, and learning. Effective strategies scaffold student learning and provide contexts that make students' cognitive processes more transparent for the teacher. According to Jensen (2008), some aspects of student processes are open for assessment whereas others are more difficult to access. At the end of the day, he states, "it is the cognitive skills—not the content—that will be the primary measure of a student's long-term success" (p. 233). Rather than viewing the final assessment as the only measure that "counts," we can maximize our strategies and time during the lesson to assess those aspects of student progress that often are overlooked.

The use of systematic and structured interaction to help students make public how they are processing and applying

the information being taught is crucial for assessment during the lesson. Students should have multiple opportunities to interact with peers as they build on existing cultural, linguistic, cognitive, and academic knowledge and skills. This can be accomplished when the teacher is aware of and creates opportunities for student talk, as discussed in Chapter 8, where the teacher shares information and then releases it to the class for discussion, clarification, or elaboration. These opportunities can take the form of partner talk that allows students to discuss for a short period what was read or said by the teacher, small-group talk that is structured around solving a problem or coming to consensus on some aspect of the topic, or individual responses to a question that will demonstrate what each student is thinking with regard to the concepts and vocabulary of the lesson.

Such opportunities for students to convey their thoughts and ideas provide us with numerous chances to informally assess and document their application of learning. Furthermore, they provide us with the information we need to actively accommodate our students' assets and needs in our instruction. For example, we often make accommodations for learners based on their demonstrated level of language proficiency during a lesson. We use the information we have gathered to strategically plan for partners and grouping configurations that will provide scaffolds that ensure the best situational context for our assessment of a student's oral language development and content learning. We also consider other dimensions of the student's biography. For instance, we determine which social contexts will allow optimal levels of social and academic interaction to occur. Figure 9.6 provides a glimpse of ways student interaction can be used throughout the lesson to promote CLD students' learning.

Posing Questions That Count

> Most teachers waste their time by asking questions that are intended to discover what a pupil does not know, whereas the true art of questioning has for its purpose to discover what the pupil knows or is capable of knowing.
>
> —*Albert Einstein*

Questioning is underutilized as a tool for assessment in today's classrooms. Observe a master teacher and you will quickly see a facilitator who has perfected the questioning techniques that get students where they need to be by challenging them to link to the past, think beyond, and use questions to discover and uncover new learning. Kinsella and Feldman (2003) describe the kinds of questioning that facilitate academic talk for different purposes. Questioning has the potential to engage students in talk that allows for:

FIGURE 9.6
Student Interaction Throughout the Lesson

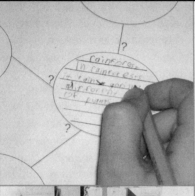

Students begin to engage with the lesson by activating their background knowledge and recording their ideas to be used during the lesson.

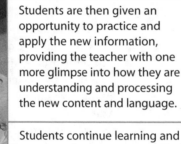

The teacher uses the information gained to inform her practice and make explanations and examples more connected to what the students brought from their own backgrounds.

Students are then given an opportunity to practice and apply the new information, providing the teacher with one more glimpse into how they are understanding and processing the new content and language.

Students continue learning and practicing both language and content in small groups. At this point, students are placed with peers that will challenge and support their academic learning and language use.

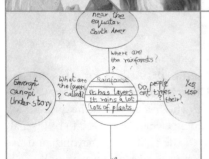

At the end of the lesson, the teacher is able to assess what students have learned and determine which accommodations and groupings were most beneficial for students, given their individual needs.

—*Denise Johnson, 2nd Grade, Kansas*

- Clarification and elaboration of learning
- Review of information as it is taught
- Rehearsal of responses before they are shared with the learning community
- Multiple opportunities for retrieval of information

Academic questions structured with a specific purpose in mind become useful for re-voicing what the students are learning in their own words, as described in Chapter 8, and thus become a tool for providing respectful feedback to CLD students. Structured academic questions promote academic dialogue between partners and within small groups; they nudge students to reach new limits with the questions they themselves pose. Releasing a question to a small group of students increases the chances that an $i+1$ response will become part of the group answer. As students negotiate answers to difficult questions, they consider others' perspectives, pose questions of the teacher that will guide them in coming to consensus, and evaluate their own lines of thought—skills that are precursors for effective self-questioning as learning occurs.

As students work together to develop responses to questions, the teacher takes on the task of reflectively observing student talk. The teacher gathers insights that will help him or her orchestrate subsequent dialogue to promote student thinking and learning. During this time, the teacher considers what he or she hears in light of what students shared in the preassessment phase and during earlier parts of the lesson. In these moments, the teacher reflects on ways he or she can scaffold to get students back on track, as necessary, by making new connections or revisiting previous connections to students' background knowledge and content understanding.

Learning Strategies as a Bridge to Summative Assessment

Student learning strategies have long been overlooked as a tool that teachers can use during formative assessment and as a bridge to summative/postinstructional assessment. Learning strategies can be a great resource for observation and documentation of thinking and learning throughout the lesson. In addition, learning strategies have the potential to promote simultaneous development of both academic knowledge and language skills. As we support CLD students in taking ownership of and monitoring their own learning, we increase the chance that what we teach will become knowledge that students can retrieve in the future.

Application of learning strategies enhances students' comprehension, motivation, and self-esteem and makes transparent for us teachers what has been learned and what needs additional rehearsal. Students who are taught to use learning strategies strategically, systematically, and consistently are empowered to utilize these tools for articulating their learning in multiple ways. The discussion that follows provides a brief introduction to the use of student learning strategies as a source of authentic, informal assessment.

Cognitive Strategies: Aiding the Brain

When teachers model and gradually release cognitive learning strategies for students to use as part of their daily routine, they create ideal conditions for students to share background knowledge and use it to accelerate learning. A natural progression follows: students use what they know, or what they surmise, to make inferences and predictions about the content or text during the lesson. Students can then use the activated schematic associations they have related to the overall topic to classify and group ideas from the new information. Mind maps, when used as a student learning strategy, provide students with a scaffold for performing all of these learning tasks as well as for summarizing what was learned at the end of the lesson.

Mind maps support CLD students in their efforts to conceptualize ideas, understand relationships among terms, make sense of their thinking, and better understand what they know (and don't know) about the content. This strategy allows each learner, regardless of biography, to represent ideas first in pictures and words. Then, with appropriate support and guidance, all students share their thinking and learning through more complex spoken and written forms of communication.

In this mind map, the student was provided the opportunity to make connections first to her own background knowledge and then to the story the class was reading, *Charlie and the Chocolate Factory*. The student's mind map of this information was then used to write a summary of the story. The teacher encourages students to use the mind map as a cognitive strategy to prompt their thinking when summarizing information.

—*Kendra Herrera, 3rd Grade, Texas*

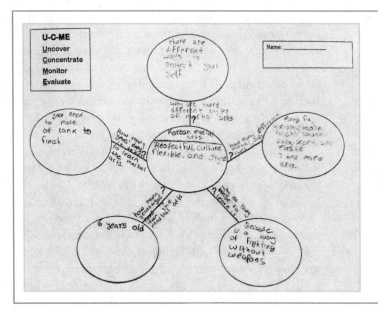

This photo illustrates how the U-C-ME strategy can be used to uncover student understandings and then connect those understandings with the new learning. Students' known knowledge was placed in the middle circle. Next, students were asked to frame questions regarding the topic and place those questions on the spokes. Students continually monitored their learning throughout the lesson, using the questions to guide their thinking. Finally, students placed their learnings in the circles at the ends of the spokes. In this way, the U-C-ME strategy was used at the end of the lesson as a way to assess student learning. (See Appendix G for a full description of the U-C-ME strategy.)

—*Kelley Ledesma, Middle School, Kansas*

Metacognitive Strategies: Thinking It Through

There's just not enough time! It seems as though we always are in such a hurry during every phase of the lesson that we forget to talk about and model how to "think through our learning" as we read and write. By habitually incorporating metacognitive strategies, we can support our students as they plan how they will learn new information. For example, we might teach students how to use their selective attention to focus on what is important or to define vocabulary and content concepts of a lesson. When students are guided to monitor their listening, reading, and writing, they are more likely to be academically successful at the end of the lesson. They can use the same metacognitive skills and strategies during assessment to think about what they know in relation to a prompt and to organize and express this knowledge. CLD students need to be able to evaluate their own learning, and to understand processes that can help them enhance their learning throughout the lesson and reveal it after the lesson. The U-C-ME strategy (see Appendix G) is a straightforward way to embed the skills of planning, focusing, monitoring, and evaluating learning as students proceed through the lesson.

Social/Affective Strategies: Finding Support

The use of social/affective strategies throughout the lesson creates situations in which learners become less dependent on the teacher as they make and elaborate on connections to the critical concepts of the lesson. Opportunities to work with one or more peers allow students to ask questions for clarification. When teachers configure groups based on students' biographies, they ensure student pairings and groupings that will result in challenging, yet low-risk and supportive environments. The Thumb Challenge (see Appendix H) is a great strategy for having students work together to rehearse vocabulary definitions as well as assess their understanding of how the vocabulary connects to the content. During strategy implementation, the teacher informally assesses learning while moving from group to group to observe. Ultimately, what we see during the lesson is the best predictor of the results we will see after the lesson. The activities and strategies we choose to use during the lesson as tools for formative assessment can become the scaffold for subsequent summative assessments. Figure 9.7 discusses how selected learning strategies can be taken into the final stage of assessment.

Teaching and modeling for students how to use positive self-talk (e.g., *I can do it; just breathe; relax*) to manage their own emotional responses and states of mind can also increase the likelihood that CLD students will achieve their learning goals throughout the lesson and be able to demonstrate learning during assessment. Figure 9.8 offers a few suggestions for providing students with ideas for self-talk.

Review, Rehearsal, and Retrieval

When the teacher holds every student accountable, language and learning are enhanced for all students.

The "after" phase of the lesson brings everything together—what has been shared, what has been taught, and what has been learned. Because all students do not start at the same place, it is common sense that they will not all end at the same place. However, every student will have gained valuable knowledge that will keep him or her moving forward.

FIGURE 9.7
Taking Strategies to the Final Stage of Assessment

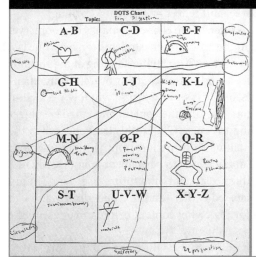

DOTS Chart

- **Preassessment:** Have students individually record their ideas and document connections between their background knowledge and the topic.
- **During the lesson:** Have students connect their known words to the target vocabulary words.
- **Summative assessment:** Have students write a summary of the topic using the words from their DOTS chart along with the target words for the topic.

See Appendix C for complete directions for employing the DOTS Chart.

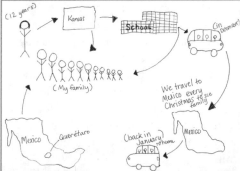

Mind Map

- **Preassessment:** Activate students' background knowledge by asking them to write/draw their schematic for the topic.
- **During the lesson:** As students use information from the text/lesson to elaborate on and add new ideas to their mind map, informally assess students' expansion of ideas.
- **Summative assessment:** Have students create a written summary of their learning, including new concepts, vocabulary, and skills.

See Appendix D for complete directions for employing the Mind Map.

Vocabulary Quilt

- **Preassessment:** Activate what the student associates with the words.
- **During the lesson:** Observe to assess student learning related to academic concepts and linguistic skills.
- **Summative assessment:** Have students use their understanding of the words on the quilt to create individual summaries, which are scored as part of final assessment.

See Appendix E for complete directions for employing the Vocabulary Quilt.

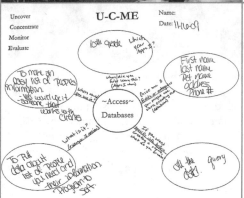

U-C-ME

- **Preassessment:** **Uncover** students' schematic connections to the topic.
- **During the lesson:** Have students create questions to better **concentrate** their learning.
- **Summative assessment:** Have students **monitor** their comprehension by answering the questions they created. **Evaluate** students by having students use their responses to the questions to summarize their learning in sequence.

See Appendix G for complete directions for employing U-C-ME.

Confirmation of Learning

Take a moment to think about one of your recent lessons. How much time did you allow at the end of the lesson to provide students with a "dress rehearsal," or final review, before their culminating performance? Did you provide students with an opportunity to voice what they had learned by talking to someone, writing about how they understood the words and concepts, or participating in an interactive activity? Did you give yourself one more chance to listen, observe, and reflect on students' learning?

Reviewing is often left to chance in many classrooms, yet it is the place in the lesson where students can have one last opportunity to confirm their understanding of the vocabulary and concepts and self-assess their overall comprehension of the lesson. It is the teacher's "window peek" into whether the class has met the content and language objectives. According to Sousa (2006), this last rehearsal is the final step for taking information from working memory (practice and application) to permanent memory, where it will be available to students for future use. The Thumb Challenge discussed earlier (and in Appendix H) also can serve as tool for reviewing content before moving into the last phase of assessment.

Remember that "anxiety is the enemy of memory" (Vail, n.d.). We help to relieve students' anxiety before the final assessment by providing them with an opportunity to review and rehearse what they have learned. In this way, we better ensure that the assessment will measure what it is intended to assess. Without time for review, our assessments are more likely to reflect the negative effects that students' emotional states can have on their performance. Review at the end of the lesson also gives us teachers one more opportunity to address any gaps that may still exist in student learning.

FIGURE 9.8
Student Self-Talk

The frequent testing and assessment of CLD students often serve to raise their affective filter. As a result, some CLD students experience mental blocks or acute anxiety, resulting in teachers misunderstanding or underestimating what CLD students really know or are able to do. Moreover, when taking a test or talking to a teacher, CLD students tend to overtly monitor their speech in English and become exceedingly self-conscious about their accent or routine grammatical errors. For these reasons, it is critical for the professional to teach CLD students how to use the self-talk strategy.

The following are examples of self-talk:

- **You can do it!**

  When taking a test or working in a group, CLD students may feel too intimidated and embarrassed to participate, because they think their English proficiency is not compatible or comprehensible to other students. Often they give up and opt to stay silent. Teachers should consistently encourage CLD students to believe in themselves. You can tell students, "You can do it!" Prompt them to think, "I can do it!"

- **Making a mistake is better than not talking at all!**

  Whether speaking to a teacher or in front of the whole class, CLD students are often intimidated. Thus, CLD students often hesitate to speak, pause frequently, or even refuse to speak at all. Teachers should let CLD students know that it is okay to make mistakes. You can help them feel safe in making mistakes by giving them plenty of compliments when they finally have the courage to answer or speak. Make it clear that what matters are their ideas and opinions, not the grammatical errors they might make.

- **So what?**

  A great way to boost confidence in CLD students is to have them repeat the words, "So what?" Yes, your answer was wrong, so what? Now you know the right answer. That's how you learn. Nobody knows everything! Yes, your opinion was challenged by others, so what? That's the fun part of the lesson. Let others know what you know.

Ms. Lynch, the learning coach, works with 6th-grade students after a lesson on Roman history. She is reviewing the vocabulary words with students and using this time to confirm/disconfirm students' understanding of the words. This opportunity for student review also allows her to see which words need to be re-taught.

—*Jackie Lynch, Elementary Resource Room, Kansas*

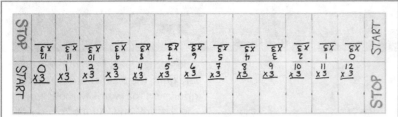

Depicted here is an example of a math concept strip Ms. Barton used with her class when implementing the Thumb Challenge strategy (see Appendix H). The students worked in pairs to review and assess the multiplication facts they had learned. Students moved their thumbs from one multiplication fact to the next taking turns. As students did this, Ms. Barton went around the room listening to her students practice and discuss their learning.

—*Cheryl Barton, Special Education Resource, Kansas*

Summative Assessment: A Celebration and Elaboration of Learning

Having made expectations for learning transparent from the beginning of the lesson, the teacher's next task is to plan a gallery of opportunities for the students to exhibit what they have accomplished during the lesson. The products that students are asked to develop might vary, based on the data gathered from formative assessments. The teacher's goal is to create opportunities to celebrate what students know and to encourage them to elaborate on their linguistic and academic learning.

Consider the following insights from three CLD students' biographies, and ask yourself how their end-of-lesson assignments might differ.

- *Alberto* is fluent in the English language for social purposes. He still has difficulty with new academic words. He enjoys reading to the class and is eager to translate when others need help. He processes information best when he is allowed to retell using his own words, rather than completing worksheets or answering end-of-chapter questions in the text.
- *Iram* can return to materials used during the lesson and produce definitions of vocabulary words and content concepts in context. He still is very much in need of a scaffold during the assessment phase. A tangible aid provides him with a sense of security as he uses his third language (English) to put his thoughts on paper.
- *Fatima* prefers to work alone and can easily generate definitions or sentences as they relate to concepts learned. She does well taking the sentences and elaborating on what was learned orally with a partner. She still has difficulty with grammar. The sentences she creates provide a tool that can be used to practice grammatical structures.

In the context of a lesson in which the teacher is using the Vocabulary Quilt strategy (described in Chapter 8; see Appendix E for a complete strategy description) to assess students' ability to use the target vocabulary to retell about the key concepts of the lesson, the three students might be asked to demonstrate their learning by completing the following tasks:

- *Alberto* is asked to write a detailed outline of what he learned about the topic, incorporating the target vocabulary, and then orally share his report with the class.
- *Iram* is asked to write what each vocabulary word means in the context of the lesson. He is allowed to use his completed vocabulary quilt as a resource, which includes his original thoughts about the words along with his new understandings.
- *Fatima* is asked to incorporate the vocabulary words as she writes a summary of what she learned about the topic. As part of the process, she will have a peer read her summary and underline in pencil any parts that are especially confusing. Fatima will then make minor revisions to enhance the clarity of her summary.

This kind of summative assessment moves beyond traditional conceptualizations of what postinstructional assessment looks like in practice. Figure 9.9 presents ideas for summative assessment tasks that can be used to help CLD students' progress toward their linguistic and academic goals.

Feedback based on summative assessments should be provided to students in ways that both acknowledge moments of excellence and recognize errors made—appreciating them as markers that indicate the route along which

---

FIGURE 9.9

Summative Assessment Tasks

Informal Summative Assessments

- Portfolios/E-portfolios
- Writing summary of concepts/topics
- Group project
- Unit grade
- Teacher-created tests

Formal Summative Assessments

- End of chapter tests
- Mid-term and final exams
- Policy-driven tests

re-teaching can occur. In this way, thinking and learning do not end with assessment. Rather, assessment provides the redirection needed for the learning process to continue as a shared responsibility between the teacher and the CLD student. The writing of Bernstein (1966) has implications for our practice today, as he describes the influence of models both of the past and of the future. We teachers continually strive to move students one step beyond their current knowledge, skills, and understandings by situating their learning within the context of past performance and helping them envision possibilities for their future endeavors.

Rethinking Our Aim: Testing and Grades Versus Teaching Through Assessment

Teachers always comment about my idealistic view as a researcher, educator, and author, given the demands and agenda of those who "control" what happens in schools and classrooms. My response is that in order to be ethical and caring educators, we must approach teaching, learning, and assessment by valuing what students know and are capable of accomplishing. When teachers only care about standardized tests and grades, we fail to value what students really know.

Merely testing provides teachers with a one-moment-in-time view of CLD students' knowledge. Most testing does not take into account the biography or the ways testing outcomes are affected by each student's starting point. Not taking into consideration the CLD student's biography makes end-of-lesson assessments inherently biased. Although there is much talk about differentiation of instruction, pressure exists in most classrooms to teach and test grade-level curriculum through a fast-paced, drill-and-practice approach that leaves behind the students most in need of differentiated instruction and assessment. Those practices stand in stark contrast to what research tells us about the need for pedagogy that validates and builds on CLD students' background knowledge and experiences.

FIGURE 9.10
Pic-Tac-Tell

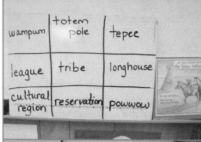

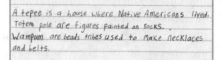

Taking the words from the vocabulary quilt, the teacher has created a grid using the words to move from the "before" and "during" phases of the lesson to one last review and then individual accountability. Using the quilt, the teacher and the students review the words together.

The teacher then moves to having the students work in groups to discuss the words in relations to the concepts that were covered during the lesson. She observes for the ways students use the words with one another, keeping in mind what she has learned about each student throughout the lesson.

Next, the teacher has students practice writing short paragraphs using their words and the target vocabulary. The words must be used correctly in the context in which they were learned.

At the end of the lesson, after multiple opportunities for practice and application, the student is ready to be held accountable for his or her learning. In Pic-Tac-Tell, students are asked to write their own paragraph related to the content. The teacher, having observed students along the way, provides a more accurate final assessment.

—*Kendra Metz, 6th Grade, Kansas*

Think about the sequence of learning and assessment employed in the Pic-Tac-Tell strategy (Herrera et al., in press) illustrated in Figure 9.10. Reflect on what can be gained from using authentic assessment throughout all three phases of instruction. Ask yourself, How might what I learn about my students throughout the lesson lead to a more accurate assessment of what they have learned as a result of my lesson?

Grades often have a negative impact on both learning and community. They frequently result in an environment that is individualistic, competitive, and detrimental to students' creative and critical thinking. A grade does not increase learning. It merely lifts some students, diminishes others, and encourages all students to view learning as a process of identifying what the teacher deems most important and then efficiently reproducing those facts and perspectives on assessment tasks. Much more can be accomplished when we strive for the development of a cohesive community of learners working together with a common mission.

CLD students experience true access to education when instruction and assessment are biography-driven and holistic in nature, rather than focused on mastery of isolated or decontextualized pieces of information. As Jensen (2008) notes, "The brain is not very good at learning isolated information, especially when it is devoid of any joy or meaning" (p. 178). By providing students with the kinds of learning contexts and situations described in this volume, we foster their intrinsic motivation and hope of success. This confidence in learning will translate into measurable academic achievement and better performance in the classroom as measured by grading systems. It is our responsibility as educators to think about what we want for our classrooms and to begin balancing school politics with what we know is right for the learners. This will require us to:

- Create an environment that provides CLD students with a safe place for making public their thoughts and ideas
- Configure groups that teach
- Orchestrate student dialogue through questions that challenge
- Move students beyond the mentality that only "correct" answers count
- Develop assessments that are focused on producing thinking and learning
- Use assessment results to provide feedback that supports students' future learning

One of our greatest challenges today is convincing students that assessment does not have to be, and indeed *should not be,* dehumanizing. We must redefine assessment as an indicator of progress that values each student's point of departure. Assessments should inform our instruction and guide us to make sound decisions regarding ways we can continue to build on CLD students' assets to increase their achievement and support their development as lifelong learners.

Reflections on Affirming Student Learning Through Assessment

Great teachers empathize with kids, respect them, and believe that each one has something special that can be built upon.

—*Ann Lieberman*

Transparency in teaching and end-of-lesson celebration and elaboration increase student engagement and create a community in which students know they can succeed. This perception alone can have a tremendous influence on the state of mind and motivation of the CLD student. It is much easier to encourage and support students who know they have been provided with all the conditions, situations, and tools to be successful. When we implement strategies throughout the lesson that provide optimal $i+1$ conditions for learning, students come to the end of the lesson ready to demonstrate their new understandings and skills on summative assessments. Such assessments take on a new look when the CLD student biography is the guiding force behind individual accountability. Postinstructional assessments culminate the lesson and provide more feedback than a grade.

A move toward biography-driven assessment will require us to revisit our own patterns and habits of teaching and assessment. By focusing more on students' thinking and learning and less on meeting externally imposed agendas (which frequently are the agendas of individuals who lack the preparation to understand culturally relevant and responsive pedagogy), we transform our classrooms into true communities of care and learning. As a result, students are more likely to experience greater academic success in the classroom and increase their achievement on standardized tests as well! As our students reap the benefits of internalized learning strategies, more in-depth comprehension of content, and lowered affective filters, enhanced performance on the "standard" measures of student achievement often results as a happy side effect. As is taught by the folk wisdom of many cultures, there are no shortcuts to the completion of a challenging goal; rather, the more we maintain our focus on the humanity and well-being of others, the more likely we are to arrive at our destination. While the long-term goals remain the same, the path I am asking you to take looks very different from those we often see followed in classrooms today.

CHAPTER 10

Culturally Responsive Teaching

Voices of Care, Hope, and Academic Achievement

Cultural pedagogy therefore creates the possibility of education being personal, and thus collective or social change, as well as intellectual challenge and the pursuit of knowledge, is possible. Recognizing and developing education as a cultural practice creates an opportunity for students to engage actively in a change process that aims to influence positively the way that they understand and relate to one another.

—*Debra Manning (2006, p. 54)*

AT THE END of this book and the end of your school day, it will be important to ask: What have I accomplished today to make the world a better place for all students? This is the question that really matters in teaching. Not long ago, before I had any thoughts of writing about my work in schools, I was being interviewed by a person who wanted to know what it would take to decrease the dropout rate, engage and motivate students, and give CLD students the "push" they needed to achieve academic success. My response was not what the interviewer expected to hear.

I explained that during my years in collaborating with both pre-service and in-service teachers, my only goal was to move them beyond the "I don't see color" perspective toward seeing the *cargas* and *regalos* (gifts and challenges) that CLD students bring to the classroom. Rather than seeing students from a "deficit" perspective, we should begin the journey toward educating them as if they were the next president of the United States. I told the interviewer that this was more important than any theory or strategy teachers would learn from participating in a course or professional development. I said that assumptions about what is possible need to be examined for their validity. What really matters is the biography of the teacher and how that influences their teaching and CLD students' learning.

The interview continued with my responses always coming back to knowing students' biographies, understanding each student's "point of departure," captivating students' hearts and minds, and knowing who they really are, including their dreams and aspirations. It was evident after 10 minutes that not only was the interviewer frustrated with my answers but also that he wanted me to provide him with some magic answer that was not so "touchy feely." Finally, the frustration with my responses got to him and he asked, "Aren't you a little too idealistic about what is possible with these students? They have so many problems in their home, they are so behind, and their parents don't really care about education."

I smiled and reminded him that it is in the "idealistic" world that teaching happens, because there are no limitations placed on what can happen. When you believe it is possible, you approach curriculum and the learner from a different perspective. As a teacher, you keep looking at what research has to say and setting up the learning environment to ensure no student is left behind. This, I have observed, happens most often in rural and urban, rich and poor schools with teachers who are "idealistic," who are passionate, and who care about their students. Through their teaching, such educators provide opportunities for everyone to have access, hold high expectations, and create low-risk environments where everyone is held accountable for learning. Then it becomes less about the curriculum and more about the student, hope, and academic achievement.

As a teacher educator, I have to ask myself if this is, indeed, too idealistic to make it part of the plan for teaching and learning. Yet, many who have committed a lifetime to writing about culturally relevant pedagogy in schools have documented through their work *how* and *when* it happens. Sonia Nieto, Guadalupe Valdés, Luis Moll, Geneva Gay, and many others continue to encourage teachers to realize that *all* students can and will learn if provided the conditions to do so.

What then is it that keeps us educators trapped in a box? Could years of research be so wrong that many in political circles discount what they have to say? I believe the alternative to be true. Politics and politicians often are driven by agendas that are economic rather than humanistic in nature. So much time is spent focusing on what does not work that CLD students are lost in the debate. Culturally relevant pedagogy begins with understanding CLD students and their families. It ends with teachers' ability to think outside the box, to think beyond limitations, to make no more excuses, and to provide equitable opportunities for CLD students to be successful in school. Teachers who are committed to proving the "status quo" wrong—and who have the necessary passion and commitment—have the potential to shift current political agendas and provide those all-important opportunities in today's schools.

A Different Type of Agenda

The complex and dynamic nature of our schools today requires a capacity to move beyond prescriptive programs and "laundry lists" of characteristics and behaviors that are to be expected from different cultural groups. Rather, educators must be prepared to understand the biographies of their students and the implications those biographies have on practice. Becoming informed is the first and most important step toward becoming a culturally responsive teacher. This means finding the time and doing what it takes to make the biography of the CLD student a priority within our classrooms and schools. As educators, we must understand the contexts in which we teach, and we must use the assets that students bring from home and community to create conditions and situations in our classrooms that value *all* knowledge.

One of the most significant goals of this book is to move teachers beyond the myth that what is presented in high-quality courses or professional development training for CLD students is "*just good teaching*" for all students. If this were true, more of our schools across the country would be performing significantly better than they currently are. Gay (2000) reminds us:

Many educators still believe that good teaching transcends place, people, time, and context. They contend it has nothing to do with the class, race, gender, ethnicity, or culture of students and teachers. This attitude is manifested in the expression "Good teachers anywhere are good teachers everywhere." Individuals who subscribe to this belief fail to realize that their standards of "goodness" in teaching and learning are culturally determined and are not the same for all ethnic groups. (p. 22)

If we continue to think, "Oh, it's just good teaching," we discount the rich diversity that students bring to our classrooms and buy into the one-size-fits-all mentality. A movement away from this, as discussed and described in this book, is about getting to know the student and family beyond superficial interest surveys, questionnaires, home language surveys, or other point-in-time snapshots of what students know, like, and can do. Our decisions and actions in our professional practice must create opportunities for us and our students to learn not only about the content, but also about each other as unique individuals.

Standards Set the Path

An examination of current standards set forth by different organizations reveals that central to the education of CLD students is the need for teachers to place the student biography—including family, community, and individual voice—into their lesson planning, delivery, and assessment. Yet, under pressure to have students achieve higher scores on standardized tests, teachers frequently place standards of effective pedagogy to the side in a rush to pursue a multitude of content standards. It is important to remember the need to slow the rush to check off a laundry list of standards and to keep our eyes on what is important for student learning. This priority is validated for us by the National Board for Professional Teaching Standards (NBPTS), Teachers of English to Speakers of Other Languages (TESOL), and other educational organizations that set excellent goals for pre-service and in-service teachers pursuing effectiveness in meeting the needs of CLD learners.

For my own professional development work, I have chosen to use the Standards for Effective Pedagogy and Learning espoused by the Center for Research on Education, Diversity & Excellence (CREDE, 2002) to highlight some of the language found among all standards developed to guide the preparation and work of teachers. CREDE's standards are the result of 25 years of working in schools, families, and communities and aligning what the research and development literature has to say is effective practice for students of all cultural, linguistic, socioeconomic, and academic backgrounds. These ideas and principles present valuable guideposts and a standard for comparison that any educator can use to reflect on and improve his or her current practice. Consider the specific words that are used to describe these ideas as they relate to the principles, tools, and ideas of this text.

I. Joint Productive Activity
Teacher and Students Producing Together

Facilitate learning through joint productive activity among teacher and students. According to CREDE, learning that occurs in "joint productive activity" toward a common goal is more likely to achieve the intended goals of the lesson. As noted in this standard's description, "Teaching and learning through 'joint productive activity' is cross-cultural, typically human, and probably 'hard-wired.'" Therefore, learning is maximized when:

- Students work in a collaborative environment to solve a problem or develop a product
- Teachers design grouping configurations based on students' biographies, including aspects such as language, academic ability, and interests
- Teachers support students by monitoring their collaborative efforts and providing feedback (e.g., through revoicing of students' ideas and knowledge)

In this way, teachers and students who may not share the same linguistic and cultural experiences begin to build a "common context of experience." This type of activity and production promotes student learning and creates ecologies in which students are more likely to risk without fear of failure.

II. Language Development
Developing Language Across the Curriculum

Develop competence in the language and literacy of instruction across the curriculum. This standard builds on the notion that a student's linguistic biography is an asset for his or her development of academic content knowledge. As CREDE notes, "culturally based ways of talking can be effectively linked to the language used for academic disciplines by building learning contexts that evoke and build upon children's language strengths." The way we ask questions, respond to student thinking, and use materials in the classroom must take into account the existing schemas and frames of reference that students bring. Teachers who do this encourage "students' use of first and second languages" and use "speaking, listening, reading, and writing activities" to support students' development of "content vocabulary." Furthermore, teachers who exemplify these principles use the language and literacy of the student as a foundation for explicit instruction of the language particular to the content area.

III. Contextualization
Making Meaning:
Connecting School to Students' Lives

Connect teaching and curriculum to students' experiences and skills of home and community. Contextualizing teaching and learning in the lives of the students we teach is paramount to their success in school. This means learning about the funds of knowledge, prior knowledge, and academic knowledge students bring to our classrooms. "What students already know from home, community, and school" can enhance our explanation of vocabulary and content concepts. Often our hurried pace in the classroom leads us to discount the value of listening, prompting, and thinking about how students are making sense of what we are teaching. As CREDE states, "'Understanding' means connecting new learning to previous knowledge." When teachers contextualize lesson activity in students' lives, they immediately increase the chances that students will engage with the lesson.

IV. Challenging Activities
Teaching Complex Thinking

Challenge students toward cognitive complexity. One of the most critical of all aspects of teaching is letting go of the myth that second language learners cannot participate in cognitively challenging activities. CLD students have the ability to participate in challenging activities when scaffolds based on their biographies are in place to guide their learning. This makes it necessary for the teacher to have the skills and knowledge to provide "responsive assistance" throughout the lesson. This standard challenges educators to move beyond "rote, repetitive, detail-level drills" and prepare lessons that are "cognitively challenging." Instruction in which students are "motivated to stretch" involves teachers "getting the correct balance" and providing curriculum that is not so challenging that it overwhelms, but challenging enough that it motivates student engagement and learning. Key to this process is providing feedback and using "meaningful assessment" that takes each student one step closer to achieving "high academic standards."

V. Instructional Conversation
Teaching Through Conversation

Engage students through dialogue, especially the instructional conversation. This standard is described as the teacher and students holding conversations that lead to unscripted sharing of ideas and knowledge. During this sharing, the teacher listens and observes for "intended meaning" and looks for opportunities to make connections between what is known by the student from his or her background knowledge ("individual, family, and community") and academic content in order to build "communities of learners" where the instructional conversation values every student's voice. During this instructional conversation, the teacher is able to engage the learner by observing, listening, and responding to what he or she has to say. When students are encouraged to become active participants, the conversation "reveals the knowledge, skills, and values—the culture—of the learner." It is in this type of conversation that that biography is valued and the teacher is able to "contextualize teaching" and take the CLD learner to $i+1$.

Voices from the Field

The following reflect the voices of administrators and teachers who have chosen to step outside the box and create ecologies that are grounded in the lives of the students they teach. Gay (2000) defines culturally responsive teaching as "using the cultural knowledge, prior experiences, frames of reference, and performance styles of ethnically diverse students to make learning encounters more relevant to and effective for them" (p. 29). I have chosen to include in this final chapter the voices of individuals who have inspired me to continue my work in schools. Through their vision, commitment, and passion, I have been affirmed in my efforts to pursue the "idealistic" world in which CLD students are supported in achieving academic success.

The reports that follow are taken from the districts with which I have worked the longest and where I have had time to see systemic transformative results. Other districts around the country, from Oregon to Pennsylvania, Texas to South Carolina, are adopting biography-driven instructional principles and tools as an overlay to the ESL programs they are using, and they, too, are beginning to feel the excitement that you will hear in reflections that follow. Readers who start incorporating biography-driven instruction and assessment also are invited to share their experiences with me.

The administrators and teachers whose voices you will hear have taken their knowledge and *acted* to do what is right for students, regardless of the consequences. For example, by going from a pull-out program to a push-in program that considered the biographies of students who represented 49 different languages, Hillcrest Elementary created an ecology of respect for their students and families. The road was not easy. Yet, through ongoing conversation and dedication to an "idealistic" goal, a new type of instructional conversation resulted for teachers and students in *all classrooms.*

Although we often hear that change cannot happen at the high school level, two administrators from Salina South High School share their journey of change. With high expectations for all, Salina South is on a journey of rethinking the education of their CLD students. Without excuses, they have moved forward in building communities of learners, where more opportunities are provided for students to learn from one another. Evident in this ecology is the value placed on all students' biographies.

The final three voices are those of educators who have lived and experienced what it means to be biography-driven. They speak with openness and honesty about the joys and struggles of finding ways to make their classrooms, schools, and districts places where every student of every background can be at home. By collaborating with students, families, and colleagues, these educators have found ways to make their professional practice relevant and responsive to the assets and needs of their CLD students.

Tammy Becker, Principal

Hillcrest Elementary, Lawrence, Kansas

Learning for All, Whatever It Takes

Transforming the curriculum for our culturally and linguistically diverse students and, as educators, rethinking our perspectives on these students was no easy task. But when we discovered we were doing an inappropriate job of instructing nearly half of our student population, we knew something had to change. Some of our teachers started thinking of how we could make our school community inclusive of all our students. As we started working with the needs of students, we found that the students do not see differences. They see each other as individuals all coming together. At our school and in the classroom we recognize our differences, but it doesn't set us apart.

The initial idea of working toward a classroom community came in 2003, when a group of our staff began taking professional development that eventually led to professional dialogue within our building about the way we handled the instruction of our students. At that time, we were pulling CLD students out of the classroom to work on materials different from what was happening in their grade-level classroom. That meant removing, at times, 300 CLD students from their 200 English-speaking peers—likely leading to stigmatization of the CLD students.

The more we worked with students, the more we realized that the Celias, Mohammeds, and Joses of the world need more than just being pulled out of the classroom and seeing a new face every 30 minutes. Not only was this a costly practice, but it also didn't recognize any of the CLD students' academic knowledge in their native language. We saw students from many Arabic countries sit in the library during the lunch hour and refuse to go to the cafeteria. We also saw that some of our students would refuse to participate in any Halloween-related activities. As we started asking "why" about many of these unfamiliar practices, we found ourselves with no answers.

The more we reflected on these challenges, the more we started thinking that since our students were being divided among so many teachers, none of our teachers really were aware of the biographies of our students. All we knew was that we had this student whose parents had filled out a home language survey and the district had done a LAS (language assessment) on them. We placed the students based on the numbers they received for their LAS scores. And when the students were pulled from their grade-level classrooms, they missed out on the content being taught, and we only continued to hinder their progress. That was a turning point in making learning a true reality for a lot of our students. We knew we needed to bring the students back into the general classroom; we needed to help them acquire academic language skills, while also exposing them to the content-area curriculum.

In 2004 we began using sheltered instruction, and within 2 years all students were included in the general classroom. This truly was the beginning of making students feel like they were a part of our community. From that time onward, we decided as a school that we can no longer make assumptions, and it is now our moral responsibility to support our students when they sit out at lunch hour during the month of Ramadan or don't participate in Halloween activities due to their cultural backgrounds.

During the process of implementing this program, I experienced resistance from both teachers and parents who thought that having ESL students in the classroom would take away from other students' learning. But by inviting parents to be a part of the school and being open about the changes and the research supporting our decisions, many parents began to see that when CLD students are in the classroom, not only do they benefit, but so does the rest of the school population. Now students work more collaboratively—across language and culture barriers—and share what they know, because now *we* know that when students work cooperatively, they enhance their ability to learn and retain what they have learned.

Every day I walk down the hallway of the school and know this is my vision, and each day I learn something new from our students. We are honored to have students in our school and classrooms who truly make our school a community of learners. Culture and language have become integral parts of our curriculum. Just the other day, our 6th-grade students together voted not to have any snacks in the classroom during Ramadan so our Muslim students don't feel excluded when the others are eating. This would not have happened in the classroom if the teachers did not share the vision of "Learning for all, whatever it takes."

Even now, 3 years after we completely implemented the program, I know that we must make a continual effort to provide culturally responsive teaching. We are working toward full implementation of a push-in-type program, wherein the students who need additional language support work with a specialist for half an hour on vocabulary development that reinforces classroom material. That means supporting our teachers and providing more than a one-time professional development session. It takes time and commitment to make sure all our teachers are able to meet the needs of every single student. All our teachers receive intensive training, including observation and feedback and ongoing professional development to learn new instructional strategies. We encourage collaboration between grade-level teachers and hold student-progress reviews, which provide a time for educators to work as a team to identify ways to help their CLD students achieve academic success.

I know that facing a classroom in which half the students are ELLs can be daunting. But I know it can be done, when we all work together to help *all* our students succeed.

Dr. George Troutfetter and Gary White, Assistant Principals
Salina South High School, Salina, Kansas

Valuing the Student Begins with Valuing the Native Language

Oliver Wendell Holmes wrote, "Every language is a temple, in which the soul of those who speak it is enshrined." As assistant principals at a school where English is a second (or third) language for a quarter of the student population, this statement highlights how important it is that educators respect students' language. When you respect language, you respect the person. From our experiences of shifting our own perspectives and redesigning programming for culturally and linguistically diverse students, we've learned the importance of respecting each student's first language.

We're almost ashamed to admit that for years we neglected the ESL population at our school. The first-year ESL students attended half days of ESL instruction and then were sent home, because we didn't know what to do with them. Students who spoke a language other than English in the general classroom were often referred for disciplinary action, because we assumed that if they weren't speaking English, they were off task. Now, after much professional development and training, we know just how wrong and culturally ignorant we were.

By understanding the difference between BICS and CALP, we came to realize that students acquire social language skills before academic language skills. Just because we might hear CLD students speaking English in the hallway to a friend doesn't mean that they will excel in the classroom. In fact, they might still struggle in an academic setting. But when we support students' L1, their second language acquisition comes faster.

Now we've created a more culturally friendly environment—one that values CLD students' first language and celebrates our diversity. For instance, we have bilingual teacher assistants to provide staff support. These assistants are often upper-level CLD students who help teachers translate and modify materials, bridge the language gap for students, and also earn credit for their work. Not only do these students gain valuable experience, but we also validate their L1 and show them the value of their language skills.

Perhaps most importantly, we've given these students a sense of hope. To be included now is to be equal; we are not going to lower the bar or let our CLD students slip through the cracks. We provide support with translation software and classroom materials in various languages. CLD students are also intentionally placed in certain classrooms. ESL instructors and counselors meet to discuss students' schedules, ensuring that CLD students are in a classroom with an ESL-certified instructor or, at the very least, that they are placed in classrooms with two or three students who speak the same language and can act as a support system. Even by utilizing content and language objectives, we move beyond thinking "I taught it and they just didn't get it." Now we reexamine *why*. And most of our teachers also realize that is good teaching for *all* our students.

Our preliminary assumptions that these students can't learn math or science until they learn English have been completely disproved. We've moved far beyond thinking we couldn't serve our CLD students in the general classroom because they'd be a detriment to the rest of the school. Having CLD students in the classroom has enriched our environment and broken down barriers between all the cultures in our community.

Scott Calder, English Teacher
Olathe North High School, Olathe, Kansas

From Self-Congratulation to Critical Self-Reflection

Every teacher believes that his or her skill level falls somewhere between good and great on the self-evaluation continuum. It is easy to understand that teachers find a comfort in the axiom that "good teaching is good teaching." Teachers honestly, but naively, insert themselves into the equation and feel a sense of satisfaction that they can meet the needs of all students in their classroom under the generic umbrella of "best practices."

I had been teaching high school English for 25 years. During all this time, I had numerous hours of self-reflection and self-congratulation, and I knew that I was a good teacher. As I did this, I never really thought about the many variables that should be considered regarding the academic and linguistic needs of CLD students. As I started working more with the needs of students, I reflected upon their linguistic and academic biographies. One of the first aspects that I reflected upon was the difference between conversa-

tional and educational English language. When I had a student in class who did not speak English at home, but did use conversational English in the classroom, I assumed that the student would understand the nuances of the educational language within the context of assignments, discussions, and written responses about the current topic. My thought was that if the student was not doing well on the task, he was just not trying hard enough. This led to several assumptions on my part as I continued with the learning process of my students.

Through coursework, however, I was guided to *critically reflect* on my professional practice. I was forced out of my "good teacher" comfort zone and started challenging myself to be empathetic with my CLD students who needed support to meet the challenges of learning content material with their age-level peers. In an effort to learn more about the academic and linguistic needs of my students, I continuously reflected upon the many issues surrounding them. The more I started working with the students, the more I started implementing scaffolding techniques for teaching my CLD students. I learned how to structure collaborative learning groups to accommodate my second language learners based on their biographies.

During all this time, I had to rethink my philosophy of working with students many times. As I implemented various methods to front-load vocabulary words when introducing difficult literature, I had to reflect upon the students and what they were bringing with themselves. During my numerous discussions with colleagues and reflections upon students' needs, I came up with the most valuable teaching device: a personal biography questionnaire. Students' responses to the questionnaire provided me with the insights I needed to support CLD students who had conversational English skills but lacked knowledge of educational terms or had not learned how to analyze content literature. An understanding of students' biographies truly led me to focus on my students and helped me think of ways to bring student voices into the classroom.

The more I thought about my students, the more my teacher's world opened up. One of the first revelations came up during my English class. Our class was reading Edgar Allen Poe's "The Black Cat," and my native English-speaking students were creating higher level and insightful literary collaborative learning group assessments about how the narrator had alcohol, domestic, and animal abuse issues. But I noticed that the CLD students were not strong contributors to the group work. After the lesson, when I reflected upon the students and the lesson itself, I realized that the book was full of specifics that related to an American context of various issues.

In my efforts to balance this situation in my room, I spoke with two of my CLD students and asked them to recommend a scary story they knew that also had a moral message. They immediately thought of "*La Llorona*." I found an English translation of the tale, and when we had class discussions and group work, my Mexican students became the leaders of class. The climate of the classroom changed immediately. The CLD students' self-confidence soared, and the native English-speaking students were empathetic to the plight of analyzing the literature of a different culture.

The Mexican students taught the class that "*La Llorona*" is more than a scary story; it is a preventive tale that teaches children to stay away from fast-flowing waters, to not talk with strangers, and to come into the house before nightfall. None of these nuances of the story were picked up on by the native English-speaking students. We had great discussions following the story. Some of my American-born learners were able to share out their own experiences of scary stories with their parents. The discussion that followed in my classroom was truly reflective of a community of learners.

I now incorporate many accommodations to aid my CLD students, but the most valuable is when I speak with the students about their native literature and infuse it into the curriculum to support my standard pieces of literature. The CLD students are gaining confidence in analyzing the standard pieces, and the native English speakers are enjoying expanding their view of literature through a whole new world of heroes and villains. This is truly what creating a sense of global community is all about.

I am glad that my CLD students are learning from the strategies I incorporate to help with academic and linguistic needs. After having implemented various techniques for a long time, I now am continually reflecting upon the many needs of my students and looking for various ways to incorporate the biographies of my students in the content. I try to make this a year-round focus for my students rather than a one-time affair, where we only talk about cultural celebrations once a year. This is something that needs to be embedded into the curriculum every single moment of the day so that the students can truly work as a community. It is this that gives me the vision to be always moving forward with the students in their academic and linguistic development. I have had several students talk to me about the connections they now are able to make with the content.

Every day our students remind us of the need for us to make instruction a reality for them. As I walk the hallways of my school and listen to the students talk in multiple languages and represent different cultures, it makes me proud to be a teacher and a member of our school community that welcomes and accepts students from every part of the world. I know that this will not be possible if we don't keep an open mind and an open heart regarding the students and their biographies.

Denise Johnson, 2nd Grade
Hillcrest Elementary, Lawrence, Kansas

Connecting with Parents— Connecting to Biographies

At Hillcrest we have gone through various cycles of transformation in understanding our students and what they bring. Going through this transformation, we have all come together now, as a school, in trying to do what's right for our students and do the best we can to educate them and make them the students of our global community. There were times when the path to reaching this goal was very challenging. At least that was my experience here at Hillcrest, when we were transitioning from a pull-out program to a push-in program. After facing and overcoming multiple challenges, we now realize what a benefit this new model has been to our CLD students.

I still remember the days when half my class would be gone for most of the day. As my students left, the rest of the class—including myself—would find it so hard to really consider the CLD students a part of our classroom community. When the students came back to the room, they felt distant and lost in the class. Now, when they're no longer being pulled out of the classroom and pulled to different places, I've seen my CLD students excel socially and academically. Keeping them in the classroom for the full day has helped their language acquisition immensely. And perhaps just as importantly, these students now feel like they are part of the classroom and part of a family. They have a home and this is something we really need to focus on.

As a result of having CLD students in the classroom, more and more teachers in our school are having dialogues regarding students and their biographies. A connection with the student's family and culture is a critical component in teaching the whole child. I think a little fear of the unknown can be an obstacle for both parents and the teacher. The parent often feels uncomfortable because of the language barrier and because they have to come into an unfamiliar environment. So, that means the teacher needs to go to the home. Home visits are important to make the connection work and ease the nervousness.

I now understand the importance of connecting with CLD students' parents. For example, we've had a student from Vietnam in our school since kindergarten. Year after year, we discussed how we could make Judy more a part of the classroom community. When Judy got to 2nd grade, we knew we had to do something different. We had to come together as a school community to find out more about Judy. At one meeting we decided to conduct a home visit. We knew it was not going to be an easy task, especially since the parents don't speak the English language, but it had to be done to help them see that we truly cared.

At the home visit, we instantly found the connection with Judy and her parents. She is now a part of the classroom the way we want her to be. From this, we learned that it's still possible to make a connection. If you can get Mom and Dad to see that you care about their child, you're already helping your students immensely. I might not be able to communicate extremely effectively in person, but by trying various methods of communication, such as e-mail, newsletters, and phone calls, I have more opportunities to show the parents how much I care.

Throughout my time at Hillcrest, I have found many other ways, in addition to home visits, to get to know my CLD students. For example, during my first year at Hillcrest, I had three students from Saudi Arabia. The three boys and their parents taught me about Islam and the traditions of their culture. I am a practicing Catholic, but understanding other religions has always intrigued me. I knew that gaining an understanding of their religion was something that I had to do in order to truly connect with their biographies. So, when I was invited to their parties, of course I said yes.

These parties were for women and children only. We talked and ate. The food was unbelievable, and I was privy to many of the ways of the Islam culture. This was truly an experience that helped me better understand one aspect of my classroom community. My students enjoyed introducing me, their teacher, to their family and friends. We had made a connection. The parents trusted me. The boys knew I cared, and I learned so much. This experience definitely paved the way for me to create a relationship and an understanding in my classroom that was appreciated by my students and their parents.

The more I have reflected on the biographies of my students, the more I have been able to get their biographies to become a part of the everyday academic experience in my classroom. One interesting experience that I recently had was when my student from Pakistan brought her father in to teach with me. He was a master teacher/principal in his country. He took notes and pictures of my lesson and activity and I took pictures and notes about his lesson. He even put together a PowerPoint presentation explaining Ramadan. The presentation fit perfectly with our cultural awareness objective. The family is now back in Pakistan and we still e-mail.

Last year, I had two American Indian children in my room. They were quiet, did not participate much, and their assessments were low. These children could have been overlooked because they are so quiet and well behaved. Yet, these students were examples of children who were not connected to school. I found out to which tribe the two children belonged, and I called the parents. Even though they had been reluctant to share in previous phone calls, this time I asked about them and their culture. I encour-

aged them to come into the classroom. One parent did. That particular parent became my connection to literature that day. She spoke about the Navajo Indian tribe, and I then read a story called "Annie and the Old One." We talked about the connections and that allowed my two quiet students to be spotlighted. We discussed the vocabulary from the story, and the mom helped me to illustrate to the students what many of the words meant. That afternoon we all learned about the Navajo people, made real connections to literature, and gained a greater understanding of the importance of everyone being a part of the class.

As we have transitioned at our building and reflected upon the needs of students, we also have experienced many challenges. For example, last summer I was given the opportunity to teach summer school to five ESL students. The money to teach was there, but transportation was not. This was becoming a true challenge for some of the families, as they wanted the students to come, but transportation was causing issues and making their participation difficult. I started talking to the moms about how to get their children to school. Only two of the parents were able to transport due to work schedules and lack of transportation. After several phone calls and introductions, we were able to work out a car pool. The connections I made with the parents were a critical component in the success of the program. At the end of the summer, I had our business partners donate massages to the two parents that drove for the car pool. It was a treat for all, knowing that we had found a way to overcome this obstacle. We had shared a vision of providing for the needs of these students and, by working together, we accomplished our goal.

Esperanza Wickert, K–12 ESL Coach

Reading School District, Reading, Pennsylvania

Hope for the Future

There always have been compassionate teachers who have pushed and encouraged and wanted to see all their students succeed, even when ESL was not a thought, much less a federal mandate. So how are things different today? Teachers continue to care, but they are more purposeful in their efforts to reach every student. With increasing numbers of CLD students, teachers are becoming better prepared to recognize students' biographies and how important they are in the scope of learning. As a K–12 ESL Coach, I have visited many classrooms and have seen purposeful teaching. I have seen how knowing the biography of students makes a difference in the classroom environment/teaching. With every classroom visit, I am reminded why I and other teachers came into the profession.

By learning the biographies of their students and validating who they are as individuals, teachers are able to connect with students and create an environment of trust and understanding. Because they are willing to reflect and reevaluate practices they may have implemented in the past, teachers are able to change their professional practice to better meet the needs of their students. Even novice teachers are able to create classroom cultures in which discussions about heated topics can be held amongst a group of teens that respect one another as well as each group member's beliefs and opinions. For such teachers, this is about more than just good teaching. It's about knowing their students.

I am blessed every day that I get to spend time with the teachers in my district. They are full of passion and conviction. They consider student biographies in their lesson planning. They listen and observe to make connections to the students' lives. Their students are actively engaged and know that they are valued. It is an honor and privilege to work with them. I am hopeful that by validating our students' cultures, values, and beliefs, and with meaningful planning, our CLD students can experience success.

Final Reflections

Every day, educators across the country enter their classrooms ready to achieve what they have spent a lifetime preparing to do—educate *all* students regardless of the challenges they may face. As discussed earlier, too often political agendas and school dynamics complicate our efforts to move forward and do the best work we can with students and families. Still, we must continue to forge new paths that will lead to the classrooms, schools, districts, and world we envision for our children.

Knowing a good story when they see one, in recent decades those in Hollywood have dramatized the lives of educators who have succeeded in spite of overwhelming odds. Some of these stories are based on real teachers who saw their students not as empty vessels waiting to be filled with academic content mandated by benchmarks or standardized tests, but as individuals who need meaningful educational experiences to succeed. By taking the responsibility to learn about their students, the students' families, and the community in which they taught, these teachers were able to look at their students as individuals and recognize that each has unique academic potential. Armed with this background information, the teachers were able to passionately advocate for the right to approach instruction in a way that would not punish the student but instead would awaken, challenge, and motivate the learner.

Not surprisingly, this same thread runs through the academic literature, as well as our own lives as students. The teachers who knew us first as individuals changed our lives.

Decades of study, working in classrooms, and my own life experiences have shown me that the only effective approach to meeting the needs of all learners—especially those who are culturally and linguistically diverse—is to accept responsibility for learning about the individuality of each one of them. In this book, I have addressed several key considerations that successful teachers can intentionally act upon to enhance student motivation, engagement, and learning. These considerations include (a) critically reflecting on our own socialization to identify assumptions, (b) understanding how these assumptions affect how we teach, (c) translating the theoretical fundamentals into our own practice, (d) planning effective strategies that link students' background knowledge to new learning, and finally (e) using appropriate assessments to determine academic progress. Such considerations effectively enable teachers to integrate their differentiated practices with models, curriculums, and frameworks currently in use within the school.

The consequential impact of such actions cannot always be operationalized or measured in numbers. We must embark on a journey *with* our students. The first step is to check for roadblocks—attitudes and assumptions that might impede our own motivation, engagement, and learning. Such roadblocks may result from our own socialization or may be the natural result of working under the harsh and confining conditions prevalent in many of our schools. Too often we are led to believe that certain students can only be motivated if we threaten their existence, remind them daily of their failure to learn, and ultimately push them out of school. We can help clear these roadblocks for ourselves and for others by continuing to build our own knowledge and skills, creating networks with other teachers and community members, and then advocating for the rights of our students.

Defensibility of practice takes place at two levels, head (research) and heart (passion). The head takes theory into practice, using methods such as those described in this book, and devising creative new approaches as unique as the classroom environment and as individual as each teacher. The heart is touched by the eagerness and potential each student brings to the classroom. We develop a connection and affection for our students as we work toward a common goal. Care and concern guide us in employing the methods and strategies we have learned to ensure that *all* students have access to academically challenging and individually meaningful educational experiences. In challenging the status quo and becoming advocates, we can make a difference in the way our students and classrooms accommodate the different learning needs of all of our students. The heart takes care never to forget the calling to become a teacher—and the strength of love in that call.

Appendices

Appendices B–H are available for free download and printing from www.tcpress.com

Lau v. Nichols: U.S. Supreme Court Decision (1974)

First filed as a class action lawsuit on behalf of Chinese-speaking children in the San Francisco Unified School District, the case of *Lau v. Nichols* progressed to the U.S. Supreme Court. Plaintiffs alleged that Chinese-speaking students were not receiving equal access to educational opportunities within the school system and that their Fourth Amendment Rights were therefore being violated. Referring to the Civil Rights Act of 1964, the U.S. Supreme Court issued the following ruling:

There is no equality of treatment merely by providing students with the same facilities, textbooks, teacher, and curriculum; for students who do not understand English are effectively foreclosed from any meaningful instruction.

Basic English skills are the very core of what these public schools teach. Imposition of a requirement

that, before a child can effectively participate in the education program, he must have already acquired those basic skills is to make a mockery of public education. We know that those who do not understand English are certain to find their classroom experiences wholly incomprehensible and in no way meaningful. (*Lau v. Nichols,* 1974)

Consequences for CLD Students' Educational Opportunities: The decision in favor of the Chinese-speaking students had "a direct and immediate impact on the proliferation of bilingual education programming in the United States" (Herrera & Murry, 2005, p. 118). Additionally, the ruling caused the U.S. Office of Civil Rights (OCR) to enact improved oversight of federally funded programs that are designed for CLD students.

Castañeda v. Pickard: Federal Court Decision (1981)

Parents of Mexican American children alleged that the Raymondville Independent School District (Texas) had violated their children's civil rights by (a) "ability tracking" Hispanic students, causing them to be segregated from other students; (b) discriminating against Mexican Americans when hiring and recruiting school personnel; and (c) failing to provide bilingual programs for language minority students. The Fifth Circuit Court of Appeals ruled in the parents' favor, reversing the initial district court decision. The ruling in favor of Mexican American plaintiffs in the *Castañeda v. Pickard* case was an important step forward concerning the rights of CLD students under the provisions set forth by the Equal Educational Opportunity Act (EEOA). The EEOA (1974) prohibits discrimination against any member of a school district including faculty, staff, and students due to race, skin color, or national origin. It also requires school districts to "take action to overcome students' language barriers that impede equal participation in educational programs" (U.S. Department of Justice, 2008).

Consequences for CLD Students' Educational Opportunities: This ruling resulted in the creation of the Castañeda Test, which is used to measure the degree of school district compliance with the EEOA. Evaluation of the effectiveness of programming is based upon three specific criteria:

- *Theory:* The school program must be based on sound educational theory.
- *Practice:* The program must be implemented effectively with adequate resources and personnel.
- *Results:* The program must be evaluated and proved effective, not only in the teaching of language, but also in access to the full curriculum—math, science, social studies, and language arts. (Herrera & Murry, 2005, p. 119)

Plyler v. Doe: U.S. Supreme Court Decision (1982)

The U.S. Supreme Court ruled that schools are prohibited from denying students access to a free public education regardless of the students' or parents' immigration status, invoking the Equal Protection Clause of the Fourteenth Amendment. This ruling not only sets a judicial precedent protecting undocumented students' rights to a public education but it also intends to provide CLD students with access to "quality programming that meets the Castañeda Test as the benchmark standard" (Herrera & Murry, 2005, p. 119).

Consequences for CLD Students' Educational Opportunities: In addition to providing undocumented students with access to public education, the *Plyler v. Doe* ruling prohibits school districts from requiring students or their parents to provide information pertaining to their immigration status, such as a green card or a social security card, as criteria for admission to public schools (Alexander, Alexander, & Alexander, 2000; Carrera, 1989). Public schools, therefore, are forbidden from acting in the capacity of immigration enforcement agents (Mid-Atlantic Equity Consortium, 1995).

English-Only Movements (1983–present)

According to the "U.S. English" Web site, "Declaring English the official language means that official government business at all levels must be conducted solely in English. This includes all public documents, records, legislation and regulations, as well as hearings, official ceremonies and public meetings" (www.us-english.org). Another English-only movement, English First, describes its organization as "the only pro-English group to testify against bilingual ballots in 1992 and the only pro-English group to lead the fight against bilingual education in 1994" (http://englishfirst.org). Thirty states have passed some type of legislation declaring English the official language; however, many people are surprised to learn that, at the national level, no "official language" exists.

Consequences for CLD Students' Educational Opportunities: While declaring English the official language of the United States might seem like an insignificant act, those in opposition are concerned that it could actually have far-reaching and negative consequences for CLD students, especially those in bilingual programs across the country. Many contend that legislation mandating English as the official language conflicts with the Courts' rulings in *Lau v. Nichols* and *Castañeda v. Pickard.* Both of these rulings afford CLD students access to bilingual education opportunities, and English-only legislation threatens to impede these rights.

California's Proposition 227 (1998)

The passage of California's Proposition 227 in 1998 dealt a powerful blow to advocates and supporters of bilingual education across the United States. Despite the outcry against the initiative from California Teachers of English to Speakers of Other Languages (CATESOL) and many respected researchers in the education field—including Collier, Cummins, Crawford, Krashen, Ramirez, and Thomas, whose research supports the effectiveness of bilingual education—the passage of Proposition 227 (also called the "English for the Children" initiative) illustrated how politics often takes precedence over sound educational theory. Playing into voters' misconceptions about bilingual education, the chief sponsor of the initiative, businessman Ron Unz, insisted that bilingual education was not effective for educating CLD students and that its implementation should be greatly curtailed.

Consequences for CLD Students' Educational Opportunities: Greatly restricting the access of CLD students to bilingual education, Proposition 227 includes the following provisions:

- Outlaws the use of bilingual instruction for LEP (limited English proficient) students unless the district is petitioned by at least 20 parents seeking bilingual classes for children in the same grade level at the same campus. The process is repeated every year that parents request bilingual instruction.
- Implements the use of sheltered English immersion for LEP and non-English speaking-children up to age 10 for 1 year.
- Places LEP children into mainstream classes after 1 year of intensive English instruction. (Romero, 1998)

Given what research tells us regarding the process of second language acquisition, it is unrealistic to expect that CLD students will acquire in 1 year the English language skills needed for grade-level content. Even with additional language support, the majority of CLD students require 5 or more years to develop the academic language skills needed for success in the grade-level classroom (Cummins, 1979).

Proposition 203, Arizona's version of the "English for the Children" initiative, which was again spearheaded by Ron Unz, places even greater restrictions on bilingual education, especially at the local level. The key features of Proposition 203 may be outlined as follows:

- Prohibits any "teaching of reading, writing, or subject matter" and the use of "books and instructional materials" in a language other than English.
- Restricts "waivers" of the English-only rule, for children under age 10, to those with "physical or psychological handicaps" (i.e., special education students); only for older children would schools be given flexibility to exercise their "informed belief" about what is best for the student.
- Allows parental waiver requests to be denied "without explanation or legal consequence."
- Requires English learners to be reassigned to mainstream classrooms once they have acquired "a good working knowledge of English" (a standard that remains undefined).
- Repeals all Arizona statutes governing the education of English language learners, including standards of student assessment, teacher training, program accountability, parental choice, and other civil rights guarantees.
- Mandates English language achievement tests for all Arizona students, regardless of their English proficiency.

- Invites lawsuits to enforce the initiative by any "parent or legal guardian of any Arizona school child."
- Holds educational administrators and school board members who violate the law liable for personal financial damages, which could not be paid by an insurance policy or other third party.
- May never be repealed by the Arizona legislature; while amendments to "further the purposes" of the law will require a three-fourths "super majority" vote in both houses, substantive changes will require passage of another statewide ballot measure. Crawford (2000/2001, "Tightening the Screws")

Consequences for CLD Students' Educational Opportunities: In describing the repercussions of the legislation, Crawford makes it known that passage of this initiative in 2000 has resulted in a "two-tier system of education," one for fluent English speakers and another for CLD students, by "restricting teachers' ability to address their [students'] individual needs." Researchers (e.g., Jimenez, Garcia, & Pearson, 1996; Nagy, Garcia, Durgunoglu, & Hancin-Bhatt, 1993) have long discussed the benefits of students' transfer of native language skills and knowledge to their process of learning English. Yet because Proposition 203 bans native language materials in public schools, CLD students in Arizona must attempt to learn a second language without the advantage of using their native language as a resource.

For detailed instructions for filling out the Biography Card, see pages 64 and 65.

Name:

Age:

Grade:

Country of Origin:

Time in USA:

L1: _____
R: _____
W: _____

L2 Proficiency
(LAS/IPT/Other):
O: _____
R: _____
W: _____
SLA: _____

Student Processing:

Learning Style:

Prior Academic Experiences:

Preferred Grouping:

School-Situated

Sociocultural Dimension
Home + Community + School =
♡ **Background**
Knowledge

Linguistic Dimension
Valuing L1 & L2

Cognitive Dimension
Implications for Practice

Academic Dimension
+   State of Mind   –
⟷

Biography-Situated

C.1. Overview

The DOTS Chart provides a window that allows students, through pictures and words, to make public their immediate connections with a topic. Used throughout the lesson, the DOTS Chart helps students link new learning to build on existing knowledge.

Phase	Directions	Benefits to CLD Students
Before the Lesson **D** **Determine** what I know	• Give students a blank DOTS Chart before the lesson begins. • Have students place the name of the topic/concept that will be taught at the top of the chart. • Start by asking students to write things they know about the topic/story, putting each word, term, or phrase in the box of the letter with which it starts. • Students can be encouraged to write in their native languages or to draw to show their understanding. • Allow only 3–5 minutes for students to write/draw.	• Empowers students to tap into their background knowledge and bring information they can share. • Can be applied to any content area.
During the Lesson **O** **Observe** and make connections to what I am learning from teacher/text **T** **Talk** to peers	• Have students write the target vocabulary around the outside of the chart as the words are introduced during the lesson. • Have students make associations with the words inside their charts with those outside the chart to demonstrate connections to the vocabulary words and extend learning. • Students can demonstrate associations physically by drawing lines between the words that they connect. • Have students share their associations with a partner or small group, because such discussion helps to solidify connections. • Students can add words that come up during the lesson, as well as words from text used for a reading.	• Helps students connect the DOTS by linking and building on what they already know to develop and reinforce target vocabulary. • Gives students something concrete to hold on to throughout the lesson.
After the Lesson **S** **Summarize** what I have learned	• Ask students to use their chart to do the following types of tasks depending on their language proficiency: • Use the chart as a tool to write definitions. • Use the vocabulary to complete a fill-in-the-blank/cloze exercise. • Use the vocabulary to write a paragraph. • The teacher can create a checklist or a rubric to assess students' understanding of the vocabulary words or the paragraphs they created.	• Provides students with a scaffold with which to strengthen connections and demonstrate their learning.

Name: _____

DOTS Chart
(<u>D</u>etermine, <u>O</u>bserve, <u>T</u>alk, <u>S</u>ummarize)

Topic: _____

A–B	C–D	E–F
G–H	**I–J**	**K–L**
M–N	**O–P**	**Q–R**
S–T	**U–V–W**	**X–Y–Z**

Mind Map

D.1. Overview

The Mind Map is an instructional strategy that can be used as a tool for documenting students' linguistic and academic growth throughout the lesson. Mind maps can be extremely helpful in providing students with a way to express their understanding through linguistic and nonlinguistic representations.

Phase	Directions	Benefits to CLD Students
Before the Lesson	• Before the lesson, ask students to create a mind map where they can put everything they know about the concept through linguistic and nonlinguistic representation (i.e., words and pictures). • Once the students have created their mind maps, encourage them to share with each other what they have drawn or written. • Observe as students share, to gain insights about their background knowledge about key concepts.	• Provides students with a means to focus on their prior knowledge in a meaningful way. • Allows students to make linguistic and nonlinguistic connections to new information.
During the Lesson	• Have students add new information and make connections between the things already on their mind maps and the new material they are learning. • Monitor students' understanding by closely observing the new connections they are making during the lesson.	• Helps students learn how to discover meaning on their own and how to make meaning out of new concepts.
After the Lesson	• At the end of the lesson, have students once more add to their mind maps by summarizing key points of their new learning—through pictures as well as words. • As a way of extending students' learnings, have them share their mind map with a peer, a small group, or even the whole class. • As a further extension, after the students have completed their mind maps, ask them to use that information to create persuasive or expository paragraphs that summarize what was learned during the lesson. • The teacher can create a rubric to assess students' understanding as demonstrated in their work with their mind maps.	• Provides students with a scaffold with which they can document and summarize key learning and concepts.

Mind Map

Student Academic Behavior Rubric

Name: _____   Topic: _____   Total Score: _____

Criteria	Beginning 1–2	Developing 3–4	Accomplished 5
Creative Use of Information	Student takes information from the mind map and uses it to create simple sentences. The ideas on the map have been depicted using a minimal combination of pictures and words.	Student uses information from the mind map to write sentences that summarize the important ideas of the topic. The ideas on mind map have been explained using a good combination of visuals and words.	Student uses the information from the mind map to write sentences that depict an in-depth understanding of the topic. The topic is being explained through extensive use of pictures and words.
Connections to the Map	Minimal link made between the concepts on the map and the paragraph.	Some connections made between the concepts on the map and the paragraph.	Extensive connections made between the concepts on the map and the details of the paragraph.
Knowledge of Topic	Student has basic information that reflects only a part of the discussion conducted during the class.	Student paragraphs show many facets of the learning gained during the class.	Extensive connections made between the concepts on the map and the details of the paragraph. Student examples and connections made represent the critical concepts learned as well as links to outside resources (past learning, prior experiences, and personal connections).

Comments

—Developed by Classroom Teachers

E.1. Overview

The Vocabulary Quilt lets students activate background knowledge about vocabulary they will need for new learning. By updating their quilts throughout the lesson, students will strengthen connections with newly acquired information.

Phase	Directions	Benefits to CLD Students
Before the Lesson	• Choose eight vocabulary words based on their relevance to the lesson. • Create blank vocabulary quilts by folding a large sheet of paper horizontally and vertically to produce eight boxes. • Divide students into groups of four or five and give each group a vocabulary quilt. • Have students write each vocabulary word in a separate box on the quilt. • Explain to students that each individual should quick-write (in English or their native language) and/or draw in the box for each vocabulary word whatever comes to mind when he or she reads the word. • Give students 3–5 minutes to write something for each word. It may be helpful to have each student use a marker or pen of a different color. • Provide students with the opportunity to discuss in their groups the rationales for the associations they made.	• Provides students with the opportunity to share based on their background knowledge. • Incorporates both linguistic and nonlinguistic representations. • Allows for use of the native language. • Talk with peers allows for associations to be made.
During the Lesson	• Post the vocabulary quilts to make "interactive word walls" that students can continually revisit during the lesson. • Give students sticky notes they can use to write down additional information about the key vocabulary words as they encounter them in class readings or in the text. • Have students add to their quilts new information gleaned from class or small-group discussion. • Working as a facilitator, refer to students' vocabulary quilts and revoice the connections between students' initial associations and added text-related knowledge. • Confirm/disconfirm associations from preassessment.	• The focus on key vocabulary allows learners to selectively attend to the targeted words in relation to the content/standard. • Revisiting the students' words/images written before the lesson reminds students that what they know can often be associated with what they are learning.

After the Lesson	• Have students work together in small groups to define an assigned subset or all of the vocabulary words one last time.
	• Have groups share with the class the definitions they generated.
	• Have students individually or in pairs write a paragraph summarizing what was learned.
	• For limited English speakers, the following adaptations can be made to the writing activity:
	  • Have students dictate the sentences to a teacher, paraprofessional, or peer who can write them.
	  • Allow students to write in their native language.
	  • Pair the students with more proficient peers who can help them write the paragraph in English.
	• The teacher can create a checklist or a rubric to assess students' understanding of the definitions or the paragraphs they created.
		• Allows students to demonstrate their integrated knowledge of the vocabulary and content.
		• Allows accommodation for students who have limited ability to write English.

Vocabulary Quilt

Student Academic Behavior Checklist

Student Name: _____

Descriptors	Yes	No	Comments
Pronounces the target word orally before putting the picture or the word in the box			
Relates to words using prior experiences and background knowledge			
Uses descriptive words for the target vocabulary			
Connects to the words using the native language			
Infers meaning of the words beyond the text			
Attends to every word on the quilt			
Predicts what the story will be about based on the words on the quilt			

—Developed by Classroom Teachers

F.1. Overview

The IDEA strategy enables the teacher to activate students' background knowledge and then guide them in navigating the content-area curriculum. The strategy promotes synthesis and application of vocabulary, rather than rote memorization.

Phase	Directions	Benefits to CLD Students
Before the Lesson **I Ignite**	• Select five to seven key vocabulary words that are related to the same concept. • To **ignite** students' understandings of these words, have them think about what they already know about the words. • Showing students visuals of the words will help to activate their understandings of the words. • Have students discuss what they already know with a partner or in a small group.	• Uses students' prior knowledge as the basis for "igniting" understanding of new vocabulary.

During the Lesson
 	
D   Discover
	• Students **discover** the meaning of the words as they are taught in context by:
	  • Talking about the words within the context of the lesson.
	  • Reading a text/story in which the words appear.
	  • Generating and writing definitions of the words within the context of the lesson.
	• Be sure to have students make connections back to their initial ideas discussed during the "Ignite" phase.
		• Helps students learn how to discover meaning on their own and make meaning out of the new concepts.

After the Lesson **E Extend** **A Affirm**	• As a way to **extend** students' learning, have them create links between individual words by creating a vocabulary chain, where they organize vocabulary word cards (one vocabulary word per card) to show a connection/link between the vocabulary words/concepts. • Students can first do this orally, by sharing the links with peers and then with the teacher to **affirm** their understanding. • Have students independently use all of the vocabulary words to write a paragraph that shows their understandings. Allow students to draw their connections if they are in the preproduction or early production phase of second language acquisition. • The teacher can create a rubric to assess students' understandings of the words, as demonstrated in the paragraphs students wrote.	• Helps students extend on their learnings through listening, speaking, reading, and writing.

I̲gnite, D̲iscover, E̲xtend, A̲ffirm (IDEA)
Student Academic Behavior Rubric

Student Name: _____

Group: _____

Category	Below Standards 1	Meet Standards 2	Above Standards 3	Score
Group Work				
Vocabulary Chain	Vocabulary connections unclear. The vocabulary words are wrongly placed in the chain.	Vocabulary connections made to students' prior experiences. Some vocabulary words are placed in order to show the connections that exist between them.	Vocabulary connections contain numerous details that relate to prior experiences of students. All of the words are appropriately placed in the chain to show the connections that exist between them.	
Supporting Details / Group Discussion	No details added to the word chain. No evidence of student discussion.	Some details added to the word chain. Students in the group discussed word chain details with each other.	Many details added to the word chain. Extensive student discussion evident from the added details.	
Individual Work				
Individual Paragraph	The paragraph shows no connection with prior knowledge. Details not presented in a logical manner.	The paragraph shows some connections with prior knowledge. Details presented in a manner that shows some logic.	The paragraph shows evidence of thoughtful connections with prior knowledge. Details presented in a clear and logical order that shows thoughtful connections.	
Creative Use of Information	None of the sentences constructed include the vocabulary words in the chain.	A few sentences well constructed and follow the sequence of the vocabulary words in the chain.	All sentences well constructed and follow the sequence of the vocabulary words in the chain.	
Comments				

G.1. Overview

The Thumb Challenge allows learners to practice language through interaction and to support each other in extending understanding of the target vocabulary or concepts. During strategy implementation, the teacher has the opportunity to informally assess learning by observing student interactions.

	Directions	Benefits to CLD Students
Alliteration　Simile　Metaphor　Onomatopoeia　／　Onomatopoeia　Metaphor　Simile　Alliteration	• Take two sentence strips or a piece of paper and write the key vocabulary words or critical concepts on both sentence strips or sides of the paper. If sentence strips are used, tape them together after the vocabulary words have been written on them. • Make sure to write the same words/key concepts on both sides so the students are practicing the same words. • Have students sit facing each other, with the sentence strips/paper between them. • Ask both students to hold the sentence strips/paper together with a thumb and index finger with a thumb on the first word on each side. (Note: The words should be the same and in the same order for both students. For example, Alliteration would be the first word on the strips shown at the left.) • Have one student start by reading the first word/concept and then stating the definition/meaning of the word/concept. • If the student who began first struggles or does not know a word/concept, the other student starts sharing from the very first word. As the second student shares his or her definition/meaning, the first student's comprehension is stretched to the next level. • If the second student cannot complete the words/concepts, the first student begins again with the first word. • The student who finishes first is the winner. • Be sure to tell students that if at any point they are both unable to figure out a word, they can raise their sentence strip in the air as a signal that they need help from the teacher. • As the students are sharing, the teacher can go around and listen to students' comments and check for understanding. • If many students struggle with a certain word, bring the whole group back and review that particular word again with the entire class. • **Teacher Tip:** Laminate sentence strips with key vocabulary so they can be used repeatedly.	• Provides a great review/ assessment activity for students across content areas. • Students do not have to rely on their ability to write their responses. Instead, they can state them orally. • The fact that students can challenge each other at any point stretches them to a higher cognitive level as they must justify their responses. • The focus is on engaging students and moving beyond factual knowledge to demonstrate learning in a participatory manner. Such participation makes thinking public and extends student learning and use of content-based English vocabulary.

Thumb Challenge

Student Academic Behavior Rubric

Name: _____   Topic: _____

Category	Below Standards 1	Meet Standards 2	Above Standards 3	Score
Oral Explanation of Words	No explanations are provided, or explanations are unrelated to the topic.	Explanations are vague, somewhat related to text. Explanations include verbal and nonverbal representations.	All explanations for words are appropriate, detailed, and specific, using verbal representations.	
Student Interaction	No interaction is taking place between students.	Interaction is only related to the oral production of vocabulary words.	Student interaction is meaningful regarding word explanation, and there is turn-taking between students.	
Summary Sentence	No sentence is submitted or sentence is incomplete and unrelated to the text.	Sentences are accurate but simple.	Sentences accurately express the major ideas in the text and are meaningfully elaborated.	

Comments

—Developed by Classroom Teachers

APPENDIX H
Uncover, Concentrate, Monitor, Evaluate (U-C-ME)

H.1. Overview

U-C-ME is a tool that allows students to demonstrate their prior knowledge and connections to the particular topic or concept by writing down everything they know or have experienced that is related to the topic or concept before the lesson. During the lesson, students' attention is focused on specific information, and growth is monitored at the end of the lesson.

Phase	Directions	Benefits to CLD Students
Before the Lesson **U Uncover**	• Give students a blank U-C-ME template before the lesson. • Have students write the name of the topic/concept that is the focus of the lesson around the outside of the center oval. • Ask students to write down everything they "bring to the table" or know about the topic/concept inside the center oval. • Encourage students to write down information in their native language if they prefer. • Allow only 2–3 minutes for students to write.	• Uncovers what students already know, enabling them to build from the *known* to the *unknown*.
During the Lesson **C Concentrate**	• Once students have finished with the uncovering phase, have them think of specific questions they may have about the topic. Model this first by posing sample questions for two or three of the spokes. • Generate questions that require students' higher order thinking skills. • Have students pose their own questions on the remaining spokes. These questions will become the guide for student learning. • During instruction, make sure to concentrate on information that can be used to answer students' questions. • To guide students, it may be helpful to create a whole-class U-C-ME template on which key learning can be documented.	• Helps students learn how to focus on critical concepts during the lesson.

After the Lesson
 	
M   Monitor
 	
E   Evaluate
	• Have students monitor their learning by placing responses to each of the questions posed in the corresponding ovals.
	• Final evaluation of student understanding can be done by having students use what was in the ovals to summarize what they learned about the topic or concept:
	  • In written form (persuasive or narrative paragraph).
	  • In oral conversations with a peer (discussing what was learned and where or how it was learned).
		• Provides students with a scaffold they can use to document and summarize key learning.

Uncover, Concentrate, Monitor, Evaluate (U-C-ME)
Student Academic Behavior Rubric

Teacher Name: _____

Student Name: _____

Category	Below Standards 1	Meet Standards 2	Above Standards 3	Score
Sequencing	Many of the support details or arguments are not presented in an expected or logical manner.	Arguments and support are provided in a fairly logical order and are easy to follow.	Arguments and support are provided in logical order using the discussions from the class.	
Paragraph Narrative	Only a few arguments are specific to the chart.	Arguments are specific to the U-C-ME chart but do not go beyond the class discussion.	Arguments in the paragraph are specific to the U-C-ME chart and some even go beyond the class discussion.	
Sentence Structure	None of the constructed sentences follow the sequence of the U-C-ME chart.	A few sentences are well constructed and follow some sequence of the U-C-ME chart.	All sentences are well constructed and follow the sequence of the U-C-ME chart.	
Connections to Prior Knowledge	The paragraph shows no connection with the prior knowledge.	The paragraph shows some connections with the prior knowledge as shown through the U-C-ME chart.	The paragraph shows evidence of thoughtful connections with prior knowledge as shown on the U-C-ME chart.	

Comments

—Developed by Classroom Teachers

U-C-ME

Name: _____

Date: _____

Uncover
Concentrate
Monitor
Evaluate

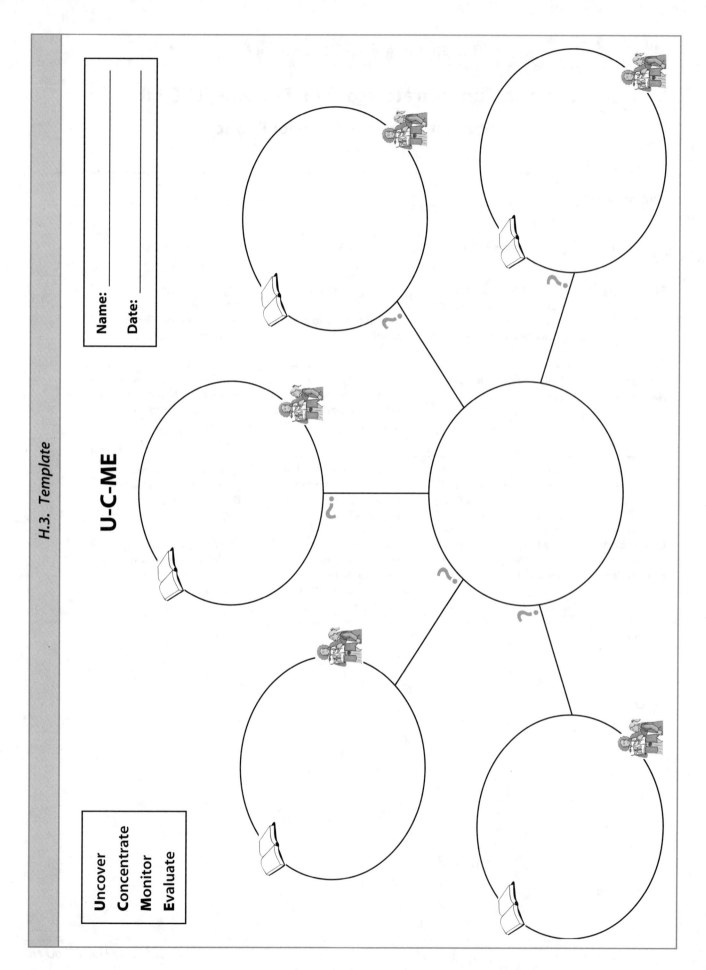

References

Afflerbach, P., Pearson, P., & Paris, S. G. (2008, February). Clarifying differences between reading skills and reading strategies. *The Reading Teacher, 61*(5), 364–373.

Alexander, B. (2003). (Re)visioning the ethnographic site: Interpretive ethnography as a method of pedagogical reflexivity and scholarly production. *Qualitative Inquiry, 9*(3), 416–441.

Alexander, K., Alexander, M. D., & Alexander, D. (2000). *American public school law* (5th ed.). Belmont, CA: Wadsworth.

Aljaafreh, A., & Lantolf, J. P. (1994). Negative feedback as regulation and second language learning in the zone of proximal development. *The Modern Language Journal, 78*(4), 465–483.

Allen, B. A., & Butler, L. (1996). The effects of music and movement opportunity on the analogical reasoning performance of African American and White school children: A preliminary study. *Journal of Black Psychology, 22*(3), 222–232.

Anderson, J. R. (1976). *Language, memory, and thought.* Hillsdale, NJ: Erlbaum.

Anderson, J. R. (1983). *The architecture of cognition.* Cambridge, MA: Harvard University Press.

Anderson, J. R. (1985). *Cognitive psychology and its implications* (2nd ed.). New York: Freeman.

Anderson, L. W. (Ed.), Krathwohl, D. R. (Ed.), Airasian, P. W., Cruikshank, K. A., Mayer, R. E., Pintrich, P. R., et al. (2001). *A taxonomy for learning, teaching, and assessing: A revision of Bloom's Taxonomy of Educational Objectives* (Complete edition). New York: Longman.

August, D., Carlo, M., Dressler, C., & Snow, C. (2005). The critical role of vocabulary development for English language learners. *Learning Disabilities Research & Practice, 20*(1), 50–57.

Babad, E. (1993). Teachers' differential behavior. *Educational Psychology Review, 5*, 347–376.

Ballard & Tighe. (2004). *IDEA Proficiency Test (IPT).* Brea, CA: Author.

Beck, I. L., McKeown, M. G., & Kucan, L. (2002). *Bringing words to life: Robust vocabulary instruction.* New York: Guilford.

Bennett, C. I. (1995). *Comprehensive multicultural education: Theory and practice* (3rd ed.). Boston: Allyn & Bacon.

Berman, P., Chambers, J., Gandara, P., McLaughlin, B., Minicucci, C., Nelson, B., et al. (1992). *Meeting the challenge of language diversity: An evaluation of programs for pupils with limited English proficiency* (Executive summary, Vol. I). Berkeley, CA: BW Associates.

Bernstein, N. A. (1966). *Essays on the physiology of movement and physiology of activity.* Moscow: Meditsina. (In Russian)

Biemans, H. J. A., & Simons, P. R. (1996). Contact-2: A computer-assisted instructional strategy for promoting conceptual change. *Instructional Science, 24*(2), 157–176.

Bloom, B. S. (Ed.), Engelhart, M. D., Furst, E. J., Hill, W. H., & Krathwohl, D. R. (1956). *Taxonomy of educational objectives: The classification of educational goals. Handbook I: Cognitive domain.* New York: David McKay.

Boggs, S. T. (1985). The meaning of questions and narratives to Hawaiian children. In C. B. Cazden, V. H. John, & D. Hymes (Eds.), *Functions of language in the classroom* (pp. 299–327). Prospect Heights, IL: Waveland.

Bowers, C. A., & Flinders, D. (1990). *An ecological approach to classroom patterns of language, thought, and culture.* New York: Teachers College Press.

Bransford, J. D., Brown, A. L., & Cocking, R. R. (2000). *How people learn: Brain, mind, experience, and school.* Washington, DC: National Academy Press.

Brock, C. H., & Raphael, T. E. (2005). *Windows into language, literacy, and culture: Insights from an English language learner.* Newark, DE: International Reading Association.

Brophy, J. E. (1982). How teachers influence what is taught and learned in classrooms. *Elementary School Journal, 83*(1), 1–13.

Brown, A. L. (1980). Metacognitive development and reading. In R. J. Spiro, B. C. Bruce, & W. F. Brewer (Eds.), *Theoretical issues in reading comprehension* (pp. 453–481). Hillsdale, NJ: Lawrence Erlbaum.

Bruner, J. (1996). *The culture of education.* Cambridge, MA: Harvard University Press.

Buzan, T. (1983). *Use both sides of your brain: New techniques to help you read efficiently, study effectively, solve problems, remember more, think clearly.* New York: E. P. Dutton.

Byers, P., & Byers, H. (1985). Nonverbal communication and the education of children. In C. B. Cazden, V. P. John, & D. Hymes (Eds.), *Functions of language in the classroom* (pp. 3–31). Prospect Heights, IL: Waveland.

Caine, R. N., & Caine, G. (1991). *Making connections: Teaching and the human brain.* Alexandria, VA: Association for Supervision and Curriculum Development.

Calderón, M. (2007). *Teaching reading to English language learners, grades 6–12: A framework for improving achievement in the content areas.* Thousand Oaks, CA: Corwin Press.

California State Department of Education. (1994). *Building bilingual instruction: Putting the pieces together.* Sacramento: Bilingual Education Office. Retrieved July 10, 2009, from http://pubs.cde.ca.gov/tcsii/documentlibrary/englishlearners.aspx#fn4

Carlo, M. S., August, D., McLaughlin, B., Snow, C. E., Dressler, C., Lippman, D., et al. (2004). Closing the gap: Addressing the vocabulary needs of English-language learners in bilingual and mainstream classrooms. *Reading Research Quarterly, 39*(2), 188–215.

Carrera, J. W. (1989). *Immigrant students: Their legal right of access to public schools.* Boston: National Coalition of Advocates for Students.

Center for Research on Education, Diversity & Excellence (CREDE). (2002). *The Standards for Effective Pedagogy and Learning.* Retrieved January 5, 2010, from http://gse.berkeley.edu/research/credearchive/standards/stand_indic.shtml

Chamberlain, S. P. (2005). Recognizing and responding to cultural differences in the education of culturally and linguistically diverse learners. *Intervention in School and Clinic, 40*(4), 195–211.

Chamot, A., & O'Malley, J. M. (1994). *The CALLA handbook: Implementing the cognitive academic language learning approach.* New York: Addison-Wesley.

Chapin, S. H., O'Connor, C., & Anderson, N. C. (2003, Fall). Classroom discussions using math talk in elementary classrooms. *Math Solutions Online Newsletter, 11.* Retrieved June 18, 2008, from www.mathsolutions.com/documents/0-941355-53-5_L.pdf

Charney, R. S. (2002). *Teaching children to care: Classroom management for ethical and academic growth, K–8* (Rev. ed.). Greenfield, MA: Northeast Foundation for Children.

Chater, N., & Manning, C. D. (2006). Probabilistic models of language processing and acquisition. *TRENDS in Cognitive Sciences, 10*(7), 335–344.

Christensen, L. (2000). *Reading, writing, and rising up: Teaching about social justice and the power of the written word.* Milwaukee, WI: Rethinking Schools.

Clandinin, D. J., & Connelly, F. M. (1995). *Teachers' professional knowledge landscapes.* New York: Teachers College Press.

Conant, B. (n.d.). *Learning: What we've learned.* Retrieved February 9, 2009, from http://users.stargate.net/~cokids/article learning.html

Cooper, H., & Good, T. (1983). *Pygmalion grows up: Studies in the expectation communication process.* New York: Longman.

Cooperstein, S. E., & Kocevar-Weidinger, E. (2004). Beyond active learning: A constructivist approach to learning. *Reference Services Review, 32*(2), 141–148.

Crawford, J. (2000/2001, Winter). Bilingual education: Strike two. *Rethinking Schools Online, 15*(2). Retrieved July 30, 2009, from www.rethinkingschools.org/archive/15_02/Az152.shtml

Cremin, L. A. (1976). *Public education.* New York: Public Books.

Cummins, J. (1979). Cognitive/academic language proficiency, linguistic interdependence, the optimum age question and some other matters. *Working Papers on Bilingualism,* No. 19, 121–129.

Cummins, J. (1981). The role of primary language development in promoting educational success for language minority students. In C. F. Leyba (Ed.), *Schooling and language minority students: A theoretical framework* (pp. 3–49). Los Angeles: Evaluation, Dissemination and Assessment Center, CSULA.

Cummins, J. (1996). *Negotiating identities: Education for empowerment in a diverse society.* Los Angeles: California Association for Bilingual Education.

Cummins, J. (1998). Language issues and educational change. In A. Hargreaves, A. Lieberman, M. Fullan, & D. Hopkins (Eds.), *International handbook of educational change* (pp. 440–459). Dordrecht, Netherlands: Kluwer Academic.

Cummins, J. (2000). *Language, power, and pedagogy: Bilingual children in the crossfire.* Clevedon, UK: Multilingual Matters.

Cushner, K., McClelland, A., & Safford, P. (2006). *Human diversity in education: An integrative approach* (5th ed.). New York: McGraw-Hill.

Delgado-Gaitan, C. (1987). Traditions and transitions in the learning process of Mexican children: An ethnographic view. In G. Spindler & L. Spindler (Eds.), *Interpretive ethnography of education: At home and abroad* (pp. 333–359). Hillsdale, NJ: Lawrence Erlbaum.

Delpit, L. D. (1988). The silenced dialogue: Power and pedagogy in educating other people's children. *Harvard Educational Review, 58*(3), 280–298.

Delpit, L. (1996). *Other people's children: Cultural conflict in the classroom.* New York: The New Press.

Deutsch, M. (1949). A theory of cooperation and competition. *Human Relations, 2,* 129–152.

Dewey, J. (1897). My pedagogic creed. *The School Journal, LIV*(3), 77–80.

Dewey, J. (2007/1916). *Democracy and education: An introduction to the philosophy of education.* Sioux Falls, SD: NuVision.

Díaz-Rico, L. T. (2008). *Strategies for teaching English learners* (2nd ed.). New York: Allyn & Bacon.

Dickson, S. V., Chard, D. J., & Simmons, D. C. (1993). An integrated reading/writing curriculum: A focus on scaffolding. *LD Forum, 18*(4), 12–16.

Duncan, S. E., & DeAvila, E. A. (1990). *Language Assessment Scales.* Monterey, CA: CTB/McGraw-Hill.

Duncan, S. E., & DeAvila, E. A. (1998). *Pre-Language Assessment Scale 2000.* Monterey, CA: CTB/McGraw-Hill.

Dunn, R., & Dunn, K. (1993). *Teaching secondary students through their individual learning styles: Practical approaches for grades 7–12.* Boston: Allyn & Bacon.

Dunn, R., & Dunn, K. (1999). *The complete guide to the learning styles inservice system.* Boston: Allyn & Bacon.

Echevarría, J., & Graves, A. (2003). *Sheltered content instruction: Teaching English-language learners with diverse abilities* (2nd ed.). Boston: Pearson Education.

Echevarría, J., Vogt, M., & Short, D. J. (2000). *Making content comprehensible for English language learners: The SIOP model.* Boston: Allyn & Bacon.

Echevarría, J., Vogt, M., & Short, D. J. (2004). *Making content comprehensible for English language learners: The SIOP model* (2nd ed.). Boston: Allyn & Bacon.

Echevarría, J., Vogt, M., & Short, D. J. (2008). *Making content comprehensible for English language learners: The SIOP® model* (3rd ed.). Boston: Allyn & Bacon.

Eisner, E. W. (1998). *The kind of schools we need: Personal essays.* Portsmouth, NH: Heinemann.

Ellis, N. C. (2002). Frequency effects in language processing. *Studies in Second Language Acquisition, 24,* 143–188.

Ellis, N. C. (2006a). Language acquisition as rational contingency learning. *Applied Linguistics, 27,* 1–24.

Ellis, N. C. (2006b). Selective attention and transfer phenomena in L2 acquisition: Contingency, cue competition, salience, interference, overshadowing, blocking, and perceptual learning. *Applied Linguistics, 27,* 164–194.

Ellis, N. C. (2007). The associative-cognitive CREED. In B. VanPatten & J. Williams (Eds.), *Theories in second language acquisition: An introduction* (pp. 77–95). Mahwah, NJ: Lawrence Erlbaum.

Ellis, R. (1997). *SLA research and language teaching.* Oxford: Oxford University Press.

Engel, G. (1977). The need for a new medical model: A challenge to biomedicine. *Science, 196*(4286), 129–136.

Faltis, C. J., & Hudelson, S. J. (1998). *Bilingual education in elementary and secondary school communities: Toward understanding and caring.* Boston: Allyn & Bacon.

Forman, E. A., Larreamendy-Joerns, J., Stein, M. K., & Brown, C. A. (1998). "You're going to want to find out which and prove it": Collective argumentation in a mathematics classroom. *Learning and Instruction, 8*(6), 527–548.

Freeman, Y. S., & Freeman, D. E. (2002). *Closing the achievement gap: How to reach limited-formal-schooling and long-term English learners.* Portsmouth, NH: Heinemann.

Gaddy, B. (Ed.). (1999). *Including culturally and linguistically diverse students in standards-based reform: A report on McREL's Diversity Roundtable 1.* Aurora, CO: Mid-Continent Research for Education and Learning. (ERIC Document Reproduction Service No. ED455335)

Garcia, E. E. (2003). *Student cultural diversity: Understanding and meeting the challenge.* Boston: Houghton Mifflin.

Gardner, H. (1993). *Multiple intelligences: The theory in practice.* New York: Basic Books.

Gates, M. L., & Hutchinson, K. (2005). *Cultural competence education and the need to reject cultural neutrality: The importance of what we teach and do not teach about culture.* Paper presented at the College of Education, Criminal Justice, and Human Services (CECH) Spring Research Conference, University of Cincinnati, OH. Retrieved May 10, 2005, from www.education.uc.edu/SRC2005/abstracts/gates_hutchinson.pdf

Gay, G. (2000). *Culturally responsive teaching: Theory, research, & practice.* New York: Teachers College Press.

Gay, G. (2002). Preparing for culturally responsive teaching. *Journal of Teacher Education, 53*(2), 106–116.

Gee, J. (1990). *Social linguistics and literacies: Ideologies in discourses.* New York: Falmer Press.

Gee, J. P. (2001). A sociocultural perspective on early literacy development. In S. Neuman & D. Dickinson (Eds.), *Handbook of early literacy research* (pp. 30–42). New York: Guilford.

González, N., Moll, L., & Amanti, C. (Eds.). (2005). *Funds of knowledge: Theorizing practices in households, communities, and classrooms.* Mahwah, NJ: Lawrence Erlbaum.

González, N., Moll, L. C., Tenery, M. F., Rivera, A., Rendon, P., Gonzales, R., et al. (1995). Funds of knowledge for teaching in Latino households. *Urban Education, 29*(4), 443–470.

Good, T. L. (1987). Teacher expectations. In D. C. Berliner & B. V. Rosenshine (Eds.), *Talks to teachers* (pp. 159–200). New York: Random House.

Gregorc, A. F. (1984). *Gregorc style delineator: Development, technical and administration manual.* Columbia, CT: Gregorc Associates.

Gronlund, N. E. (2004). *Writing instructional objectives for teaching and assessment* (7th ed.). Upper Saddle River, NJ: Pearson.

Guerra, C. (1996). Krashen's *i+1* issue revisited from a Vygotskian perspective. *TESOL-GRAM (The Official Newsletter of Puerto Rico TESOL), 23,* 7–8.

Guild, P. B. (2001). *Diversity, learning style and culture.* Retrieved January 4, 2010, from www.newhorizons.org/strategies/styles/guild.htm

Guild, P. B., & Garger, S. (1985). *Marching to different drummers.* Alexandria, VA: Association for Supervision and Curriculum Development.

Gutiérrez, K. D. (2008, April/May/June). Developing a sociocritical literacy in the Third Space. *Reading Research Quarterly, 43*(2), 148–164.

Gutiérrez, K. D., Baquedano-López, P., & Tejeda, C. (2003). Rethinking diversity: Hybridity and hybrid language practices in the Third Space. In S. Goodman, T. Lillis, J. Maybin, & N. Mercer (Eds.), *Language, literacy, and education: A reader* (pp. 171–187). Trent, UK: The Open University.

Gutiérrez, K., Rymes, B., & Larson, J. (1995). Script, counterscript, and underlife in the classroom: James Brown versus *Brown v. Board of Education. Harvard Educational Review, 65*(3), 445–471.

Harcourt Assessment. (2003). *Stanford English Language Proficiency (SELP) test.* San Antonio, TX: Author.

Heath, S. B. (2000). Linguistics in the study of language in education. *Harvard Educational Review, 70,* 49–59.

Herrera, S. (2007). *By teachers, with teachers, for teachers: ESL Methods course module.* Manhattan, KS: KCAT/TLC.

Herrera, S. (2008). *By teachers, with teachers, for teachers: ESL Assessment course module.* Manhattan, KS: KCAT/TLC.

Herrera, S., Kavimandan, S., & Holmes, M. (in press). *Biography-driven strategies for academic literacy development.* New York: Teachers College Press.

Herrera, S. G., & Murry, K. G. (2005). *Mastering ESL and bilingual methods: Differentiated instruction for culturally and linguistically diverse (CLD) students.* Boston: Allyn & Bacon.

Herrera, S. G., Murry, K. G., & Morales Cabral, R. (2007). *Assessment accommodations for classroom teachers of culturally and linguistically diverse students.* Boston: Allyn & Bacon.

Herrera Terry, D. (with BESITOS students). (2004). *Student voices: Two short plays on the Latin@ educational experience* [DVD]. Manhattan, KS: Kansas State University.

Hiebert, E. H. (1991). Introduction. In E. H. Hiebert (Ed.), *Literacy for a diverse society: Perspectives, practices, and policies* (pp. 1–6). New York: Teachers College Press.

Honig, B., Diamond, L., & Gutlohn, L. (2008). *Teaching reading sourcebook* (2nd ed.). Berkeley, CA: Consortium on Reading Excellence.

Howard, E. R., & Christian, D. (2002). Two-way immersion 101: Designing and implementing a two-way immersion education program at the elementary level. Center for Research on Education, Diversity & Excellence (CREDE), Santa Cruz: University of California.

Howard, E. R., Sugarman, J., Christian, D., Lindholm-Leary, K. J., & Rogers, D. (2007). *Guiding principles for dual language education* (2nd ed.). Washington, DC: Center for Applied Linguistics.

Howe, M. A. (1984). *A teacher's guide to the psychology of learning.* New York: Blackwell.

Hymes, D. H. (1972). On communicative competence. In J. B. Pride & J. Holmes (Eds.), *Sociolinguistics: Selected readings* (pp. 269–293). Harmondsworth: Penguin.

Jensen, E. (2000). *Brain-based learning* (Rev. ed.). San Diego: The Brain Store.

Jensen, E. (2006). *Enriching the brain: How to maximize every learner's potential.* San Francisco: John Wiley & Sons.

Jensen, E. (2008). *Brain-based learning: The new paradigm of teaching* (2nd ed.). Thousand Oaks, CA: Corwin Press.

Ji, L., Zhang, Z., & Nisbett, R. E. (2004). Is it culture or is it language? Examination of language effects in cross-cultural research on categorization. *Journal of Personality and Social Psychology, 87*(1), 57–65.

Jimenez, R. T., Garcia, E. G., & Pearson, P. D. (1996). The reading strategies of bilingual Latina/o students who are successful English readers: Opportunities and obstacles. *Reading Research Quarterly, 31*(1), 90–112.

Johnson, D. W., & Johnson, R. T. (1989). *Cooperation and competition: Theory and research.* Edina, MN: Interaction Book.

Johnson, D. W., Johnson, R. T., & Holubec, E. (1994). *Cooperative learning in the classroom.* Alexandria, VA: Association for Supervision and Curriculum Development.

Johnson, D. W., Johnson, R. T., & Maruyama, G. (1983). Interdependence and interpersonal attraction among heterogeneous and homogeneous individuals: A theoretical formulation and a meta-analysis of the research. *Review of Educational Research, 53*(1), 5–54.

Johnson, R. T., & Johnson, D. W. (1994). An overview of cooperative learning. In J. S. Thousand, R. A. Villa, & A. I. Nevin (Eds.), *Creativity and collaborative learning: A practical guide to empowering students and teachers* (pp. 31–44). Baltimore: Paul H. Brookes Publishing.

Jussim, L., Smith, A., Madon, S., & Palumbo, P. (1998). Teacher expectations. In J. E. Brophy (Ed.), *Advances in research on teaching: Expectations in the classroom* (Vol. 7, pp. 1–48). Greenwich, CT: JAI Press.

Kagan, S. (2000, Fall). Kagan structures—not one more program: A better way to teach any program. *Kagan Online Magazine.* Retrieved January 4, 2010, from www.kaganonline.com/Kagan Club/FreeArticles/ASK10.html

Keefe, S., & Padilla, A. M. (1987). *Chicano ethnicity.* Albuquerque: University of New Mexico Press.

Kelleher, A. (2008a). Who is a heritage language learner? In J. K. Peyton (Ed.), *Frequently asked questions about heritage languages in the United States* (Vol. I, pp. 5–7). Center for Applied Linguistics. Retrieved January 5, 2010, from www.cal.org/ heritage/research/faq.html

Kelleher, A. (2008b). What is a heritage language program? In J. K. Peyton (Ed.), *Frequently asked questions about heritage languages in the United States* (Vol. I, pp. 8–11). Center for Applied Linguistics. Retrieved January 5, 2010, from www.cal.org/ heritage/research/faq.html

Kim, S. (2007). *Exploring the self-reported knowledge and value of implementation of content and language objectives of high school content-area teachers.* Unpublished doctoral dissertation, Kansas State University, Manhattan. Available at http://hdl.handle .net/2097/357

Kindler, A. L. (2002). *Survey of the states' limited English proficient students and available educational programs and services: 2000– 2001 summary report.* Washington, DC: National Clearinghouse for English Language Acquisition and Language Instruction Educational Programs.

Kinsella, K., & Feldman, K. (2003). *Narrowing the language gap: Strategies for vocabulary development.* Retrieved from http:// www.fcoe.net/ela/pdf/Vocabulary/Narrowing%20Vocab%20 Gap%20KK%20KF%201.pdf

Knowles, M. S. (1970). *The modern practice of adult education: Andragogy versus pedagogy.* New York: Association Press.

Kolb, D. (1984). *Experiential learning: Experience as the source of learning and development.* Englewood Cliffs, NJ: Prentice Hall.

Krashen, S. D. (1981). *Second language acquisition and second language learning.* London: Pergamon Press.

Krashen, S. D. (1982). *Principles and practice in second language acquisition.* London: Pergamon Press.

Krashen, S. D. (1984/2002). Bilingual education and second language acquisition theory. In C. F. Leyba, *Schooling and language minority students: A theoretical framework* (2nd ed., pp. 47–75). Los Angeles: Legal Books.

Krashen, S. D. (1985). *The input hypothesis: Issues and implications.* London: Longman.

Krashen, S. D., & Terrell, T. (1983). *The natural approach: Language acquisition in the classroom.* Oxford: Pergamon Press.

Krussel, L., Springer, G. T., & Edwards, B. (2004). The teacher's discourse moves: A framework for analyzing discourse in mathematics classrooms. *School Science and Mathematics, 104*(7), 307–312.

Kuhrt, L. (2007, Fall). The forgotten half: Those who do not succeed in American schools. In D. Allen, P. O'Shea, J. Kaufman, & P. Baker (and the students of Old Dominion University's ECI 301), *Social and cultural foundations of American education* (3rd ed., Chapter 7). Retrieved July 1, 2009, from http://en .wikibooks.org/wiki/Social_and_Cultural_Foundations_of _American_Education

Kulesz, P. P. (2007). Transparent teaching: A pedagogy for success. *Scholarship and Creativity Online: A Publication of the Texas College English Association.* Retrieved June 12, 2009, from www .english.txwes.edu/tcea/documents/PritchardKuleszEssay.pdf

Kwon, O. N., Ju, M. K., Rasmussen, C., Park, J. H., & Cho, K. H. (2008, July). *Roles of teacher's revoicing in an inquiry-oriented mathematics class: The case of undergraduate differential equations.* Paper prepared for a Topic Study Group of the 11th International Conference on Mathematical Education, Monterrey, Mexico. Retrieved May 26, 2009, from http://tsg.icme11 .org/document/get/541

Lacina, J., New Levine, L., & Sowa, P. (Eds.). (2006). *Helping English language learners succeed in pre-K–elementary schools.* Alexandria, VA: TESOL.

Lackney, J. A. (1998, June). *12 design principles based on brain-based learning research.* Paper presented at the CEFPI Midwest Regional Conference. Retrieved February 7, 2009, from www .designshare.com/Research/BrainBasedLearn98.htm

Ladson-Billings, G. (1994). *The dreamkeepers: Successful teachers for African-American children.* San Francisco: Jossey-Bass.

Ladson-Billings, G. (1995). But that's just good teaching! The case for culturally relevant pedagogy. *Theory into Practice, 34*(3), 159–165.

Ladson-Billings, G. (1998). Who will survive America? Pedagogy as cultural preservation. In D. Carlson & M. W. Apple (Eds.),

References

Power/knowledge/pedagogy: The meaning of democratic education in unsettling times (pp. 289–304). Boulder, CO: Westview Press.

Langer, J. A. (1991). Literacy and schooling: A sociocognitive perspective. In E. H. Hiebert (Ed.), *Literacy for a diverse society: Perspectives, practices, and policies* (pp. 9–27). New York: Teachers College Press.

Laosa, L. M. (1977). Cognitive styles and learning strategies research: Some of the areas in which psychology can contribute to personalized instruction in multicultural education. *Journal of Teacher Education, 28*(3), 26–30.

Larkin, M. (2002). *Using scaffolded instruction to optimize learning.* Available online at www.ccc.spcd.org

Lau v. Nichols, 414 U.S. 563 (1974).

Lewin, K. (1935). *A dynamic theory of personality.* New York: McGraw-Hill.

Lewis, J. P. (2006). *The project manager's desk reference* (3rd ed.). New York: McGraw-Hill.

Linquanti, R. (1999). *Fostering academic success for English language learners: What do we know?* San Francisco, CA: WestEd. Retrieved January 4, 2010, from www.wested.org/policy/pubs/fostering

Mager, R. F. (1962). *Preparing instructional objectives.* Palo Alto, CA: Fearon Press.

Manning, D. (2006). Constructing meaning and metaphor for cultural pedagogy. *International Journal of Pedagogies and Learning, 2*(1), 48–62.

Marzano, R. J. (2004). *Building background knowledge for academic achievement: Research on what works in schools.* Alexandria, VA: Association for Supervision and Curriculum Development.

Massey, A. (1998, September). *The way we do things around here: The culture of ethnography.* Paper presented at the Ethnography and Education Conference, Oxford University Department of Educational Studies (OUDES).

Mays, L. (2008). The cultural divide of discourse: Understanding how English-language learners' primary discourse influences acquisition of literacy. *The Reading Teacher, 61*(5), 415–418.

McCarthey, S. J. (2000). Home-school connections: A review of the literature. *Journal of Educational Research, 93,* 145–152.

McDaniel, E. R., Samovar, L. A., & Porter, R. E. (2009). Understanding intercultural communication: The working principles. In L. A. Samovar, R. E. Porter, & E. R. McDaniel (Eds.), *Intercultural communication: A reader* (12th ed., pp. 6–17). Boston: Wadsworth Cengage Learning.

Mehan, H., Hubbard, L., & Villanueva, I. (1994). Forming academic identities: Accommodation without assimilation among involuntary minorities. *Anthropology & Education Quarterly, 25*(2), 91–117.

Met, M. (1991). Learning language through content; learning content through language. *Foreign Language Annals, 24*(4), 281–295.

Mid-Atlantic Equity Consortium. (1995). *Legal responsibilities of education agencies serving language minority students.* Retrieved July 30, 2009, from www.maec.org/pdf/legale.pdf

Mohr, K. A. J., & Mohr, E. S. (2007). Extending English-language learners' classroom interactions using the response protocol. *The Reading Teacher, 60*(5), 440–450.

Moll, L. C., Amanti, C., Neff, D., & González, N. (1992). Funds of knowledge for teaching: Using a qualitative approach to connect homes and classrooms. *Theory into Practice, 31*(2), 132–141.

Moll, L. C., & Greenberg, J. (1990). Creating zones of Combining social contexts for instruction. In L. C. *Vygotsky and education* (pp. 319–348). Cambridge, bridge University Press.

More, A. J. (1989). Native Indian students and their learnin Research results and classroom applications. In B. J. (Ed.), *Culture, style, and the educative process* (pp. 150- Springfield, IL: Thomas.

Nagy, W. E., Garcia, E. G., Durgunoglu, A. Y., & Hancin-Bhatt (1993). Spanish–English bilingual students' use of cognates English reading. *Journal of Reading Behavior, 25*(3), 241–259.

National Clearinghouse for English Language Acquisition (NCELA). (2007). *The growing number of limited English proficient students, 1995/96–2005/06.* Washington, DC: Author. Retrieved November 12, 2009, from www.ncela.gwu.edu/files/uploads/4/GrowingLEP_0506.pdf

National Research Council and the Institute of Medicine. (2004). *Engaging schools: Fostering high school students' motivation to learn.* Committee on Increasing High School Students' Engagement and Motivation to Learn. Board on Children, Youth, and Families, Division of Behavioral and Social Sciences and Education. Washington, DC: The National Academies Press. Available at www.nap.edu/openbook/0309084350/html/R1.html

Newmann, F. M. (Ed.). (1992). *Student engagement and achievement in American secondary schools.* New York: Teachers College Press. (ED371047)

Nieto, S. (2000). *Affirming diversity: The sociopolitical context of multicultural education* (3rd ed.). New York: Addison Wesley Longman.

Nieto, S. (Ed.). (2005). *Why we teach.* New York: Teachers College Press.

Numelin, K. (1998). The importance of sequencing and planning when integrating language and content. *ACIE Newsletter, 2.* Retrieved June 12, 2009, from www.carla.umn.edu/immersion/ACIE/vol2/Bridge2.1.pdf

Nyikos, M., & Hashimoto, R. (1997). Constructivist theory applied to collaborative learning in teacher education: In search of ZPD. *Modern Language Journal, 81,* 506–517.

O'Connor, M. C., & Michaels, S. (1993). Aligning academic task and participation status through revoicing: Analysis of a classroom discourse strategy. *Anthropology and Education Quarterly, 24*(4), 318–335.

O'Connor, M. C., & Michaels, S. (1996). Shifting participant frameworks: Orchestrating thinking practices in group discussion. In D. Hicks (Ed.), *Discourse, learning, and schooling* (pp. 63–103). New York: Cambridge University Press.

O'Dwyer, S. (2006). The English teacher as facilitator and authority. *TESL-EJ, 9*(4). Retrieved June 12, 2009, from http://tesl-ej.org/ej36/a2.pdf

Ogbu, J., & Simons, H. D. (1998). Voluntary and involuntary minorities: A cultural–ecological theory of school performance with some implications for education. *Anthropology and Education Quarterly, 29*(2), 155–188.

O'Malley, J. M., & Chamot, A. U. (1990). *Learning strategies in second language acquisition.* New York: Cambridge University Press.

Ormrod, J. E. (1995). *Human learning* (2nd ed.). Englewood Cliffs, NJ: Prentice Hall.

Ortega, L. (2009). *Understanding second language acquisition.* London: Hodder Education.

Ovando, C. J., Combs, M. C., & Collier, V. (2006). *Bilingual and ESL classrooms: Teaching in multicultural contexts* (4th ed.). Boston: McGraw Hill.

Oxford, R. L. (1990). *Language learning strategies: What every teacher should know.* New York: Newbury House/Harper Collins.

Palincsar, A. S. (1998). Social constructivist perspectives on teaching and learning. *Annual Review of Psychology, 49,* 345–375.

Park, J. H., Park, J. H., Kwon, O. N., Rasmussen, C., Ju, M. K., & Marrongelle, K. (2007, February). *Roles of revoicing in an inquiry-oriented mathematics class: The case of undergraduate differential equations.* Paper presented at the Conference on Research in Undergraduate Mathematics Education, Mission Valley, CA. Retrieved May 26, 2009, from www.rume.org/crume2007/papers/park-park-kwon-rasmussen-ju-maron gelle.pdf

Pepitone, E. (1980). *Children in cooperation and competition.* Lexington, MA: Lexington Books.

Phelan, P., Davidson, A. L., & Yu, H. C. (1998). *Adolescents' worlds: Negotiating family, peers, and school.* New York: Teachers College Press.

Porter, R. E., & Samovar, L. A. (1991). Basic principles of intercultural communication. In L. A. Samovar & R. E. Porter (Eds.), *Intercultural communication: A reader* (6th ed., pp. 5–22). Belmont, CA: Wadsworth.

Quinn, N., & Holland, D. (1987). *Cultural models of language and thought.* New York: Cambridge University Press.

Ramirez, J. (1992). Executive summary. *Bilingual Research Journal, 16*(1–2), 1–62.

Ramírez, M., III, & Castañeda, A. (1974). *Cultural democracy, bicognitive development and education.* New York: Academic Press.

Reid, D. K. (1996, Summer). 1995 CLD distinguished lecture: Narrative knowing: Basis for a partnership on language diversity. *Learning Disability Quarterly, 19*(3), 138–152.

Romero, A. A. (1998, January). Bilingual education under attack: Misconceptions fuel the fire. *IDRA Newsletter.* Retrieved July 20, 2009, from www.idra.org/IDRA_Newsletter/January_1998 _Bilingual_Education/Bilingual_Education_Under_Attack/

Rubie-Davies, C., Hattie, J., & Hamilton, R. (2006). Expecting the best for students: Teacher expectations and academic outcomes. *British Journal of Educational Psychology, 76*(3), 429–444.

Saleebey, D. (2001). *Human behavior and social environments: A biopsychosocial approach.* New York: Columbia University Press.

Säljö, R. (1996). Mental and physical artifacts in cognitive practices. In P. Reiman & H. Spada (Eds.), *Learning in humans and machines: Towards an interdisciplinary learning science* (pp. 83–96). Oxford: Pergamon/Elsevier.

Sapir, E. (1968). The status of linguistics as a science. In D. G. Mandelbaum (Ed.), *Selected writings of Edward Sapir in language, culture, and personality* (pp. 160–166). Berkeley: University of California Press.

Schifini, A. (1994). Language, literacy, and content instruction: Strategies for teachers. In K. Sprangfenberg-Urbschat & R. Pritchard (Eds.), *Kids come in all languages: Reading instruction for ESL students.* Newark, NJ: International Reading Association.

Segalowitz, N. (2003). Automaticity and second languages. In C. J. Doughty & M. H. Long (Eds.), *Handbook of second language acquisition* (pp. 382–408). Malden, MA: Blackwell.

Shade, B. J. (1989). The influence of perpetual development on cognitive style: Cross-ethnic comparisons. *Early Child Development and Care, 51,* 137–155.

Snow, M., Met, M., & Genesee, F. (1989). A conceptual framework for the integration of language and content in second/foreign language instruction. *TESOL Quarterly, 23*(2), 201–217.

Snyder, C. R., Harris, C., Anderson, J. R., Holleran, S. A., Irving, L. M., Sigmon, S. T., et al. (1991). The will and the ways: Development and validation of an individual-differences measure of hope. *Journal of Personality and Social Psychology, 60*(4), 570–585.

Sousa, D. A. (2006). *How the brain learns* (3rd ed.). Thousand Oaks, CA: Corwin Press.

Sternberg, R. J., & Grigorenko, E. L. (1997). Are cognitive styles in style? *American Psychologist, 52,* 700–712.

Stevens, K. C. (1980). The effect of background knowledge on the reading comprehension of ninth graders. *Journal of Reading Behavior, 12*(2), 151–154.

Straits, W. (2007). "She's teaching me": Teaching with care in a large lecture course. *College Teaching, 55*(4), 170–175.

Strike, K. A., & Posner, G. J. (1985). A conceptual change view of learning and understanding. In L. H. T. West & A. L. Pines (Eds.), *Cognitive structure and conceptual change.* New York: Academic Press.

Swartz, R., & Perkins, D. (1987). *Teaching thinking skills: Theory & practice.* New York: Freeman.

Sylwester, R. (1998). *Student brains, school issues: A collection of articles.* Arlington Heights, IL: Skylight Training and Publishing.

Tang, G. M. (1993). Teaching content knowledge and ESOL in multicultural classrooms. *TESOL Journal, 2*(2), 8–12.

Thomas, W. P., & Collier, V. P. (1995). Language-minority student achievement and program effectiveness studies support native language development. *NABE News, 18*(8), 5, 12.

Thomas, W. P., & Collier, V. P. (1997). *School effectiveness for language minority students* (NCBE Resource Collection Series No. 9). Washington, DC: National Clearinghouse for Bilingual Education. Retrieved October 7, 2002, from http://www .ncela.gwu.edu/files/rcd/BE020890/NCBE_School_Effective ness.pdf

Thomas, W. P., & Collier, V. P. (1999). Accelerated schooling for English language learners. *Educational Leadership, 56*(7), 46–49.

Thomas, W. P., & Collier, V. P. (2002). A national study of school effectiveness for language minority students' long-term academic achievement. Santa Cruz, CA: Center for Research on Education, Diversity & Excellence (CREDE). Retrieved February 5, 2003, from http://gse.berkeley.edu/research/credearchive/ research/llaa/1.1_final.html

Tomlinson, C. A., & McTighe, J. (2006). *Integrating differentiated instruction and understanding by design.* Alexandria, VA: Association for Supervision and Curriculum Development.

Tompkins, G. E. (2004). *Fifty literacy strategies: Step by step.* Upper Saddle, NJ: Pearson.

Torgesen, J. K., Myers, D., Schirm, A., Stuart, E., Vartivarian, S., Mansfield, W., et al. (2007). Closing the achievement gap: Second year findings from a randomized trial of four reading interventions for striving readers. Washington, DC: The Corporation for the Advancement of Policy Evaluation.

Touchstone Applied Science. (2001). *Maculaitis Assessment of Competencies II (MAC II)*. Brewster, NY: Author.

Triplett, N. (1898). The dynamogenic factors in pacemaking and competition. *American Journal of Psychology, 9*, 507–533.

Tsai, Y., Kunter, M., Lüdtke, O., Trautwein, U., & Ryan, R. M. (2008). What makes lessons interesting? The role of situational and individual factors in three school subjects. *Journal of Educational Psychology, 100*(2), 460–472.

Tse, L. (1996). The effect of language brokering on home-school communication. *Journal of Educational Issues of Language Minority Students, 16*, 225–233.

Tylee, J. M. (1992). *Nursing education in the tertiary sector in New South Wales, 1986–1989: An analysis of ideological orientations of curriculum, with particular reference to one institution.* Unpublished doctoral thesis, The University of Newcastle.

Tylee, J. (1999). *Teacher as facilitator: One of the face-to-face teacher's roles.* Retrieved June 3, 2009, from www.education4skills.com/jtylee/teacher_as_facilitator.html

Urdan, T., & Schoenfelder, E. (2006). Classroom effects on student motivation: Goal structures, social relationships, and competence beliefs. *Journal of School Psychology, 44*(5), 331–349.

U.S. Department of Justice. (2008). *Educational opportunities section: Frequently asked questions.* Retrieved July 30, 2009, from www.usdoj.gov/crt/edo/faq.php#4

Vail, P. L. (n.d.). *The role of emotions in learning.* Retrieved February 13, 2009, from http://www.greatschools.org/LD/managing/the-role-of-emotions-in-learning.gs?content=751

Valdés, G. (2000). Spanish for native speakers. AATSP Professional Development Series Handbook for Teachers K–12. Fort Worth, TX: Harcourt College Publishers.

Valdés, G. (2001). Heritage language students: Profiles and possibilities. In J. K. Peyton, D. A. Ranard, & S. McGinnis (Eds.), *Heritage languages in America: Preserving a national resource* (pp. 37–77). Washington, DC: Center for Applied Linguistics.

Vaughn, S., & Linan-Thompson, S. (2004). *Reading: Effective instructional activities for elementary students.* Alexandria, VA: Association for Supervision and Curriculum Development.

Vélez-Ibáñez, C. G., & Greenberg, J. B. (1992). Formation and transformation of funds of knowledge among U.S.-Mexican households. *Anthropology and Education Quarterly, 23*(4), 313–335.

Verplaetse, L. S. (2002). How content teachers interact with English language learners. *TESOL Journal, 7*(5), 24–28.

Vygotsky, L. S. (1956). *Selected psychological investigations.* Moscow: Izdatel'stvo Akademii Pedagogicheskikh Nauk SSSR.

Vygotsky, L. S. (1962). *Thought and language.* Cambridge, MA: MIT Press. (Original work published 1934)

Vygotsky, L. S. (1978). *Mind in society: The development of higher psychological processes* (M. Cole, V. John-Steiner, S. Scribner, & E. Souberman, Eds.). Cambridge, MA: Harvard University Press.

Vygotsky, L. S. (1986). The genetic roots of thought and speech. In A. Kozulin (Trans. & Ed.), *Thought and language* (pp. 68–95). Cambridge, MA: MIT Press.

Walqui, A. (2000). *Strategies for success: Engaging immigrant students in secondary schools.* (EDO-FL-00-03) Retrieved June 15, 2009, from www.cal.org/resources/Digest/0003strategies.html

Waxman, H. C., & Tellez, K. (2002). *Research synthesis on effective teaching practices for English language learners.* Philadelphia: Mid-Atlantic Laboratory for Student Success. (ERIC Document Reproduction Service No. ED474821)

Weinstein, R. S. (2002). *Reaching higher: The power of expectations in schooling.* Cambridge, MA: Harvard University Press.

Wertsch, J. V. (1998). *Mind as action.* New York: Oxford University Press.

Wessels, S. (2008). *IBA vocabulary framework: **I**gnite, **B**ridge & **A**ssociate vocabulary development for culturally and linguistically diverse students.* Unpublished doctoral dissertation, Kansas State University, Manhattan.

West, L. H. T., & Pines, A. L. (Eds.). (1985). *Cognitive structure and conceptual change.* New York: Academic Press.

Willis, J. (2006). *Research-based strategies to ignite student learning.* Alexandria, VA: Association for Supervision and Curriculum Development.

Wlodkowski, R. J., & Ginsberg, M. B. (1995). A framework for culturally responsive teaching. *Educational Leadership, 53*(1), 17–21.

Woodcock, R., Muñoz-Sandoval, A. F., Ruef, M., & Alvaredo, C. G. (2005). *Woodcock–Muñoz Language Survey Revised (WMLS-R).* Itasca, IL: Riverside.

Wright, W. E. (2007). Heritage language programs in the era of English-only and No Child Left Behind. *Heritage Language Journal, 5*(1), 1–26.

Young, T. A., & Hadaway, N. L. (Eds.). (2006). *Supporting the literacy development of English learners: Increasing success in all classrooms.* Newark, DE: International Reading Association.

Index

Subjects

academic dimension of student's biography, 18, 26, 29, 57–68, 72, 75, 130

academic knowledge, 16, 33, 57, 83–84, 85, 115

academics, 22, 23, 57–58, 62–63, 66, 68, 69

academic vocabulary, 96, 101

access for CLD learners, 62

accommodation, 7, 48, 58, 76, 104, 127, 131, 132, 148, 158

accountability, 56, 99, 103, 113–115, 128, 138, 139

acculturation, 24–25, 48, 82, 130

acquisition, of language, 31, 34

acquisition–learning hypothesis, 32–33

activation, 15, 66, 75, 77, 84, 87, 93, 99, 100, 102–103, 116, 120–122, 126, 158, 160

activities, vs. strategies, 106–107

additive language instruction programs, 6, 9

affective filter hypothesis, 33

affective influences, in biography-driven instruction, 22

affective strategies, 10, 51, 52, 109–110, 134

affirmation, 15–16, 74–76, 77, 123, 126

anxiety, 73–74, 125, 136

application, 111

Arizona, Proposition 203 in, 8, 152

assessment
 affective strategies and, 134
 as celebration of learning, 137–138
 cognition and, 43, 125–127, 133
 continuum of, 128
 as elaboration, 137–138
 emotion and, 125–127
 formative, 127–132
 grades vs., 138–139

to inform instructional practice, 2, 35, 43, 71–72

of language proficiency, 35, 36

learning strategies and, 132–135

metacognitive strategies and, 134

with P-EP-S-I Ahh!, 129

postassessment, 129, 135

preassessment, 127–129, 135

questioning in, 131–132

school-situated, 127

social/affective strategies and, 134

standardized, 15, 35, 63, 66, 127, 138, 141

summative, 128, 132–134, 137–138

teaching through, 138–139

testing vs., 138–139

background knowledge, 17, 30, 32, 34, 76–78, 83–85, 98–100, 102–106, 113–117, 120–122, 124, 126, 128, 142, 154, 156, 158, 160

basic interpersonal communication skills (BICS), 32

behaviorism, cognition in, 43

BICS, 32

biography card, 64–68, 153

biography-driven instruction
 academic knowledge and, 83–84, 85
 acculturation and, 82
 action model, 74–84
 affirmation in, 74, 76
 background knowledge and, 84
 biological aspects in, 20
 biopsychosocial history and, 19–20
 classroom community and, 73–74
 classroom ecology and, 69–70
 cognitive academic language learning approach and, 11
 community climate and, 72–73

concepts, 126

context and, 69–72

cooperative learning in, 114

facilitation in, 74, 76

foundation of, 7–16

funds of knowledge in, 78–81, 85

grouping configurations in, 112–114

home visits and, 24–26

input hypothesis and, 7, 10

knowledge systems and, 84, 85

observation in, 74, 76

prior knowledge and, 81–83, 85

psychological aspects in, 20–21

school-initiated responses in, 23–26

sheltered instruction observation protocol and, 13

situational processes and, 69, 70–71

situational teaching and, 71–72

sociocultural dimension in, 22–30, 26

sociological aspects in, 21

specially designed academic instruction in English and, 12

student biography in, 22–30

teacher as participant observer in, 76–84

transparency and, 87–88

vocabulary and, 91–101

biological factors, in biography-driven instruction, 20

biopsychosocial history, 19–21

Bloom's taxonomy, 45, 48, 118, 121

California
 "English for the Children," 5, 151, 152
 Proposition 227, 151
 Unz Initiative, 5

CALLA, 6, 10–11

CALP, 8, 9, 32

Castañeda v. Pickard, 150, 151

Cited Authors

About the Author

SOCORRO HERRERA is a professor in the Department of Elementary Education and serves as Executive Director of the Center for Intercultural and Multilingual Advocacy (CIMA) in the College of Education at Kansas State University. As a keynote speaker, district consultant, and trainer of trainers, she has helped teachers across the country find new paths to academic success for culturally and linguistically diverse learners. Dr. Herrera has authored several books, including *Mastering ESL and Bilingual Methods: Differentiated Instruction for Culturally and Linguistically Diverse Students; Assessment Accommodations for Classroom Teachers of Culturally and Linguistically Diverse Students;* and *Teaching Reading to English Language Learners: Differentiated Literacies.* Recent articles by Dr. Herrera have appeared in the *Bilingual Research Journal, Journal of Hispanic Higher Education, Journal of Research in Education, Journal of Latinos and Education,* and *Journal of Teaching and Learning.*